SOUND

BEHIND
THE SILVER
SCREEN

BEHIND THE SILVER SCREEN: A Modern History of Filmmaking

When we take a larger view of a film's "life" from development through exhibition, we find a variety of artists, technicians, and craftspeople in front of and behind the camera. Writers write. Actors, who are costumed and made-up, speak the words and perform the actions described in the script. Art directors and set designers develop the look of the film. The cinematographer decides upon a lighting scheme. Dialogue, sound effects, and music are recorded, mixed, and edited by sound engineers. The images, final sound mix, and special visual effects are assembled by editors to form a final cut. Moviemaking is the product of the efforts of these men and women, yet few film histories focus much on their labor.

Behind the Silver Screen: A Modern History of Filmmaking calls attention to the work of filmmaking. When complete, the series will comprise ten volumes, one each on ten significant tasks in front of or behind the camera, on the set or in the postproduction studio. The goal is to examine closely the various collaborative aspects of film production, one at a time and one per volume, and then to offer a chronology that allows the editors and contributors to explore the changes in each of these endeavors during six eras in film history: the silent screen (1895–1927), classical Hollywood (1928–1946), postwar Hollywood (1947–1967), the Auteur Renaissance (1968–1980), the New Hollywood (1981–1999), and the

Modern Entertainment Marketplace (2000–present). *Behind the Silver Screen: A Modern History of Filmmaking* promises a look at who does what in the making of a movie; it promises a history of filmmaking, not just a history of films.

Jon Lewis, Series Editor

1. ACTING (Claudia Springer, ed.)
2. ANIMATION (Scott Curtis, ed.)
3. CINEMATOGRAPHY (Patrick Keating, ed.)
4. COSTUME, MAKEUP, AND HAIR (Adrienne McLean, ed.)
5. DIRECTING (Virginia Wright Wexman, ed.)
6. EDITING AND SPECIAL VISUAL EFFECTS (Charlie Keil and Kristen Whissel, eds.)
7. PRODUCING (Jon Lewis, ed.)
8. SCREENWRITING (Andrew Horton and Julian Hoxter, eds.)
9. ART DIRECTION AND PRODUCTION DESIGN (Lucy Fischer, ed.)
10. SOUND: DIALOGUE, MUSIC, AND EFFECTS (Kathryn Kalinak, ed.)

SOUND
DIALOGUE, MUSIC, AND EFFECTS

Edited by Kathryn Kalinak

I.B. TAURIS

LONDON · NEW YORK

Published in 2015 by I.B. Tauris & Co. Ltd
London • New York
www.ibtauris.com

ISBN: 978 1 78453 404 2 (HB)
ISBN: 978 1 78453 405 9 (PB)
ISBN: 978 0 85773 927 8 (ebook)

A full CIP record for this book is available from the British Library

Printed and bound in the United States of America

CONTENTS

SOUND

INTRODUCTION   Kathryn Kalinak

Sound has played an important role in the cinematic experience across the entire history of moving images. Audiences experienced sound in the earliest exhibitions of motion pictures, most of it produced live. But it would be technology that provided the means for motion pictures to transform from a silent to a sound medium. In addition to the technological, there were institutional, economic, aesthetic, and ideological factors driving the revolution in synchronized sound, a complex nexus that continued to influence sound's evolution across the century. As the twentieth century drew to a close and the twenty-first century dawns, film sound is evolving for the future with new and ever-changing technologies fundamentally transforming sound both in terms of its production and its reception. The subject of film sound is a continuing, vibrant, and essential point of interrogation for any complex understanding of film.

What distinguishes this approach from other histories of sound, however, is its attention to what transpired behind the silver screen, its emphasis on the workers who collaborated in Hollywood (and before Hollywood) to produce sound for motion pictures. A set of questions beckons. Who was responsible for the musical accompaniment for the Silent Screen? Who was manning (and they were always men) the microphones in Classical Hollywood? Who was winning Academy Awards for scoring in Postwar Hollywood and why? Who were the agents of change in film sound during the Auteur Renaissance? Where was the influx of new composers in the New Hollywood coming from? In the Modern Entertainment Marketplace, what are the innovations in sound and who is instituting them? These are just some of the questions that find answers in the chapters of this book. The organization is chronological and each essay covers the important developments in film sound during a specific historical period, from the inception of motion pictures to the present. Here in the introduction I provide an overview, the big picture, if you will, of the history of film sound (and here I mean dialogue, sound effects, and music), filling in some prehistory and making connections between and among the different periods covered by the individual essays.

Let me begin with another question. Why was early film dubbed "silent" film? "Silent film," as it turns out, was a label created during the industry-wide conversion to synchronized sound and projected back onto an era that generally used the term "moving pictures" to describe the phenomenon. Early film, in fact, often had a sonic component: speech provided by lecturers who talked audiences through the new experience; dialogue provided by actors who appeared either in front of or concealed from audiences; musical accompaniment and sound effects, provided both by live musicians and recordings; and even mechanically synchronized sound and image. Even in the era before any of these sounds became commonplace, viewers in Kinetoscope parlors were surrounded by extraneous sounds produced by other patrons. Audiences for projected images, before conventions for audience behavior were in place, heard each other chattering away during screenings (as in the cinematic viewing spaces of today minus the cell phones). As contributor James Wierzbicki argues, "The audience's vocalized reactions of course do not belong to whatever is on display, but they belong very much to the aural content of the entertainment as a whole." The screen may have been silent in silent cinema, but if we consider sound to be any sound available, not just reproduced, during the screening of moving pictures and heard by the audience, the experience of cinema was anything but silent.

Along these lines, consider how many early films visualized sound. Think of Annabel dancing, John Rice talking to May Irwin as a prelude to their kiss, or Annie Oakley firing her shotgun in early Edison Company motion pictures. Audiences often watched the production of sound taking place in early film, whether or not that sound was reproduced in the viewing space. In fact, the visualization of sound was the point of some of these early films. Why film Fred Ott's sneeze, as W.K.L. Dickson did for Edison in 1894, if not to capitalize on the sound produced? Early filmmakers, it would seem, were not reluctant to draw attention to the very thing that modern audiences find so awkward: images divorced from the sounds they produce. But images were not divorced from all sound in early film; sound was often present, and increasingly so, in one form or another, in early cinematic viewing spaces. But early film did not duplicate the sounds seemingly produced by the images, and the images—and the nascent art form of which they were a part—were not yet tied by sound to reality.

Films weren't the only moving image phenomena to exploit sound. Motion pictures can be thought of as the latest (and far from the culmination) of a long history of moving images paired with sound. Asian shadow-puppet theater, elaborate spectacles where the shadows of intricately moveable puppets were projected onto a screen and whose heyday was between 800 and 1500, was accompanied by gamelan orchestras in Java. Étienne-Gaspard Robertson's various *Phantasmagoria* beginning in the 1780s in Paris, complex magic lantern shows that presented moving images via mechanically moving slides and mobile projectors, featured spooky music and various unearthly sound effects. Charles-Émile Reynaud, having developed a magic lantern device that could show a series of moving images, presented *Pantomimes lumineuses* in Paris in 1892 accompanied by a piano player. Camera obscura and magic lantern shows throughout the nineteenth century were accompanied by lecturers. Photographic images and stereopticons, on the other hand, as well as those forms of moving image entertainment designed for the individual viewer—the zoetropes, Kinetoscopes, and Mutoscopes—did not necessarily trigger the presence of sound. But when moving images became a form of mass entertainment, what Wierzbicki has termed "sonic *accoutrements*" were there.

Early moving-picture entrepreneurs who projected images to mass audiences crafted some striking examples of audio-visual performances. The Lumière brothers billed a pianist, Émile Maraval, for presentations of their films in a Paris cafe. The Edison Company booked their large-scale projection system into a vaudeville theater in New York City with an orchestra in the pit. Whether or not the music on hand preceded the screenings, followed them, or accompanied them can be difficult at this point in time to determine. But in choosing these venues, these early filmmakers seized the opportunity to exhibit film as part of a multimedia experience. Soon music would materialize at screenings, produced mechanically by phonographs or live by musicians.

Barkers, lecturers, and actors provided another form of sound—the human voice—that found its way into early screening venues. Barkers hailed potential customers. Lecturers offered commentaries. Actors provided dialogue. One or all of these forms of human intervention might have provided some rudimentary sound effects. In any case, the sound, largely, was not representational, that is, it did not duplicate, although it might approximate, the sounds the images would seem to produce. (Think of actors trying to reproduce dialogue for which they had no scripts.) Intertitles changed all that, replacing the lecturers and actors who accompanied early films. Dialogue became a visual rather than an aural element, another example of the way that early cinema visualized sound.

When cinema transformed into a narrative medium, musical accompaniment took on an increasingly important role. Eventually phonographs would be replaced by the human musicians with whom they competed. Arrayed in a variety of configurations, which expanded as the decades passed, musicians ranged from a single instrumentalist, a pianist or an organist, to a symphony orchestra. Organists had at their disposal a vast array of sonic possibilities in terms of sound and music, a result of the extraordinary range of sound the instrument was capable of producing. By the end of the era, musical accompaniment and the occasional added sound effects had become an expected part of the filmic experience, touted by enterprising theater owners to lure audiences to their theaters and spur ticket sales. There was little incentive in the major Hollywood studios, enjoying unprecedented profits in the 1920s, to synchronize sound.

It was left to scrappy Warner Bros. to herald the massive shift in production from silence to sound. In an attempt to garner a larger share of the market (and thus advance into the upper echelon of major Hollywood studios), Warner Bros. (along with the Fox Film Corporation) synchronized musical accompaniment (and some sound effects) to their features using technologies that had been available for some time. Warner Bros. had intended to better control and ultimately upgrade the quality of musical accompaniment for its pictures by recording and synchronizing a musical score for their feature films. *Don Juan* (Alan Crosland, 1926), Warner Bros.' first synchronized feature, was shot silent, but its score was recorded by the New York Philharmonic and synchronized live to the film during screenings via a complex system of projectors and phonograph discs overseen by human operators. *Don Juan*'s soundtrack, which reproduced the typical continuous music and select sound effects of silent cinema, did not fundamentally change the relationship of sound to image. It was the human voice that did. *The Jazz Singer* (Alan Crosland, 1927), built on the same technology as *Don Juan*, featured interpolated performances by its star Al Jolson singing in synchronization to his musical accompaniment. Jolson famously added improvised dialogue into two of those performances. With Jolson's voice, synchronized sound reproduced experiential reality. That's Al Jolson actually singing "Toot Toot Tootsie, Goodbye," recorded live along with the band conducted by Lou Silvers behind him.

The success of *The Jazz Singer* ushered in a new mode of production that incorporated synchronized sound. That mode of production also marked a shift in responsibility for what the audience heard. In the silent era, sound was determined by theater exhibitors and the music directors they hired. With the conversion to synchronized sound, control over sound shifted to the makers of film and would come firmly under the control of the studios. But most fundamentally, synchronized sound changed the relationship between image and sound as it precipitated an aesthetic shift toward realism. Sound would soon anchor the image in as faithful a representation of reality as the technology could muster.

That privileging of realism, however, posed some formidable challenges. At first, the only way to record sound was to capture it—live on set. The earliest synchronized sound films utilized a single microphone and thus all sound—dialogue, sound effects, and music—had to be captured simultaneously. Dialogue had to be delivered in proximity to the microphone, and sound effects and music, too, had to be within the microphone's range. This necessitated hiding the sound effects men and their equipment, and sometimes an entire orchestra. Since any extraneous sound would be captured right along with the dialogue, films became very static in order to accommodate the capturing of sound—noisy cameras were immobilized in sound blimps, actors were practically glued to their marks near the microphone, musicians and sound effects men were positioned offscreen, and nobody moved when the camera and sound equipment were running.

It didn't take long, however, for technology to evolve that allowed for the capture of sound to be divorced from the production of sound, opening up a space for sound to be constructed rather than reproduced. The advent of postproduction sound and, most importantly, rerecording and mixing techniques in the early 1930s made possible increasingly realistic sound through increasingly artificial means. Now dialogue could be rerecorded in postproduction (in a process known as looping) for a clean, perfect delivery; sound effects could be produced independent of the actual production of the sound, often from so-called "noise libraries" where sound effects were collected, catalogued, and stored; musical performances could be recorded before filming for playback and synchronizing on the set; and musical accompaniment could be recorded in postproduction after the film had been edited. And it could all be mixed in postproduction to achieve a proper balance of sound. In some cases, rerecorded sound accounted for the entire soundtrack of some films from this era. As early as 1931 at some studios, by the mid-1930s at most studios, and by the late 1930s at the rest, technology was in place to allow separate tracks for dialogue, sound effects, and music, recorded at different times and in different places (and often with little or no relationship to onscreen sources) to be mixed in postproduction after the film had been edited. What these advances in sound technology facilitated, as I argue in chapter 2, was nothing less than classical filmmaking itself, "a combination of technology and aesthetics informed by economics, enacted through style, and shared among workers at the various studios."

Music experienced a revolution of its own. With the advent of sound film, music that was not visibly produced within the filmic world posed a challenge to Hollywood's new realist aesthetic. Gone was the background score—replaced with interpolated songs and musical performances no matter what the genre. Eventually the background score came roaring back (75 minutes of the 100-minute running time of Merian C. Cooper and Ernest B. Schoedsack's King Kong [1933] was scored), at about the same time as technological changes allowed it to be recorded separately and mixed in postproduction.

In 1946, immediately following the end of World War II, Hollywood enjoyed one of its most successful years in terms of audience attendance. But with the growth of television, automobile ownership, suburbanization, and the new teen culture, Hollywood studios would soon find themselves under siege. Sound was one of the ways postwar Hollywood fought back, promising ever more realistic sound through ever more technically sophisticated and artificial means. One of the most important advances after the war was the adoption of magnetic tape for recording and rerecording, a technology that replaced the optical soundtracks in use at the time. Magnetic tape made editing easier, playback more immediate, and, since it could be reused, more cost effective. Magnetic tape facilitated many aspects of production and postproduction, saving time and therefore money. But importantly, it held the promise of increased fidelity, a promise it delivered on by positioning the soundtrack at yet another remove from the image track. Although costs and studio resistance to magnetic tape prevented its wide adoption in the postwar era, magnetic tape opened the door to constructing sounds and visual images completely separately.

Something of this same "disconnect," to borrow a phrase from contributor Nathan Platte, can be seen in the phenomenon of the soundtrack album, which began in earnest in the postwar era. Albums of music containing cues from a film's musical score, known somewhat misleadingly as soundtracks, allowed for, indeed promoted, the opportunity to listen to a film's score separate from the images, an attempt to improve the musical experience of a film without the distraction of the images. These soundtracks, often recorded in the stereophonic sound that was not yet commonplace in movie theaters, sometimes included music not heard in the film, increasing the disconnect between the image track and the soundtrack.

Stereophonic sound extended improvements in the production of sound into the cinematic auditorium itself, changing the way sound was produced in theaters. Although it would be at least another decade before stereo became commonplace in theaters, various competing systems of stereophonic sound positioned speakers both behind the screen (and thus in front of the audience) and behind the audience, thus enveloping it in sound. While studio promotional campaigns frequently invoked the naturalness of stereophonic sound, its production was anything but natural, the product of increasingly sophisticated technological systems in combination with decisions about what constituted realistic sound. The promotion of stereophonic sound as natural, by the way, was a perception not always echoed in film marketing. Nathan Platte, in his contribution, offers us this example, an advertisement for *Beneath the 12-Mile Reef* (Robert D. Webb, 1953): "The marvel of CinemaScope's stereophonic sound engulfs you in excitement you've never known."[1] What begins to germinate with the advent of stereophonic sound is the idea that cinematic sound could be an aural experience that exceeds, not duplicates, reality. Cinematic sound improving upon reality, eventually exceeding the bounds of reality, becomes an ever-expanding quest in the post-studio era.

During the years known as the Auteur Renaissance (roughly from the breakup of the studio system in the 1960s through 1980), technological advances improved noise reduction, enhanced sound clarity, extended the range of sound frequencies, and produced equipment that made location sound more efficient and cost effective. These improvements allowed filmmakers to "pack in," as contributor Jeff Smith describes it, more and more aural information, creating a soundtrack rich with possibilities.

Those possibilities exploded onto soundtracks in the 1970s, a decade that saw the birth of the sound designer, a single individual responsible for the realization of a director's sound vision across all phases of a film's production, from the planning stages to postproduction. Many of the creative and forward-thinking directors who were the first to employ sound designers had little interest in using sound simply to duplicate reality. Contributors Jay Beck and Vanessa Theme Ament point to Walter Murch's experience working as a sound designer for Francis Ford Coppola on *Apocalypse Now* (1979): Coppola wanted the "soundtrack to partake of the psychedelic haze in which the war had been fought, not only in terms of the music . . . but in general, kind of far-out juxtaposition of imagery and sound; for the soundtrack not to be just a literal imitation of what you saw on the screen but at times to depart from it."

The ever-widening gap between cinematic sound and experiential reality can be heard in Dolby Stereo, a sound system that began to be widely used for motion pictures by the 1980s. Dolby incorporated sophisticated noise reduction that produced startlingly clear sound, but its innovation extended into the cinematic auditorium itself where it enveloped the audience in a 360-degree field. So-called surround sound presented enormous opportunities for what Beck and Ament describe as "enhanced realism." Dolby created a new experience of sound, the sonic spectacle, that could only be experienced in a cinematic auditorium. By the 1990s, refinements in multichannel digital technologies allowed filmmakers to locate sound anywhere in the theater, furthering the development of the cinematic auditorium as a unique sonic space and the soundtrack as a field of hyper-reality. Not all filmmakers were comfortable with this departure from a realist aesthetic. Contributor Mark Kerins points to Mark Andrews, the director of *Brave* (Mark Andrews and Brenda Chapman, 2012), who explained, "When they were pitching me the idea of kind of encapsulating sound, this dimensional sound, I was like, but wait a minute, the screen is there, why would I have sounds behind me or above me or underneath me, it's going to be weird."[2] Nevertheless, this type of sonic activity, dimensional sound, has come to characterize big-budget action films produced in Hollywood.

In the twenty-first century, technological refinements facilitated the industry-wide conversion from analog to digital sound technology and allowed for increasingly layered and detailed soundtracks. What this has sometimes produced, however, is soundtracks that play at increased volumes and are filled with more sonic information than can be processed by audiences. Changes in exhibition, which seemed to be taking place at warp speed after the turn of the century, have changed the game for sound, too, digital projection in particular. Now sound can be customized to a particular space and sound system; the experience of sound for the same film can differ from one exhibition space to another. What these refinements have facilitated is a fundamental change in the relationship of sound and image that is taking place on the soundtrack and in the cinematic auditorium, a move toward conceiving of soundtracks, and constructing the sonic landscape of auditoriums where they are experienced, as increasingly hyper-real. The construction of sonic spectacles on the soundtrack, a growing dependence on what Kerins describes as "aggressively spatialized mixes [and] dramatic variations in loudness" is drawing film closer and closer to a soundscape in which soundtracks no longer attempt to reproduce the sounds the images seemingly produce, and audiences no longer expect soundtracks to do so.

Something along these lines has happened to a film's score as well. Increasingly as the current century progresses, film music is being synthesized, which means that the music we hear in films is often computer-generated sound produced to simulate the sounds of actual instruments. Like the soundtrack, the contemporary film score finds itself increasingly in the domain of hyper-reality. Except in big-budget films, the orchestra we hear, for example, is most often not being produced by the recording of acoustic instruments but through a complex technological process that simulates (with ever more increasing accuracy) the sounds of acoustic instruments. Soon it may be necessary to check the credits to see what you have actually heard.

As we ponder the future of film (if that is even the correct word to use at this point in time), we should not fail to take into account the increasing role of hyper-reality in film sound, and I mean by this both in the production of a film's soundtrack and in the experience of sound during a film's theatrical exhibition. Ironically, something of this disconnect between the visual source of sound on the screen and the sound experienced in the cinematic viewing space was routinely experienced in silent cinema, raising the question of whether film's future might lie in its past.

About This Volume

Each of the contributors to this volume summarizes the important developments in sound across a specific historic era, analyzes attendant changes in technologies, economics, institutional practices, reception, and film style, and highlights the creative lives of the workers behind the silver screen who contributed to the soundtrack. Each also brings to this project an individual perspective that illuminates various aspects of the soundtrack and its history in fascinating and sometimes unexpected ways. Because technological change does not obey clean and sharp divisions, there is some inevitable overlap between chapters as contributors fully explore, say, Dolby surround sound, which emerged in the late 1960s but was not fully deployed in Hollywood until the 1980s. Career arcs, too, defy historical demarcations. Sound designers such as Walter Murch, Ben Burtt, and Alan Splet began to leave their mark on the industry in the 1970s but continued to do important work in later decades. Composer John Williams spurred the rebirth of the classical symphonic film score in the late 1970s with several breakout film scores, but as anyone who has been to the movies in the twenty-first century knows, he is still an active film composer to this day.

James Wierzbicki, in "The Silent Screen, 1894–1927," begins not so much by debunking the old chestnut that silent film was never truly silent but by interrogating it, throwing open new avenues of thought about the very definition of cinematic sound itself. As he asserts, "Literally speaking, what we call 'the screen' is, and always has been, silent." Sound doesn't emanate from the screen itself, but in early cinema audiences experienced a sonic component that emanated from a variety of places in the proximity of the screen. There was other sound, too, a type of sound that is rarely addressed. As Wierzbicki points out, "Patrons of such entertainments typically also hear something else: along with the deliberately constructed sounds that are a part of the entertainment, patrons hear spontaneous sounds made by themselves." Exploring exactly what was heard in early cinema's first viewing spaces, Wierzbicki tosses preconceived notions of silence and sound on their heads with a startling but illuminating series of comparisons between patrons in a silent film viewing space, families watching silent home movies in the 1960s, parents using finger puppetry to create moving shadows on the walls at bedtime, shadow puppet theater in Asia, and "whatever might have been witnessed by the imaginary denizens of Plato's Cave." Wierzbicki's philosophical inquiry leads him to a provocative conclusion: "The human activity that involves groups of people attending to what is depicted on a screen, however, has likely never been silent. Indeed, it would seem that sound—generated not just by the presenters of the screened material but also by the audiences—has always been a part of public screenings."

Wierzbicki's resistance to writing a conventional history of sound in silent film informs his entire chapter: look for his theoretical exploration of what we mean by the term "the silent screen" (and how could a screen be anything else?); his discussion of pictures that do not move (the illustrations for *Alice in Wonderland*, a Vermeer painting, friezes on ancient Greek pottery) for insights on pictures that do; his analysis of the musical cues from an early cue sheet for a forgotten Edison short, *Why Girls Leave Home* (1909); his attention to a little-known Warner Bros. sound film, *The Better 'Ole* (Charles Reisner, 1926), made between two more famous films, *Don Juan* and *The Jazz Singer*; his inclusion of the early Fox talkie *Mother Knows Best* (John G. Blystone, 1928), which garners almost as much space in his coverage of the transition to sound as *The Jazz Singer*. For these and many other reasons, Wierzbicki's chapter is an illuminating read both for those familiar with this era of film history and for those who are coming to it for the first time.

My chapter, "Classical Hollywood, 1928–1946," treats the development of the studio system as it recalibrated for sound. Of particular interest, here, and what fascinated me the most in researching this chapter, was the fallout for studio workers. For some the coming of sound proved career-ending and for others a lucky break, while many, across a wide range of jobs affected by the new technology, retooled, reeducated, and adapted their careers for sound. Dialogue proved the engine of the sound revolution in Hollywood. Actors now had to memorize and deliver dialogue cleanly and naturally (and, yes, Rin Tin Tin was one of silent film's stars who negotiated the transition successfully). Screenwriters had to reimagine a story in verbal terms and write dialogue. Directors had to coach actors without being able to talk them through a scene and they had to create for the microphone as well as for the camera. Producers had to figure out what to do with spoken dialogue for foreign markets. A legion of new craftspeople evolved to help them do so: elocution experts, dialogue coaches, specialists in the writing of dialogue, specialists in the direction of dialogue, actors proficient in foreign languages for export versions, and more.

No new professions, however, were more critical to the sound revolution than those that evolved to provide films with sound and music. Sound recording personnel, often recruited from the radio and telephone industries, had to capture and record sound; composers, along with songwriters, orchestrators, arrangers, and musicians, many lured from concert and Broadway stages, were charged with the production of both musical numbers performed in the film and the background score performed for the film.

Hollywood adapted to sound quite successfully, as it turns out, but that was not the case with all the professionals on the front lines. There were many for whom the transition to sound proved catastrophic: the actors who could not adapt to the microphone or whose voices didn't translate well in recording or who were simply so well known as silent stars that the public lost interest in them as sound stars; the silent film scenarists displaced by playwrights and writers who could produce snappy dialogue; silent film directors pushed aside by dialogue directors and stage directors from New York; and the musicians, who were the hardest hit of all. Employed in silent film theaters to accompany the films (and on sets to provide mood music), musicians watched in trepidation and then in horror as their profession disappeared. *Variety* grimly predicted, "Over 50,000 musicians may be thrown out of work."[3] My chapter reminds us that the revolution in sound resolved itself in and through the lives of industry professionals who toiled behind the silver screen.

Nathan Platte's chapter, "Postwar Hollywood, 1946–1967," uses the development of professional film music criticism as the entry point into a volatile era for sound and music. He begins by quoting the critic Page Cook on the kind of film scores that were beginning to fill Hollywood soundtracks by 1967: "Music has all but disappeared from films. Noise has replaced it."[4] Cook's diatribe is clearly directed at contemporary scoring practices—jazz, pop, rock 'n' roll—that diverged from classical scoring principles. Yet his perception that Hollywood soundtracks had been radically transformed between 1946 and 1967 moves Platte to ask: "How exactly did changes in technology, marketing, and aesthetics transform the music and sound of postwar Hollywood cinema to such a radical degree?"

Platte's answer begins with the Academy Awards for 1946, when *The Best Years of Our Lives* (William Wyler, 1946) dominated the awards, including an Oscar for its score by studio veteran Hugo Freidhofer, and concludes with the Academy Awards for 1967, when the nominated scores "bore little resemblance in sound to films of the 1930s and 1940s that had been made on studio lots, scored by studio composers, and recorded onto optical track with studio orchestras." In between, Platte's chapter fills in the important developments that help to explain the change.

The postwar years were an unstable era for Hollywood, as Platte notes, with depressed attendance figures, increased competition from independent studios and Hollywood's nemesis, television, and with inevitable cutbacks in the studio system as a result. (Music departments were hit particularly hard.) With Hollywood looking over its shoulder at its rival, the studio system responded in ways that impacted the soundtrack. As Platte details, "Studio attempts to overshadow television with heightened spectacle brought forth larger orchestras heard in stereophonic sound. Filmmakers—many enjoying greater independence from the studio system—looked beyond the symphonic style entirely to jazz, electronic, and popular music." Although studio downsizing (and the jettisoning of expensive studio contracts) was decried in many quarters, such streamlining made it easier to bring in new musical talent from outside Hollywood. It "also gave sound personnel more independence, both contractually and aesthetically." Developments such as these fostered experimentation.

Driving these changes, as Platte points out, was the development of magnetic tape, which improved and simplified production and postproduction sound, and stereophonic sound, both of which transformed the sonic landscape. Although magnetic recording and stereophonic sound would "outstrip the playback capabilities of most theaters" until the 1970s, these developments raised the public's awareness of the soundtrack. As Platte concludes, it would be the Dolby system with its "noise-reduction and stereo technologies [that] would give filmmakers, sound designers, and composers of the Auteur Renaissance an entirely new palette of sonic possibilities."

Those sonic possibilities are taken up by Jeff Smith in his chapter, "The Auteur Renaissance, 1968–1980." Smith analyzes the technological and aesthetic changes in film sound throughout the era—the increased adoption of magnetic tape; the development of lightweight, portable recorders, such as the Nagra, which revolutionized location shooting; and the birth of Dolby sound, among other things. But what I find so fascinating are Smith's portraits of what he calls "sound 'auteurs,'" innovators who "made the soundtrack a more layered, more textured, and more visceral component of the overall cinematic experience."

Dubbing director Robert Altman, sound designers Walter Murch, Ben Burtt, and Alan Splet, and composer John Williams "sound stylists," Smith shines the spotlight on those who made important contributions in sound behind the silver screen with detailed portraits of their work: Altman, who "pushed the boundaries" of overlapping dialogue in an effort "to capture something of the actual buzz and din of groups engaged in conversation" and in the process created "a new kind of aural realism"; Murch, who essentially redefined what it meant to do sound recording and mixing "by rather ingeniously crafting low-tech solutions to the problem of creating high tech sounds"; Burtt, who created innovative sound effects (rather than recycling from a sound library), over 250 for *Star Wars* (George Lucas, 1977) alone and over 1,000 for *The Empire Strikes Back* (Irvin Kerschner, 1980); Splet, who used ambient sound to create arresting soundscapes by "using environmental sounds to add atmosphere and mood to a film's setting"; and Williams, who "revived the fortunes of the classical Hollywood score, an idiom that began to seem increasingly anachronistic after the infusion of modernist styles and pop sounds."

The creative freedoms enjoyed by sound stylists such as Murch, Burtt, and Splet were not widely experienced in the industry, however. Working largely outside Hollywood, these innovators perfected their craft in films that lacked big budgets (and it may come as a surprise how comparatively modest the budget for *Star Wars* was). When Hollywood headed into the era of the blockbuster, budgets soared, creative stylists gave way to sound teams, and the industry itself experienced a retreat to more conventional labor hierarchies and less experimental and innovative soundtracks. Ultimately, the innovations of the Auteur Renaissance "now appear more like a blip on the cultural radar than a sustained reimagining of the soundtrack's aesthetic possibilities." As Smith sums up, "Hollywood would wait at least another decade for a period that would show a similar level of creative ferment."

Jay Beck and Vanessa Theme Ament, in their chapter "The New Hollywood, 1981–1999," explore that creative ferment. In the 1980s and 1990s, a number of new sound roles—sound designers, sound effects creators, and Foley artists—proved "indications of the growing significance of film sound in the history of American cinema." Like Smith, Beck and Ament articulate these roles through an analysis of several key sound practitioners and in fact revisit some of the people introduced in Smith's chapter, namely, Murch, Burtt, and Splet.

Most important is the sound designer, a single individual who was responsible for sound through all phases of production and thus could execute the director's vision, a role made possible by the labor system in Hollywood losing its grip and the studio system continuing its decline. These conditions, however, "created a space for these 'acoustic auteurs' who developed new aesthetic strategies and introduced new technologies to serve their individual needs": Murch, who forged creative partnerships with Francis Ford Coppola and George Lucas to realize the "conceptual resonance" between the film and its soundtrack; Burtt, who transcended the job of creating sound effects on films such as the *Star Wars* and *Indiana Jones* trilogies; and Splet, who practiced "audio expressionism," sound that "simultaneously augmented the visual materials while heightening the dramatic import." Each exemplifies the ability to unify sound with the demands of the narrative.

New methods and new technologies were impacting the creation of a film's score as well. Well through the 1970s, a group of composers trained in classical Hollywood scoring were dominant, among them John Williams, Jerry Goldsmith, and Alfred Newman. Although Williams and Goldsmith would enjoy long careers in Hollywood (Newman was at the end of his), the orchestral style of scoring that they exemplified would be challenged in the 1980s by new composers schooled in the pop music industry, new technologies (such as synthesized music) and styles derived from pop music (especially rock 'n' roll), and a new form of scoring, the compilation score, a collection of preexisting pieces of music, usually songs, and usually rock 'n' roll, to accompany a film. A new role developed: the music supervisor, whose job it was to clear copyright on preexisting music and help the director realize his or her vision for the film score. These innovations would prove "a sea change" that continue to impact film scoring today. Finally, Beck and Ament continue the saga of Dolby sound in the 1980s and detail the analog to digital transition in the 1990s that has transformed film sound. They leave us poised on the brink of a new century.

Mark Kerins opens his chapter, "The Modern Entertainment Marketplace, 2000–Present," noting the sense of stability that the new century seemed to portend for the soundtrack: established labor practices were settling into place after the advent of computer-based sound editing and mixing in the 1990s; exhibition practices with regard to sound were becoming increasingly standardized after the transition from analog to digital sound; digital surround sound appeared "poised to remain the theatrical exhibition standard for the foreseeable future"; and home theaters and sound systems that could reproduce those of theatrical exhibition seemed "tantalizingly close." But as Kerins warns us, "In actuality, the film sound industry saw significant changes in the first decade of the new century. This chapter focuses on the root of many of these shifts: the exponentially increasing pace of technological change, both within the film industry and outside it." Kerins's chapter details these changes that "forced film sound professionals to adapt established practices based on control and standardization to a new reality of flexibility and adaptation."

In terms of production, the Nagra portable sound recorder, for decades the workhorse of the industry, was replaced by digital audio recorders, themselves soon to be replaced by file-based hard drive and flash drive recorders. Postproduction sound, which was similarly impacted by the shift from analog to digital, went through a variety of systems before settling on Avid's ProTools, which itself continued to expand its capabilities as the century progressed (from 64 tracks in the early 2000s to over 800 in 2013). These technological changes allowed for soundtracks that were more layered. The transition to digital nevertheless had several unfortunate consequences, including the tendency toward complicated and busy soundtracks with literally hundreds of sound effect tracks.

Kerins makes the case that the most tumultuous changes in film sound in the new century came in exhibition, however: "From digital projection to a multitude of new surround formats to 3-D, theatrical exhibition technology may have undergone more, and more fundamental, changes in the last twenty years than it had over all the rest of cinema history." Since sound data could now be stored on a hard drive instead of the film print itself, sound could be customized to individual cinematic auditoriums and "moving a film from one theater to another would involve merely selecting a different soundtrack file, not shipping a different print." New, more flexible surround-sound systems were also transforming exhibition space, creating "heavily spatialized sound environments" which forced audiences to adjust to new kinds of cinematic sound.

Kerins brings us up to date in his conclusion, pondering the future of cinematic sound given the cultural shift in exhibition from cinematic auditoriums to iPods, computer screens, and smart phones. Will small-screen film viewing "prove to be a passing fad, with consumers eventually deciding they prefer big screens and big sound, or perhaps the reverse will happen and filmmakers will have to design their soundtracks to play best over earbuds or on tinny laptop speakers"? For Kerins, "Film sound production, exhibition, and consumption all remain in flux, and no one within or outside the industry can say for sure where they will go next."

Above all, the essays contained here establish the soundtrack as a crucial and defining element of a film and lay out, in detail, how the elements of sound that the soundtrack comprises are produced and by whom. The discussions of individual films throughout these chapters articulate the transformative powers of sound as they are harnessed to shape the specific ways that meaning is made in individual texts. It is my hope that this volume will make it hard to "see" films in quite the same way as before.

1

THE SILENT SCREEN, 1894–1927   James Wierzbicki

A commonplace that permeates the popular literature on cinema suggests that the screen was never silent, and someone browsing through a library can easily find a bounty of statements that not only boldly make that claim but also offer reasons as to why films, right from the start, were fitted with musical accompaniment.[1] It has not escaped the attention of historians that most of these clichéd statements date from the 1930s and later, or that most of them come from persons who had vested interests—as producers, directors, and composers—in the making of commercial films that boasted music-rich soundtracks. Thus a second common-place, albeit confined to the writings of scholars, involves a proper debunking of the first; the standard argument has it that music and film were not comfortably wedded until almost two decades after the motion picture had proved itself to be a viable form of entertainment, and that before this time, film's sonic *accoutrements,* musical or otherwise, ranged from hit-or-miss to nonexistent.

Because it makes sense, and because it is based on increasingly solid research, that standard argument is supported here. Following the approach I took in my 2009 book *Film Music: A History,* this chapter on the silent screen divides the era of so-called silent film into three distinct periods: the exploratory initial period (1894–1905) that Tom Gunning has dubbed the "cinema of attractions";[2] the formative years of narrative cinema (1905–1915) during which films were shown—probably most often with supporting music and sound effects, sometimes even with spoken words—in small venues colloquially known as nickelodeons; and the mature medium's glorious heyday (1915–1928) during which films featuring star-studded casts were exhibited in capacious movie palaces and invariably accompanied from start to finish by music either from a large orchestra or from the recently invented theater organ. After this historical survey, in the manner of an epilogue, comes a section on experiments with sound film that date back to the very dawn of cinema. Readers for whom the term "early cinema" equates to films from the mid-1930s will, I hope, find this annotated chronology to be if not illuminating then at the very least clarifying; for readers already steeped in the history of cinema and its evolving relationship with sound, I can at best offer here, in lieu of new facts, perhaps a few new insights.

The story of sound and the silent screen has already been told, by me and by others.[3] Before launching into yet another of the story's iterations, however, I will pause for a moment to consider the key words of this chapter's title.

Literally speaking, what we call "the screen" is, and always has been, silent. That is to say, to date no sound-producing vibrations have ever issued from any flat surface on which images actually do move or on which, in the case of cinema, still images only seem to move. With the so-called sound film, the sonic phenomena that audiences experience emanate not at all from the screen itself but *primarily* from loudspeakers placed in the vicinity of the screen, and it is the same with examples of silent film with recorded soundtracks. In the case of silent films presented in the traditional manner, the sonic phenomena consist (today as much as in the 1920s) *primarily* of whatever sounds are produced—live, in the exhibition space, while the showing of the film transpires—by the accompanying musicians, actors, and/or sound effects crew. Similarly, in the case of camera obscura exhibits, whose reflected/projected images of the real world attracted viewers long before the idea of photographed moving pictures was even a twinkle in anyone's eye, the sounds consist *primarily* of the host's narration.

Three times in the preceding paragraph I used the adverb "primarily," and on each occasion—as if rhetorical repetition were not enough—I emphasized the word by setting it in italics. Indeed, with modern camera obscura exhibits and accompanied silent film as much as with the fare that we experience on a regular basis in cinemas and on television, most of what is heard is the sonic component of what patrons fully expect to be a multimedia entertainment. But patrons of such entertainments typically also hear something else: along with the deliberately constructed sounds that are a part of the entertainment, patrons hear spontaneous sounds made by themselves.

Nowadays probably very few of us laugh or gasp or shriek out loud when, quite on our own, we absorb films in the comfortable privacy of our living rooms or in the cramped confines of an economy-class seat on a transcontinental airliner. But for most of us, I suspect, all it takes is just one other person sharing in the

real-time viewing to turn the filmic experience from something solitary and pas-
sive into something communal and participatory. As was discovered more than a
half-century ago by pioneering television producers, giggles trigger giggles, and
so even today slickly edited TV sitcoms are peppered with canned laugh tracks.
No such artifice is necessary for the potential blockbusters that regularly premiere at modern cinemas during holiday seasons. If a much-promoted and thus
well-attended comedy is at least somewhat funny, unrestrained laughter from
just a portion of the audience will likely convince the rest of the audience that
the film is *very* funny. Likewise for films whose content is arguably thrilling, or
sentimental, or tragic. The audience's vocalized reactions of course do not belong
to whatever is on display, but they belong very much to the aural content of the
entertainment as a whole.

One can only speculate (because reports from newspapers, letters, diaries,
and so on have yet to surface) as to what sorts of sounds emanated from the
mouths of persons who patronized Edison's Kinetoscope parlors circa 1894–95.
These first venues for motion pictures consisted of roomfuls of machines, each of
them approximately the size of a small refrigerator, at which individual viewers
stood and, with their eyes pressed to peepholes, watched whichever brief films
(most of them less than a minute in duration) had been loaded into a particular
machine.[4] My personal guess is that during the viewings, because the experiences
were private, patrons made very few sounds. Surely the Kinetoscope parlors were
abuzz with human noise, but this would likely have been a combination of the
loud yammering of barkers calling attention to this or that new film clip and the
quiet yet constant din of individual patrons saying to their friends something
along the lines of "Hey, you just *gotta* see this."

Likewise, one can only speculate as to the sounds contributed by patrons who
in Paris in December 1895 attended the very first exhibition of moving pictures
not viewed through peepholes but projected onto screens, or who, in the years
immediately following, witnessed public exhibitions of projected motion pictures in music halls and vaudeville theaters. For these, my guess is that the sound
of the audience would have been both concerted and considerable. One should
remember that most persons ca. 1895–96 had never before witnessed a moving
picture. Because of the nature of the film stock on which they were recorded,
films from this period were of necessity quite short, and most of them did little
more than *show* one arguably interesting event or another. But the sheer novelty
of projected images that in effect came to life, no matter how mundane their
subject matter, would have been enough to elicit, one supposes, loud choruses of
oohs and aahs; for the relatively few early films whose content was overtly comic
or dramatic, the vocal reactions of the audience must have been stentorian.

What we call the screen is, almost by definition, silent. The human activity
that involves groups of people attending to what is depicted on a screen, however,
has likely never been silent. Indeed, it would seem that sound—generated not

just by the presenters of the screened material but also by the audiences—has always been a part of public screenings. Briefly mentioned above were the various types of silent film that are the focal points of this chapter. But the generalization also includes camera obscura exhibits and tent-based magic lantern entertainments of the sort that regularly took place on fairgrounds throughout Europe and the United States during the second half of the nineteenth century. The generalization includes showings of home movies like those that at least twice a year I experienced, in the often boisterous company of my immediate or extended family, during my childhood in the 1950s and early 1960s. And it includes various forms of shadow play, ranging from the finger-based images of bunnies and doggies that clever parents cast upon the walls of their kids' rooms at bedtime to the more or less formal genres of shadow-puppet theater common to traditional Asian cultures[5] and to whatever might have been witnessed by the imaginary denizens of Plato's Cave.[6]

Sound in the Cinema of Attractions

Lack of evidence, of course, is proof of nothing, and so it is impossible to state with certainty that the first projected films—at least from the point of view of their presenters—were indeed silent. But the absence of information regarding sonic *accoutrements* for these earliest public screenings, in contrast to a plethora of accounts that attest to how astoundingly sensational were these screenings' visual elements, leads one to conclude that the first showings of motion pictures were not accompanied by sounds other than announcements generated deliberately by the presenters or vocalizations generated spontaneously by members of the audience. This is not to say, however, that organized sound was not in the screenings' near vicinity.

Because a poster exists, we know that a professional musician was somehow involved, at some point, in the exhibitions of motion pictures that the brothers Auguste and Louis Lumière offered to paying audiences in Paris beginning on December 28, 1895. But we have no idea what music the *pianiste-compositeur* Émile Maraval played on his highly touted Gaveau instrument, or how—or even if—his playing figured into the actual show. The venue was small, a basement salon that seated approximately 100 persons,[7] and the program was short, a twenty-minute entertainment that featured just ten or so films. In contrast to the smallness of the venue and the program, the box office—once word of the attraction had spread—was huge. With thousands of patrons experiencing the screenings each day, it is at least within the realm of possibility that M. Maraval provided music simply to usher crowds in and out of the viewing room.[8]

Similarly, because playbills and newspaper advertisements from the day are abundant, we know that bands and orchestras were typically on hand when

Lumière films and their Edison-made equivalents found their way onto the agendas of music halls and vaudeville houses in Paris, London, and various American cities in the first six months of 1896.[9] One should remember, however, that in the vaudeville house a short sequence of films would typically share space, and compete for the audience's attention, with a host of variety-show acts that included the likes of comedians, singers, magicians, acrobatic dogs, and dancing girls. Because their routines were inherently musical, doubtless the singers and the dancing girls were accompanied by music served up by the pit bands; because the films were just brief exhibitions of one motion-picture attraction after another, probably all the musicians did was loudly herald the start of the show and then, when it was over, just as loudly signal "the end."

The much-scoured paper trail of early film showings in the vaudeville houses does lead to instances of music, sound effects, or spoken words transpiring while the films were being shown. An August 1896 showing in Philadelphia of a film that depicted "a sham battle scene," for example, was reportedly made to seem all the more realistic not just by "noise and battle din" but also by a sounding of the French national anthem;[10] a film titled *Tearing Down a Wall* (1896) shown in Providence, Rhode Island, in September of that year reportedly began with backstage assistants shouting "Look out!" and ended with a behind-the-scenes crash of bricks; exhibited in the same venue a few days later, a film depicting a cavalry brigade was enlivened by a bugle call and the fake noise of horses' hooves.[11] In October 1896 the New York showing of a film titled *McKinley at Home* involved a tenor singing one of presidential candidate William McKinley's campaign songs;[12] in 1897, in Philadelphia, a film that purported to show scenes from a German passion play was exhibited in conjunction with "unseen organ music,"[13] and in 1898 a similar film exhibited in New York was decorated with "music by organ and choristers."[14]

The passion play attractions, invariably filmed not at Oberammergau but at various locales on the eastern seaboard, are of special interest. Not only were they, along with films depicting boxing matches, among "the most popular productions of the early cinema industry"; they were also, writes Rick Altman, "the most likely to be presented by a lecturer."[15] It should be noted, however, that even John J. Lewis, an evangelical entrepreneur who billed himself as the "apostle of the Passion Play in America" and who claimed to have delivered his lectures to more than two million audience members, did not speak his weighty words simultaneous with the showing of motion pictures. Lectures combined with projected images were indeed common during this period. But regardless of a lecture's content, "one of the lecturer's primary tasks—and powers—was to provide transitions *between* film and slide material."[16] This use of projected pictures—whether moving or still—primarily to illustrate the verbal content of a lecture was a carry-over from the "[magic] lantern trade" that in the "early and mid-1890s . . . was at its most commercially developed" stage but which endured into the first decade of the twentieth century,[17] and which endures even today in the PowerPoint presentations of many a university professor.

In contrast to illustrated lectures featuring the sound of spoken words in alternation with the soundless exhibition of projected images, examples of moving pictures accompanied by sound of any sort were relatively rare. Tracked down as carefully in Europe as in the United States, they seem to have been so unusual that they support the generalization offered above. By and large, public screenings during cinema's first half-decade were indeed noisy affairs probably introduced or somehow framed by music, but hardly ever were they offered together with music or other deliberately constructed sounds. And this stands to reason.

The early films did not tell stories (examples of fictional films, so few as to support another generalization, include Edison's 1895 *The Execution of Mary, Queen of Scots,* a fifteen-second horror film showing—by means of trick photography—the chopping off of a head, and the Lumière brothers' 1895 *L'Arroseur Arrosé* [The Squirter Squirted], a comedy of forty-three seconds during which a hose-wielding gardener has a prank wetly played upon him by a young boy). The vast majority of the early films were, rather, miniature documentaries that attempted nothing more than to show renowned persons in action or, more mundanely, to depict what were sometimes called "actualities." On the one hand, early films showed a famous belly dancer or a famous sharpshooter doing whatever it was that made them famous; on the other hand, and much more common, they showed the likes of workers exiting a factory (see figure 1), a train rolling

FIGURE 1: The first frame of the Lumière brothers' 1895 *La Sortie d'Usines Lumière* (Exit from the Lumière Factory), an early example of a picture that moved

into a station, a boat sailing out of a harbor, an aging elephant being electro-cuted, or a fire brigade rushing down a city street. Musical accompaniments for such films, including those whose subject matter involved dancing, would have been superfluous. This is only in small part because of the films' extreme brevity, which meant that any music applied to them would have to have been heard as an aurally unsatisfying fragment. The main reason why these films did not need, or want, musical accompaniment is the nature of the films' content.

The ancestor of the earliest examples of the moving picture was the picture that did *not* move. Not until the late 1870s were there cameras and film stock that allowed for the fast-exposure photography that led to the idea for and then to the realization of cinema. But photography had been part of Western culture for at least fifty years before that, and before that—for thousands of years—there had existed drawings and paintings. The persons who first contemplated the illustrations in Lewis Carroll's 1865 *Alice's Adventures in Wonderland* or the seventeenth-century canvases by Vermeer, like the persons who first contemplated the figurative friezes on ancient Greek pottery or the prehistoric decorations on the walls of the caves at Lascaux, saw only still pictures. If there was a message to be conveyed, it was con-veyed by the pictures alone, and the pictures did not need the support of music. It was quite enough for the viewers merely to *see* two-dimensional images of white rabbits or Dutch landscapes or battling warriors or wooly rhinos. Likewise, it was quite enough for the viewers of the earliest films merely to *see* two-dimensional projected images that gave the illusion of movement.

In contrast, the ancestor of the storytelling films that began to come to prom-inence around 1902–03 was enacted drama. Made possible by technological advances in the manufacture of film stock that allowed for single reels to hold as much as ten or twelve minutes' worth of material, and instigated by filmmakers and exhibitors who knew that once the novelty had worn off their customers would demand more than just pictures that moved, the early narrative films were modeled on various forms of theater. These models range from highbrow Shakespeare and Molière to lowbrow melodrama and Punch-and-Judy puppet shows, from word-filled opera and oratorio to wordless yet musically rich ballet and pantomime. As different as these models are in terms of balance between visual and aural/verbal content, what they have in common is a blend of stimuli for the ear as well as for the eye. Taking a cue from centuries-old predecessors that told stories by means of a combination of action and sound, the exhibitors of the first storytelling films would have known straightaway that, in order to convey their products' messages, sonic accompaniment was not just appropriate but necessary.

Thus as the silent screen evolved from a cinema of attractions into a cinema of narrative, so did cinema's concomitant sound evolve from audience noise into more or less organized music, sound effects, and spoken words. The sounds of nickelodeon-style cinema were by and large dramatically purposeful; until the end of the twentieth century's first decade, however, they were hardly uniform in content or practice.

Sound in the Nickelodeon-style Cinema

The transition from the cinema of attractions to narrative cinema was gradual, and different historians of American film describe the change in different ways. Citing a careful survey of copyrights, Tom Gunning informs us that "in the U.S. . . . actuality films outnumbered fictional films until 1906." James Lastra writes that "after approximately 1907, narrative films dominated not only in sheer numbers but as the form around which the emerging industry grew." John Belton states that "by 1908, 96 percent of all American films tell stories."[18]

These American films from around 1908 that "tell stories" were for the most part one-reel efforts that lasted no more than ten or twelve minutes. A few filmmakers from this time indeed aspired to tell multi-reel stories whose exposition of characters and development of plot required, as did the plays of Shakespeare and Molière, several hours in which to unfold, and these filmmakers' perseverance led to the heyday of the silent film whose sonic elements are discussed later in this chapter. Through most of the twentieth century's first decade, however, their efforts were strongly—sometimes violently—discouraged by the leading manufacturers of films exhibited in the relatively small venues that eventually came to be known as nickelodeons.[19] Nine of these manufacturers, all based in New York or New Jersey, in 1908 banded together to form an organization called the Motion Picture Patents Company;[20] along with sharing technological information and collectively securing exclusive rights to the best-quality film stock, the MPPC made their products available only to exhibitors who promised to eschew films made by independent filmmakers. The cartel's obviously monopolistic practices were not declared to be illegal until 1915, by which time most of their competitors had relocated from the East Coast to Southern California, in the general neighborhood of the Los Angeles suburb of Hollywood. But until that time, and beginning around 1902, the nickelodeon suppliers held powerful sway.

There is no technological reason why any film, regardless of its vintage, could not be exhibited in a cavernous auditorium; to expand a projected image simply required the proper lens and the proper distance between projector and screen, and—indeed—examples of the cinema of attractions were often shown in large vaudeville houses. Likewise, there is no technological reason why any film from 1902 onward, when developments in the manufacturing of flexible celluloid allowed for reels that easily accommodated as much as twelve minutes' worth of material, could not be of infinite duration; to exhibit a longer film, all that was needed was a second projector, loaded and ready to go into operation as soon as the first projector had done its job. Likewise, too, there is no technological, or artistic, reason why any storytelling silent film from this or any other period could not be musically supported by a score as complex as those that, throughout the nineteenth century, had supported many a ballet. The nickelodeon theater's physical space and its cinematic fare—and eventually its typical accompanying music and sound effects—existed in a symbiotic relationship; the basis of this relationship was neither technological nor artistic but, rather, economic.

Multi-reel films of the sort that characterized silent film's heyday demanded that audiences pay attention to them at least for several hours. Such films were profitable only if they played in venues for extended periods and if the audiences for the individual showings were quite large; they attracted large audiences night after night, week after week, only if they were rich in production values and boasted star-spangled casts. The business model for the nickelodeon-style film, and thus its mode of presentation, was in almost every way the opposite.

Whereas the independent filmmakers who migrated to Hollywood took chances by investing heavily in only a handful of *big* pictures each year, the various makers of nickelodeon films had almost a sure thing with their steady production and efficient distribution of several inexpensive *small* films each week. Whereas the elegant multi-reel films from Hollywood were truly at home only in the sumptuous movie palaces that started to be built in the commercial centers of large cities on the eve of World War I,[21] the humble one-reel nickelodeon films from America's eastern seaboard were perfectly comfortable in makeshift theaters set up in the narrow and long storefronts that since the 1880s had figured into the commercial life not just of American cities but also of American small towns. Whereas a two- or three-hour Hollywood film behooved its entire audience to be present at a specific starting time, an evening of ten- or twelve-minute nickelodeon films—perhaps in combination with performances by a vocalist who sang to the accompaniment of both a piano and projected slides[22]—had five or six starting times an hour. And whereas a feature-length film shown in a movie palace required a musical accompaniment played either by an organist or, more typically, by an orchestra, a program of short nickelodeon-style films could be easily serviced, with minimal preparation, by a single pianist.

We do not know if the earliest nickelodeon films were indeed accompanied by pianists, or if these films had any sonic support at all; as with the era of the cinema of attractions, there is a frustrating paucity of solid information regarding music and sound at the dawn of the nickelodeon period.[23] We do know, however, that a piano accompaniment was the norm for the nickelodeon theater beginning around 1908–1910. We also know quite a bit about the actual music that was played during the mid- to late nickelodeon period and—significantly—about how this music was played, that is, about how the music and various sound effects were used for the purposes of furthering a film's theatrical goals.

Our knowledge about the actual music for nickelodeon-style films comes mainly from two sources. One of these sources, with its information in musical notation, is the vast array of published collections of generic music from which a dutiful pianist might have chosen when planning an accompaniment for a one-reel nickelodeon-era film; the other source, with its information in prose, is the sizeable literature of published cue sheets, or "suggestions for music," that indicate which specific musical compositions, or what type of generic music, should be played starting at specific points in particular films. Our knowledge of how music and sound effects were used in the nickelodeon theater comes for the most part from advice columns that began to appear, in 1910, in trade journals.

Collections

Of the published collections, the earliest—and one whose lengthy title perfectly summarizes the volume's content and purpose—seems to be Gregg A. Frelinger's 1909 *Motion Picture Piano Music: Descriptive Music to Fit the Action, Character, or Scene of Moving Pictures.* The collection that is best known today—perhaps because it is the most easily accessible, but also perhaps because its content is so exquisitely crafted—is the *Sam Fox Moving Picture Music* series launched in 1913 by the eponymous Cleveland-based publisher and featuring music by the Cleveland-born but Prague-educated John Stepan Zamecnik.[24]

The seventy original compositions for piano that make up the first three volumes (1913–1914) of the *Sam Fox Moving Picture Music* series are masterpieces of both simplicity and cliché. Distilled from a century's worth of musical stereotypes drawn as much from lofty opera and symphonic tone poem as from lowly British and American melodrama,[25] each of J. S. Zamecnik's pieces instantly communicates whatever basic idea (a battle or a storm, a cowboy or a fairy, a mysterious "oriental veil dance" or an equally mysterious "burglary") is mentioned in its title. Following a brief introductory passage, typically each of Zamecnik's pieces settles into a series of eight-bar phrases that end either with a half cadence suggestive of repetition or a full cadence suggestive of stopping or moving on. There is no development of material here, no dramatic complication along the lines of what happens midway through a composition in the classical sonata form. Instead, there is just one section after another, each self-contained.

Zamecnik's compositions are remarkable not just because they so immediately communicate their theatrical messages and because they are, as piano music goes, relatively easy to play. They are also remarkable because their deliberately simple designs, in terms of both phrase structure and key relationships, make it possible for even a moderately competent pianist to shift smoothly—at a moment's notice—from one piece to another.[26]

The *Sam Fox Moving Picture Music* volumes contain just a fraction of the generic material that a nickelodeon pianist, anywhere in the country, might have purchased during the years preceding World War I. It is certainly true that a different kind of cinema, and with it a very different kind of cinematic experience, was coming to the fore during the prewar years; it should be remembered, though, that the feature-length film and its glamorous movie palace at first affected culture only in the largest metropolitan areas, and that elsewhere—which is to say, throughout most of the United States—the nickelodeon-style film with its piano accompaniment enjoyed an extended twilight. Proof of this can be found in the leases and licenses that document the existence, even into the 1920s, of nickelodeon-style theaters in hundreds of American cities and towns. More easily, proof can be found in libraries that house such keyboard-focused collections as John L. Bastien's several *Dramatic and Moving Picture Music* volumes (1913), *Denison's Descriptive Music Book for Plays, Festivals, Pageants, and Motion Pictures* (1913), the *Remick Folio of Moving Picture Music* (launched in 1914), *Metzler's Original Cinema Music* (likewise launched in 1914), *Carl Fischer's Loose Leaf Motion Picture Collection for Solo Piano* (three volumes, published in 1915, 1916, and 1918), and S. M. Berg's *Berg's Incidental Series* (1916–1917).

As early as 1912 there appeared on the market collections of so-called descriptive music scored not for solo piano but for small orchestra, and a large number of similar collections were published between 1916 and 1925. Yet collections of music for keyboard alone persisted. The fourth and final volume in the *Sam Fox Moving Picture Music* series, with compositions by Zamecnik, came out in 1923. A year later, the New York–based publisher Belwin issued the large and impressively indexed *Motion Picture Moods for Pianists and Organists: A Rapid Reference Collection of Selected Pieces, Adapted to 52 Moods and Situations,* an anthology of almost 300 pieces compiled by the Hungarian-born American conductor Erno Rapee. And shortly after that Belwin began to release installments of Giuseppe Becce's *Kinobibliothek* series; launched in Germany in 1919 and continuing through 1927, the twelve volumes that constituted the *Kinobibliothek* include eighty-one pieces of music, some of them composed by the Italian-born Becce but most of them drawn from the standard classical repertoire, and all scored for solo piano.[27]

Cue Sheets

The American publisher Belwin was established in 1918 and concocted its name from letters in the surnames of its founders: the above-mentioned S. M. Berg, composer Sol Levy, and all-around musical factotum/entrepreneur Max Winkler. It is certainly a fact that Winkler was an important player in the commercialization of generic film music in the second and third decades of the twentieth century, but it is a fiction that Winkler—as he writes in his much-quoted 1951 autobiography *A Penny from Heaven*—single-handedly invented the cue sheet.

As the term suggests, a musical cue sheet for a film (or for a staged drama) is a list of cues—that is, signals contained within the script or stage directions—that indicate precisely when some sort of musical action should be undertaken. According to his self-aggrandizing account, Winkler hit upon the idea in 1912 after attending yet another nickelodeon exhibition during which the pianist failed to hit the mark. Much of his cinema-going experience, Winkler tells us, had involved accompanists just blundering through their jobs, playing this or that merely for the sake of filling an exhibition space with sound. What, Winkler supposedly wondered, would be the effect of pianists playing dramatically appropriate music at just the right moments in the unfolding of a filmed story?

Winkler in 1912 was a clerk employed by New York's Carl Fischer publishing house. As Winkler tells the story, he drew upon both his often frustrated experiences in moviegoing and his encyclopedic familiarity with Carl Fischer's holdings and concluded that nickelodeon culture could be much improved if accompanists were advised, well in advance, that at particular spots in the films they should play particular pieces of music. His thoughts were not entirely altruistic. "The hundreds and thousands of titles, the mountains of music that we had stored and catalogued and explored," he wrote, "kept going through my mind. There was music, surely, to fit *any* situation in *any* picture. If we could only think of a way to let all these orchestra leaders and pianists and organists know what we had! If we could use our knowledge and experience not when it was too late but much earlier before they ever had to sit down and play, we would be able to sell them music not by the ton but by the trainload."[28]

With such products as the *Carl Fischer Moving Picture Folio, Especially Designed for Moving Picture Theatres, Vaudeville Houses, etc.* (1912), *Carl Fischer Professional Pianist's Collection for Motion Picture Theatres, Vaudeville Houses, Theatrical Programs, and Dramatic Purposes* (1913), the *Carl Fischer's Loose Leaf Motion Picture Collection for Solo Piano* (1915–1918), and the *Carl Fischer Moving Picture Series* (1916), Winkler's employer indeed sold music "by the trainload." But Winkler's brainstorm likely happened in 1915, not in 1912, for it was in April of 1915 that Carl Fischer and Universal Studios entered into an agreement by which "musical suggestions will be published for important [Universal] films far in advance, to enable orchestra leaders to secure the music,"[29] and it was a few months after that that various journalists began to name Winkler as the cue sheets' author.

In any case, the cue sheet dates back at least to September 1909, and its likely originator is not Winkler but some anonymous employee of the Edison Company. In a two-page section of the company's promotional newsletter, musical suggestions were offered for no fewer than seven of the most recent Edison films. The suggestions name only two pieces with titles: "Home! Sweet Home!" and "For He's a Jolly Good Fellow." Following the tradition of the scripts for nineteenth-century melodramas, everything else is identified by tempo ("andante," "slow march," "allegro"), or by mood ("plaintive," "hurry," "lively"), or by some generic descriptive label ("Irish jig," "popular air," "regular overture"). While a few of the suggestions give as their cues nothing more than the number of a filmic scene, most others are more specific, and directly related to events within a film's drama. The cues for the ten-minute *Why Girls Leave Home* (1909), for example, suggest that "pizzicato" music be played during the "bridge scene" and that it continue "till gallery applauds," at which point the music should be "lively," and that the next scene—at the "heroine's home"—should feature "plaintive music."[30]

The cue sheet for an Edison film from 1910 similarly cites dramatic moments at which different bits of music should be played, but in this case most of the suggested music is identified—more or less—by title. The accompanist for Edison's twelve-and-a-half-minute *Frankenstein* is advised to play at certain moments, for example, the 1835 song "Annie Laurie," or the aria "Then You'll Remember Me" from Michael Balfe's 1843 opera *The Bohemian Girl,* or Anton Rubinstein's 1852 "Melody in F" for piano; at five different moments the accompanist is advised to play "dramatic" music (likely the dark and rumbling material that marks the "Wolf's Glen" scene) from Carl Maria von Weber's 1821 opera *Der Freischütz.* It is at the very least interesting that the compiler of the musical suggestions for Edison's 1910 *Frankenstein* reached so far back into the so-called standard repertoire; it is downright intriguing to think that the cue sheet's compiler might have supposed that the average audience of the day would have found this music to be not just affectively supportive of the scenes at hand but also, in a symbolic way, somehow meaningful.

Following the lead of the Edison Company, other nickelodeon suppliers soon enough got into the habit of sending out cue sheets in advance of their films. But by late 1910 film accompanists also found a bounty of suggestions for music, and for sound effects, in the columns that had begun to appear in the various trade journals.

Columns

As early as 1907 there were "between four and five thousand" nickelodeon theaters nationwide that attracted an audience estimated at "over two million people . . . every day of the year."[31] Trade journals were at the same time a byproduct of and a fueling source for America's burgeoning film industry. These were not publications aimed at the filmgoing public—fan magazines would come later, but only after the independent Hollywood producers had created the idea of the movie star. Rather, the trade journals were aimed at those persons involved in the nickelodeon business, primarily the East Coast filmmakers who eventually bonded to form the monopolistic Motion Picture Patents Company and the theater owners who exhibited their products, but also the manufacturers of motion-picture cameras, projectors, and film stock.

The journals began with *Views and Film Index* (1906), and after that came *Moving Picture World* (1907), *The Nickelodeon* (1909), and *Moving Picture News* (1910). At first the journals concentrated only on news of contracts and personnel changes, announcements of the various companies' latest films, descriptions and reviews of the latest technological developments, and so on. By the end of the decade, when fierce competition existed not so much between the MPPC film-makers as between the operators of nickelodeon theaters that in urban centers were often closely packed,[32] the trade journals started to run articles and even regular columns that focused on film presentation. Efficient production and fast distribution of one-reel films would be all for naught, the MPPC members knew, if patrons did not find the experience of these films to be, week after week, worth the small amount of money they spent for admission. And so writers were engaged to advise nickelodeon operators on how to maximize their audiences' enjoyment. These writers wrote about refreshments and preshow lighting, about the spacing between seats and the ordering of films into programs. Not surpris-ingly, at least a few of them wrote about films' music and sound effects.

The columnists who specifically addressed music and sound effects included such writers as Clarence E. Sinn, Louis Reeves Harrison, Clyde Martin, Ernest J. Luz, and H. L. Barnhart.[33] Sometimes they followed the example of the Edison Company's cue sheets and simply listed specific pieces, or types of generic music, that might be effectively applied to certain scenes in certain recent or forthcom-ing releases. Sometimes, and usually with a tart sense of humor, they wrote about the things that a film accompanist should definitely *not* do.[34] Accompanists are advised, for example, not to get up and go to the restroom just as a dramatic film begins its drive toward climax, or to "cut [their] chaser short" by ending their concluding music before the last patron has exited the theater,[35] or to "fun" a picture by playing a familiar tune whose lyrics perhaps related tangentially to the scene at hand but which in most ways was entirely at odds with the film's drama—for example, playing "No Wedding Bells for Me" during "a pathetic scene showing a husband mourning his dead wife,"[36] or playing "the old, friv-olous favorite 'You Made Me What I Am Today'" under a scene during which a village girl confronts the king who impregnated her and then stabs herself to death "to the heart-breaking sobs of her people."[37] And sometimes, significantly, they wrote in general terms on what film accompanists *should* do.

Accompanists should strive for continuity in their performances, the colum-nists admonished; they should "play [the] picture with just as few breaks as [they] possibly can,"[38] and their music should be "arranged [so] that not a moment is lost in changing from one theme to another."[39] Accompanists should "pick out the theme of the [entire] picture and play to it,"[40] and they should remember that "it is the general character of the picture which [they] must observe."[41] Preexisting works of music, especially of the classical sort, are indeed useful, but care should be taken because the musical structure of these works typically includes shifts of mood that might be inappropriate to the filmic scene at hand, and "the chances are a lively movement will come at the time when you should be playing a slow one."[42] Sound effects, whether played on a piano or on percussion instruments, should be used sparingly.[43] Musical gestures that are synchronized with filmic action should likewise be used sparingly. Make sure that the music does not overwhelm the film; remember that audiences come to the cinema to experience a variety of motion pictures, not to hear a concert. And so on.

Commenting on a wide range of music- and sound-centered advice columns, Rick Altman notes: "The recommendations of the trade press authors writing on film music topics are extraordinarily uniform in nature. From one publication to another and from one writer to another, only the smallest variations appear."[44] Indeed, with their contributions to the trade journals, the columnists from around 1910–1911 identified elements of what by this time was already coalescing into a common practice of film accompaniment. At least to an extent, the basic principles of this common practice were upheld even during the first quarter-century of the so-called sound film, when recorded accompanying music shared space on the soundtrack with supposedly realistic sound effects and, especially, with dialogue. Aimed primarily at pianists, the principles tentatively set out by the columnists for the trade journals certainly governed the work of musical directors whose job it was to prepare the orchestral scores that accompanied silent film during its heyday.

Sound in the Heyday of the Silent Film

Early in this chapter's previous section, the business model that allowed the nickelodeon-style film to flourish from the middle of the twentieth century's first decade until the time of World War I was contrasted with the business model that supported the feature-length silent film that emerged in the prewar years and lasted until the establishment of the sound film in the late 1920s. The contrasting business models resulted in films of a very different sort being produced by, on the one hand, the cartel of nickelodeon filmmakers who were based on America's eastern seaboard and, on the other hand, by the various independent filmmakers who either moved to or started up in the area generally known as Hollywood. In a word, the essential difference between the nickelodeon films and the feature films was one of scale.

That same word—scale—describes the essential difference between the music for the one type of film and the other. Historians have authored shelves of books that celebrate the rapid advances—in techniques of photography and editing, in screenwriting, in overall presentation of the finished product—that Hollywood filmmakers made over their relatively primitive nickelodeon forebears, and all of these are indeed part of the story. In a nutshell, the Hollywood films were simply much bigger than the nickelodeon films, and so bigger, too, had to be their musical accompaniments.

Bigger here means not just longer but louder. Almost by definition, the feature films were multi-reel affairs whose durations exceeded by far anything that the nickelodeon suppliers had to offer. One of the best-remembered of the early feature-length films is D. W. Griffith's 1915 *The Birth of a Nation;* whereas the succinct one-reel films that entertained audiences at nickelodeon theaters last just ten or twelve minutes each, the epic story told in Griffith's twelve-reel film unfolds over the course of more than three hours. Had it been exhibited in a small nickelodeon-style venue, *The Birth of a Nation* would have required that a dutiful pianist play, without stopping, for an extraordinarily long amount of time. But *The Birth of a Nation* was first exhibited in large venues, and it was accompanied not by a lone pianist but by a full orchestra.[45]

After an initial showing in Los Angeles with a score by Carli D. Elinor, *The Birth of a Nation* had its New York premiere, with the famous score composed and compiled by Joseph Breil, on March 8, 1915.[46] The accompanying ensemble was the Russian Symphony Orchestra, an ensemble that Modest Altschuler had founded in 1903 and which by 1915 perhaps had as many as ninety-five players.[47] Not all orchestras that accompanied feature-length films would have been that size, of course. But they would have been large enough to do justice to scores that, like Breil's for *The Birth of a Nation,* featured not just originally composed music and arrangements of traditional songs but also works from the standard concert repertoire. Along with such familiar items as "Listen to the Mockingbird," "Auld Lang Syne," and "Comin' through the Rye," the audiences for *The Birth of a Nation* heard partial or complete versions of, for example, the overtures to operas by Bellini, Zampa, and Weber, Tchaikovsky's *1812 Overture* and Von Suppe's *"Light Cavalry" Overture,* a movement from a Mozart mass, and—famously, for the scene in which hooded Ku Klux Klan horsemen gallop in to put down an uprising of African Americans—"The Ride of the Valkyries" from Wagner's *Die Walküre.*[48]

It was important to the score for *The Birth of a Nation*—indeed, to the scores that accompanied feature films through the rest of the silent era, and to film scores right up to the present day—that the songs and the selections from the standard concert repertoire be in the public domain. An 1897 adjustment to the American copyright law required that permission be granted (usually in exchange for a fee) from copyright holders for the use of their music in profit-making concerts or theatrical presentations. In 1917 the law was adjusted again, to require permission for the use of copyrighted material in any commercial situation, including nightclubs and movie theaters. Whereas the 1897 adjustment came about as a result of lobbying by an organization called the Music Publishers Association, the 1917 adjustment was due to lobbying by the recently formed American Society for

Composers, Authors, and Publishers (ASCAP). Led by operetta composer Victor Herbert, who in 1915 filed and eventually won a much-publicized lawsuit over a beer garden's unlicensed use of his song "Sweethearts," a veritable army of policing agents soon made it very risky for operators of highly profitable movie palaces to use ASCAP-protected music without first clearing it with ASCAP.

Music written on commission from a film studio or a movie theater, of course, was not subject to what was widely known as ASCAP's music tax. Likewise for music written—usually by composers who were not members of ASCAP, or by cash-strapped ASCAP members working under pseudonyms—upon request from a music publisher for the specific purpose of being sold as license-free library material.

Original scores were indeed composed during and even before the heyday of the American silent film, but they were few and far between. After searching the trade journals, Martin Marks was able to identify just a hundred or so nickelodeon-style American films from the 1910–1914 period that were released in tandem with arrangements for keyboard of what advertisers called "special music."[49] In the ensuing thirteen years, that is, between the sensational New York premiere of *The Birth of a Nation* in 1915 and the equally sensational premiere of Alan Crosland's recording-accompanied *The Jazz Singer* in 1927, Hollywood invested in only a few dozen films as so-called road shows. That is, ambitious producers deemed these films to be so unusual that, rather than releasing them simultaneously in venues around the country, they sent the films from city to city in the company of well-rehearsed orchestras that played scores attributed to the above-mentioned Breil and Rapee and to such other composers as William Axt, Louis F. Gottschalk, William Peters, Hugo Riesenfeld, and Louis Silvers.[50] And at movie palaces here and there throughout America, persons in charge of music sometimes took it upon themselves to compose an original score that probably was heard only in their own place of employment.[51]

Scores composed for silent films—like the celebrated score that French composer Camille Saint-Saëns wrote in 1908 for an eighteen-minute film entitled *L'Assassinat du Duc de Guise*—might well have been artistically effective, but they were not very influential. A "special" score, whether for piano or chamber ensemble or full orchestra, required not only that the music be written in advance of a film's exhibition but also that the musical notation—if it was intended for more than just a local hearing—be reproduced and distributed. "Special" music for opera was all well and good, and indeed this art form had thrived since the early seventeenth century on the idea of live presentations that were specific to certain locales and which involved certain singers who performed at just a few certain moments in time. But "special" music did not work so well in the embryonic culture of mass media, which thrived on the idea that audiences in a great many locales be exposed, more or less simultaneously, to whatever new products could be repeated over and over for as long as market interest allowed. Composed scores for silent films were perhaps praiseworthy; by and large, though, they were woefully impractical.

Not at all impractical, in contrast, were compiled scores that musical directors at individual movie theaters cobbled together for the most part from standard repertoire selections in the public domain and, significantly, from libraries of license-free material. Like the pieces that made up the *Sam Fox Moving Picture Music* volumes and other collections aimed at nickelodeon theaters, the license-free pieces that served the movie palaces were generic in their emotional or descriptive content, and they were cleverly composed so that sections could be skipped or repeated without doing damage to their musical sense. But whereas the earlier music was almost always intended for piano, the generic music that accompanied the feature film was scored for various combinations of traditional orchestral instruments or for the increasingly versatile new instrument called the theater organ.[52] With probably far more accuracy than in his account of his invention of the cue sheet, Max Winkler in his 1951 autobiography wrote: "We searched for composers who would supply what we needed and we found them. They were fine musicians, but they were specialists in just one phase of music, film music, and most of them are forgotten today. . . . And yet, in those days, gone only a few decades, their music was heard by more people in this country than the music of all the great masters combined."[53]

The commercial success of a large movie palace depended upon the ability of its musical staff not just to put together a complete and convincing score every week but to put together scores that, to the audience who attended regularly, would sound utterly new. "To achieve this," wrote Hugo Riesenfeld in 1926,

> the musical director who is obliged to prepare a new score every week must have at his disposal a limitless supply of music. For this purpose the metropolitan theaters maintain enormous libraries, some of them containing 25,000 pieces of music. These are all catalogued, not only by titles and authors, but also by the type of emotion or kind of action which they suggest. When the score [compiler] wishes a piece of music giving the atmosphere of the opening scene of *MacBeth,* he refers to the sections marked "Witch Dances" or "Ominous Music." In the same way he may instantly put his hands on music which suggests the sound of an aeroplane, anger, a runaway horse, a canoe drifting down a quiet stream.
>
> A staff of trained librarians is required to keep this stock of music constantly replenished with fresh works. . . . The compiler or arranger of scores searches down every possible alley, in every corner for something that will give just the right effect.[54]

And to help the compiler and arranger in their searches, publishers such as Carl Fischer and Belwin indeed sold license-free orchestral music "by the trainload."

The Advent of the Sound Film

The first two feature-length sound films with which Warner Bros. demonstrated its newly invented Vitaphone system—Alan Crosland's swashbuckling *Don Juan* in August 1926 and, two months later, Charles Reisner's comedy entitled *The Better 'Ole*—were accompanied by scores for the most part originally composed, not compiled in the way that Riesenfeld described.[55] But the most obvious difference between these two films and other feature films of the day was the fact that their music, instead of being performed live by a highly skilled orchestra of fifty or sixty players, was recorded on disc and then played back through an electronic amplification system. To anyone who has experienced both the rich sound of a live orchestra in a hall with reasonably good acoustics and the low-fidelity sound of scratchy phonograph recordings typical of the late 1920s, it should come as no surprise to learn that audiences for *Don Juan* and *The Better 'Ole* were not much impressed.

What the audiences at the Vitaphone demonstrations in 1926 *were* impressed by was the series of shorts that preceded these lengthy feature films. These shorts were not fictional films but, rather, true-to-life documentations of various events that the executives at Warner Bros.—apparently thinking along the same track taken thirty years earlier by participants in the cinema of attractions—hoped might catch the public's attention. In contrast to the purely visual attractions offered by their forebears, however, Warner Bros. in 1926 put forth attractions whose content was not just visual but also aural. The audio-visual attractions included a perhaps not-much-entertaining but arguably interesting introductory speech delivered by Will Hays, president of the organization called the Motion Picture Producers and Distributors of America; probably much more to the audience's liking were the attractions that featured a troupe of Russian dancers, singers of both operatic and popular persuasion, a vaudeville guitarist and a classical violinist, a comedy duo, and—significantly—the Broadway stars George Jessel and Al Jolson performing their trademark routines.

The idea of recording audio-visual attractions did not originate with Warner Bros. in 1926. It had been Thomas Edison's plan right from the start that the motion picture he supposedly invented circa 1890–91 be a companion to the phonograph that he definitely invented in 1877.[56] As early as 1891 Edison extolled the potential of what he called the "kineto-phonograph," a yet-to-be-realized device that he promised would preserve for posterity both the sound and the moving image of leading orators and actors. For the purpose of applying for a patent, Edison's engineer William Kennedy Laurie Dickson in April 1895 concocted an experimental film that linked the moving imagery of two men dancing with the sound recording of his own violin playing.[57]

Edison tried to capitalize on Dickson's work by putting on the market a device he called the Kinetophone. This was simply a Kinetoscope, as described early in this chapter, fitted out with a cylinder-based phonograph, the sounds of which a patron could listen to by means of stethoscope-like earphones while at the same viewing a motion picture through a peephole. But unlike the sounds in the Dickson experimental film, and the sounds in a film of a boxing match that Edison supposedly made but which seems not to have survived, whatever a Kinetophone customer heard had not been recorded at the same time that the camera captured the moving image; rather, it was simply a bit of music that, after the fact, had been appended to the moving image.[58] Whereas Edison in 1894 had easily secured a patent for his Kinetoscope, his efforts in June 1895 to secure a patent for the Kinetophone were not successful; the judge in charge of the hearing was apparently amused to take a peek at a forty-five-second film showing dancer Loie Fuller doing her famous "Serpentine Dance" to the tune of some arguably serpentine music, yet he dismissed the Kinetophone as not a scientific invention but, rather, "a toy."[59]

Mostly for technological reasons, although perhaps also because members of the public did not find the Kinetophone to be nearly as interesting as its inventor did, Edison's early attempts to market recorded sound combined with recorded motion-picture imagery failed.[60] Failure was experienced as well, albeit mostly for technological reasons, by the dozens of entrepreneurs who attempted, after the turn of the century, to synchronize projections of recorded imagery with the playback of recorded sound. The first of these entrepreneurs was likely Léon Gaumont, who at the Paris Exposition in 1900 demonstrated something called the Chronophone. Before the decade was out, audiences in Europe and the United States had exposure to such other novelties as the Animatophone, the Biographon, the Cameraphone, the Cinephone, the Chronophotographoscope, the Graphophonoscope, the Kinematophone, the Phoneidograph, the Photokinema, the Synchrophone, and the Vivaphone.[61] And in 1913 Edison was back on the scene, in theaters, with a much-improved version of the Kinetophone whose development almost twenty years earlier he had abandoned.

As the Greek or Latin fragments of their names suggest, these efforts amounted to pairings of a film projector with a phonograph. None of them included exhibitions of storytelling films; all of them featured audio-visual attractions whose content ranged from singers and comedians to jugglers and barking dogs, and all of them—importantly, and quite unlike Edison's Kinetophone of 1895—involved sound and imagery that had been recorded at the same time. The simultaneous recording of sound and image was relatively easy, for all that it involved was both a camera and a phonograph in effect "seeing" and "listening to" the same real-time event; the synchronized playback of the visual and aural recorded material, however, was enormously difficult, because this involved the precise coordination of two devices whose mechanisms were fundamentally different.[62] Also difficult was catering to the sonic needs of audiences in cinema's ever-larger venues; whereas a moving picture in the twentieth century's first decade and a half could easily be magnified by means of lenses, recorded sound during this same period could be amplified only by means of megaphones.

The amplification problem was handily solved early in the postwar years when the Western Electric company, the manufacturing division of American Telephone and Telegraph, perfected the electronic/electrical loudspeaker. The first public demonstration of the loudspeaker, or public-address system, took place in 1919 at an outdoor Victory Day celebration in New York; soon afterward, an elaborate PA system was installed in New York's 5,300-seat Capitol Theater, not for the purpose of enlarging the sonic components of audio-visual attractions but, rather, for the sake of amplifying radio broadcasts of boxing matches and speeches by presidential candidates.

The coordination problem was still an issue when Warner Bros., having entered into an exclusive agreement with Western Electric, in August 1926 first demonstrated its Vitaphone system with an apparently fascinating program of shorts and a perhaps not-so-fascinating exhibition of the feature-length *Don Juan*. But soon this problem, too, was solved, thanks largely to the work of German engineers who since 1919 had been working on the idea of recording sound not, as per Edison's phonograph, by having a vibrating needle cut the analogues of sound waves into the soft surface of a smoothly rotating cylinder or disc but, rather, by converting sound waves into electrical signals and then photographing, with a motion picture camera, the complex vibrations of sensitive filaments triggered by those signals. Whereas Warner Bros.' sound-on-disc Vitaphone system involved separate machines that captured image and sound on two different physical surfaces, the new sound-on-film system—called Tri-Ergon when it was patented in Germany in 1922 and then called Movietone after it was licensed by the Fox studio in 1926—involved just a single device that captured both image and sound on a single roll of celluloid.[63]

Fox's Movietone system was demonstrated to the public for the first time in May 1927 with a brief newsreel remarkable only for its precise synchronization of image and sound. In October of that year Warner Bros. released its third Vitaphone feature; like the earlier *Don Juan* and *The Better 'Ole*, *The Jazz Singer* was in essence a silent film with an orchestral accompaniment—and occasional sound effects—recorded on phonograph discs; it veered sharply from the just-established norm, however, in that it included a few segments in which the main character, played by the charismatic Al Jolson, not only sings but speaks.[64] A year later Fox brought out the first feature-length film to utilize the newly licensed Movietone system. As in *The Jazz Singer,* the main character in Fox's *Mother Knows Best* (John G. Blystone, 1928) occasionally sings;[65] significantly, throughout the film *all* the characters speak, and always their recorded sounds are precisely synchronized with their recorded images.

The Jazz Singer changed the course of cinema because its overwhelmingly enthusiastic reception made it obvious at least to everyone in the American film industry that the public very much wanted characters with voices. Although today barely remembered, *Mother Knows Best* also changed the course of cinema, because it made it just as obvious that, if a studio indeed wanted to make a credible sound film, the preferred method was not sound-on-disc but sound-on-film.

The competition between Warner Bros.' Vitaphone system and Fox's eventually victorious Movietone system played out for a few years. And Hollywood still had a long way to go before its constituents collectively figured out what to do with the capabilities of recorded sound that suddenly were at their disposal. But after *The Jazz Singer* in 1927 and then *Mother Knows Best* in 1928, it was clear that the glorious heyday of American silent film—and with it the entire idea of the silent screen—had come to an end.

2

CLASSICAL HOLLYWOOD, 1928–1946   Kathryn Kalinak

The most volatile period in American film history, in terms of the relationship between moving images and sound, was the transition between silent and sound production, in which new technologies collided with established practices and resulted in changes to film production, economics, aesthetics, and reception. This industry-wide conversion challenged and ultimately strengthened American filmmaking while marking a shift in responsibility for what the audience heard. In the silent era, sound was determined by theater exhibitors and by the music directors and accompanists they hired. With the conversion to synchronized sound, control shifted to the makers of film and would come firmly under the control of the studios. By the mid-1930s, less than a decade after the first feature-length synchronized sound films, conventions for the use of sound across all aspects of the soundtrack were in place. Sound did not alter Hollywood's dominance in the international film marketplace, and thus these conventions would provide a formidable model for filmmakers outside Hollywood to emulate, update, challenge, and revolutionize. American filmmaking today is descended from this era, and thus it behooves us to understand how synchronized sound came to be negotiated by the industry and specifically by the creative workers both in front of and behind the camera.

The Transition to Sound

As early as 1928, it was becoming clear that the future of Hollywood was tied to sound. Even mediocre sound films were outdrawing well-made silents, and the public demand for sound films, according to producer William De Mille, was outrunning the "ability of the studios to furnish it."[1] Attendance at the movies skyrocketed—from 60 million per week in 1927 to 90 million in 1930[2]—and profits surged. Sound revitalized an industry in danger of losing its edge.

Both major and minor studios pursued synchronized sound—described at the time as "the great cinematic convulsion"[3]—in a massive game of catch-up with the industry leaders—the scrappy Warner brothers and the ambitious William Fox—who took the leap into synchronized sound ahead of the rest (Warner Bros. with sound-on-disc and Fox Film Corporation with sound-on-film). In advance of the stock market crash of 1929, Hollywood financed its conversion to sound, estimated at the time at $31 million, and soon began to reap the benefits. As many film historians have noted, had Hollywood waited much longer, there would have been no ready capital for a sound revolution: "If the producers had waited until October 26, 1929—as they might well have done except for Warner Brothers and Fox—sound would have been impossible for ten more years."[4]

Although Warner Bros. exploited sound-on-disc technology, the sound-on film technology, first used by Fox, was proving the better option. In May 1928, the Big Five—MGM, Universal, First National, Paramount–Famous [Players]–Lasky (hereafter Paramount), and Producers Distributing Corp.—acting as a whole, leased Western Electric's new sound-on-film system. Other studios were right behind. The Radio Corporation of America (RCA) had devised its own competing sound-on-film system, Photophone, and when passed over by the Big Five it allied with the Film Booking Office and the Keith-Albee-Orpheum vaudeville circuit to form Radio-Keith-Orpheum (RKO) to exploit Photophone. Fox improved its sound-on-film technology, Movietone, to produce the first talkie filmed on location, *In Old Arizona* (Irving Cummings, 1928), touting a soundtrack that "not only caught and reproduced with fidelity the voices of the actors, but actually filmed and reproduced the natural sounds of the outdoors, the whispering of the wind, the song of the birds."[5] Eventually, even Warner Bros. made the switch to a sound-on-film system.

Studios continued some silent production for a number of years to accommodate small town and rural theaters and foreign markets not yet equipped for sound, and some filmmakers, such as Charlie Chaplin, tried valiantly to sustain silent filmmaking practices into the sound era. Initially, studio heads and production chiefs at the studios not yet equipped for sound, and thus with the most to lose, urged caution, such as Adolph Zukor at Paramount, Carl Laemmle Jr. at Universal, or Samuel Goldwyn, who boldly maintained that "silent films will never entirely be vanquished from the screens of the world."[6] But by mid-1929,

B. P. Schulberg, Paramount's head of West Coast production, threw in the towel. "Sound is going to be our business for a long time," he said before adding, in vintage Hollywood double-speak, "We are not going back to the silent screen ever except for occasional pictures."[7] By 1931, silent production had virtually ceased. As Harry Carr had predicted in 1929, on the front page of the *Los Angeles Times* no less, talkies would prove "the tombstone of the silent drama."[8]

Hollywood's conversion to sound must have looked like what William De Mille described as "bedlam": "New sound stages are being built. Directors, writers, and actors are all trying to learn something of the new idea and worrying about whether they are adapted to it. A complicated industry which has taken over fifteen years to develop is, to a certain extent, swept away overnight and must prepare to produce at once and in quantity a product it knows almost nothing about, with new and little understood tools and a personnel of novices."[9] Many film histories have matched his description such as this one in *The Shattered Silents*: "The shape and especially the sound of cinema movies today was decided during those few years. Not in any coolheaded, rational fashion: but amidst unbelievable confusion, stupidity, accident, ambition and greed."[10] Yet what scholars of film history have demonstrated, and here I am thinking of Douglas Gomery, Donald Crafton, Rick Altman, Alan Williams, David Bordwell, Janet Staiger, and Kristin Thompson, among others, is the ultimate adaptability of the Hollywood system. As Gomery explains, "Speed of change does not necessarily connote disorder, chaos, or confusion. The Hollywood monopolists cooperated to eliminate all-important problems, and insure maximum profits and growth for themselves. Consolidation and merger, not panic or anarchy, should be the labels we use to characterize the switch to sound by the U.S. motion picture industry."[11] Sound brought major changes in technology, aesthetics, and reception, and Hollywood as an institutional practice absorbed those changes without compromising economic security. The system ultimately prevailed and prospered.

On the Front Lines: The Sound Revolution and Studio Workers

This is not, however, to discount the havoc wreaked on the lives of studio workers. At the time it certainly looked as though "the motion picture world was being rocked to its very bottom by a revolutionary reorganization that touched every person, every element in it."[12] Hollywood adapted to sound successfully, but it was a different story on the front lines, for the established actors, directors, screenwriters, producers, and musicians who experienced the conversion as tumultuous and even career-ending. Predicted William De Mille, "There will be many heart-breaks before the studios adjust their methods and their players to new conditions."[13]

Sound shifted the focus for a number of crafts in the studio system. Actors had to adapt to a new style of acting without the declamatory postures and facial pantomime that had developed in the silent era, and they had to execute dialogue with clarity and precision. To be cast in talkies, actors had to pass a voice test. According to Jesse Lasky, "The microphone test is the one sure method" for testing the ability of actors to speak onscreen.[14] With so much at stake, "microphone fright"[15] was enough to "make strong men weep" and cause even experienced stars to make "perfect boobs of themselves."[16] Well into the 1930s a successful voice test was a paramount concern of talent scouts and casting directors.

There are many legendary stories about the inability of silent stars to negotiate the transformation to sound; some of them are actually true. Heavy foreign accents did derail the careers of Pola Negri, Vilma Banky, and Ramon Navarro (and very likely would have ruined Rudolph Valentino's had he lived); a high-pitched voice doomed John Gilbert (made even more unappealing by early sound recording and amplification that made higher, nasal voices sound particularly shrill).[17] Others may have been hurt because they were established stars of the silent cinema: Mary Pickford and Douglas Fairbanks retired from the screen; William S. Hart signed with Hal Roach, but before he could make a single talkie his contract was dissolved by "mutual consent";[18] Lillian Gish went to Broadway; Gloria Swanson and Norma Talmadge faded away. As William De Mille so aptly puts it, "In very few cases does the voice of a screen idol satisfy 'fans' who, for years, have been imagining it."[19] Some silent actors with stage experience fared better: Ronald Colman, John Barrymore, and William Powell, for instance. Others, such as Norma Shearer, Greta Garbo, Gary Cooper, and Janet Gaynor, retooled with the help of dialogue coaches and elocution experts. Rin Tin Tin, trained by vocal command in his silent films, now had to take orders via offscreen visual gestures. He proved a trouper. "They were able to get him to do anything they wanted to without saying a word. During a scene in which they were working with Rinty and little Davey Lee, they had ten times more trouble with the youngster than they did with the dog . . . and the dog had ten times more to do!"[20]

An influx of talent in the late 1920s from New York's Broadway and vaudeville stages filled the gap. Barbara Stanwyck, Bette Davis, and James Cagney, each with some minor success on Broadway, managed lengthy careers on the big screen; others from vaudeville, such as Al Jolson, experienced meteoric but relatively short-lived success. Ultimately, most New York hopefuls proved as unsuccessful in the new medium as many silent film stars had been. Actress Helen Hayes, for instance, arrived from Broadway with much ballyhoo, but worked in Hollywood for just a few short years before returning to New York. (A second wave of talent met with more success slightly later: Broadway star Fred Astaire and regionally trained actors Katharine Hepburn, Henry Fonda, and James Stewart.) Joseph Egli, casting head at Fox, maintained: "We have made good tests of inexperienced people and I can say that a number of our artists with no legitimate experience record in a very satisfactory manner. . . . The quality of the voice and not always the experience of the actor counts more than is generally known."[21] Perhaps as a publicity stunt—but who knows? Barbara Stanwyck had actually been a telephone operator—it was announced that the studios were testing young female telephone operators who might have "just the right voices for the talkies."[22] Ultimately, the public was drawn to actors who could speak naturally onscreen without "the 'high school' declamation" of many stage actors.[23] Claimed Jesse Lasky: "Ideal voices for the films are those which are natural."[24]

Screenwriters now had to be proficient in reimagining a story in verbal terms and writing snappy dialogue to carry it along. As Charles R. Condon, an early sound screenwriter, put it: "In writing scenarios [for silent film], one must explain the entire plot visually. That is the basis upon which a scenario writer primarily works—to tell the audience the story by the things the actors do. The Vitaphone and kindred devices have changed that method. Now we can explain a story by means of speeches put into the mouths of actors. By one speech we can bridge a gap which might have taken 100 feet of photography."[25] But that speech was the key. Talent scouts were sent East for "sizing up the situation" on Broadway and recruiting playwrights.[26] One studio advertised in *Variety*: "One of the biggest motion picture producing organizations has room on its staff for several of the BEST dialogue writers and stage directors in show business."[27] At one point, the studios actually sponsored a nationwide talent search for fresh young playwrights to write for the movies. Daniel Taradash, who won the contest, got the plum assignment of adapting *Golden Boy* (Rouben Mamoulian, 1939) for the screen. What he had, according to Taradash, was the "gift of verbal dialogue."[28]

Directors had to elicit clearly spoken dialogue and coach actors without the megaphones that had allowed them literally to talk actors through the scene, and they now had to create sequences for the microphone as well as for the camera. Initially, soundproof booths made the camera difficult to manage, and shooting through their glass windows posed new problems. As with actors and writers, directors from New York with legitimate stage experience flocked to Hollywood, such as William Keighley, who signed with Warner Bros., and Rouben Mamoulian and George Cukor, with Paramount. Not all New York transplants fared as well, and some of the most successful directors of early sound film, indeed of the classical studio sound era, transitioned from silent cinema where they had worked their way up the ranks: W. S. Van Dyke, Raoul Walsh, Howard Hawks, John Ford, and Alfred Hitchcock.

Producers had to figure out how to maintain world dominance in the export market now that spoken dialogue locked Hollywood films into the English language. In the silent era it was an easy matter to customize films by translating intertitles into different languages. Hollywood was at an advantage in the sound revolution, years ahead of almost all other film industries around the world. Still, producers faced what to do about dialogue for foreign markets which "want their own cultural development . . . their own traditions and ideals . . . their own language pictures."[29] Subtitling was an early attempt to solve the problem. Many producers, however, favored restaging English-language productions in foreign languages, with foreign actors stepping on the set after the English-language actors had finished, and the crew shooting scenes multiple times with different actors and languages. Fox's *The Big Trail* (Raoul Walsh, 1930) was shot—on location no less—with the dialogue scenes first in English and then in Spanish, German, French, and Italian. MGM generated the most elaborate system for such multilinguals; Paramount produced theirs in France with European actors at the Joinville studio they had purchased for this purpose. Some Hollywood stars appeared in foreign-language versions themselves: in addition to English, Adolphe Menjou was able to work in French and Spanish, Marlene Dietrich in German.[30] Dubbing was the most economical approach, having foreign actors reread the English-language actor's lines in a foreign language, and after 1931 it was technically possible to achieve an acceptable approximation of synchronization between voice and lips. Audiences worldwide, however, resisted both multilinguals and dubbed versions; in the former, audiences had to watch minor actors perform roles made famous by Hollywood stars, and in the latter they could not hear the voices of their favorite actors. As *Variety* reported: "Dubbed pictures haven't gone over so well, with the public preferring American dialogue unchanged."[31] Ultimately, subtitling would prevail overseas, an inexpensive solution that preserved the performances and voices of Hollywood's biggest asset: its stars.

The Hardest Hit of All: Musicians

No longer needed in the pit orchestras of silent film auditoriums or on the sets of silent films, musicians watched, first in trepidation and then in horror, as their profession disappeared. Headlines, such as this one from the inimitable *Variety*, told the story: "N.Y. Musicians and Organists Get Body Blow of All Time from 'Sound.'"[32] Despite organized opposition from the American Federation of Musicians to "the substitution of mechanical music, synchronized to screen action, for the personal appearance of musicians,"[33] the Loews theater chain eliminated the orchestras and organists from thirty of its New York theaters in 1928. *Variety* lamented: "Never in the record of New York union musicians has there been such a lack of work, with prospects of other circuits taking a similar course when the anticipated sound effects are finally installed."[34] Later that year, *Variety* grimly predicted, "Over 50,000 musicians may be thrown out of work within the next two years owing to the general use of talking equipment in theatres."[35] Upward of 150 musicians lost their jobs providing mood music on silent film sets. Unemployed musicians flocked to Hollywood hoping for work, and Los Angeles found itself "swamped by migration," with over 4,000 unemployed musicians vying for studio work.[36]

Yet there was plenty of music in early sound film. They were dubbed "talkies," but early sound films, musicals and non-musicals alike, were filled with copious amounts of singing. As Katherine Spring notes, more than half of the films produced in 1929–1930 featured at least one song.[37] Plans to feature opera stars in filmed operas never quite materialized in the early years of synchronized sound, though many opera stars were screen-tested and some did appear in films (John McCormack, Lawrence Tibbett, Grace Moore, Feodor Chaliapin, Lily Pons). But for the most part, it was popular music that filled the soundtrack. Actors who could sing were at an advantage. Luella Parsons proclaimed, "Players must not only Photo well, but have trained voices."[38] Even extras with musical talent had an edge. Claimed Jesse Lasky, "Those [extras] who can do any audible specialties such as singing, dancing, playing of instruments or any other added performances, are much in demand and extras who wish to rise above their present classification will do well to develop such ability."[39]

Songwriters (in Hollywood, always differentiated from composers) drawn from Tin Pan Alley and Broadway found ready work in Hollywood: Irving Berlin, Billy Rose, Walter Donaldson. Warner Bros. announced the formation of an exclusive song-writing department in 1929 with eight "song creators," including Al Dubin, all of them touted as "big-time figures in Broadway's melody lane."[40] Arrangers, orchestrators, and conductors were siphoned off from Broadway, too, such as Max Steiner and Alfred Newman. Faced with escalating music licensing fees, studios found it expedient and cost-effective to purchase music publishing houses, as in the case of Warner Bros., which bought M. Witmark and Sons. Music featured in films was cross-promoted on the radio, on the stage, and through recordings and sheet music, an early example of synergy.

With so many songs on the soundtrack, it wasn't long before producers realized that background scoring could give their films an edge in the competitive marketplace of early sound film. Luther Reed at Fox declared, "Producers will find that new music must be found and the first company to see this need and enter the field will profit greatly by it."[41] He was especially keen on original composition: "The demand of finer and original music is infinitely greater than it has ever been."[42] Initially, such scoring was quite simple: a few short musical bridges to connect sequences, mood music to create atmosphere or emotion, similar to silent film accompaniment, a quotation from a well-known piece of classical music or, more likely, a reprise of a popular song. Early on, composers from the concert hall were tapped for this work, such as Charles Wakefield Cadman, at the time a noted composer of opera and art music, who was hired by Fox. Studios began building orchestras to accommodate the new need for music. James Wierzbicki reports that by 1929 all twenty-six studios in Hollywood had an orchestra,[43] and *Variety* estimated that in 1930, 300 musicians were at work "in the film plants."[44]

Musicians were also finding work at recording studios on the East Coast, where some of the work of recording Hollywood soundtracks took place. In 1929,

United Artists announced that they would break ground for a new soundstage in Hollywood to provide synchronized scores for all their films, but until it was complete they would continue synchronizing their pictures in the East.[45] At the Camden, New Jersey, lab of the Victor Talking Machine Company, musicians were working up to fourteen hours a day "recording themes for sound pictures for all the major companies affiliated with Western Electric."[46]

Studios began to organize music departments and hire musical directors to head them. Universal appointed Joseph Cherniavsky, a Russian transplant from the concert hall, but many of the first studio music directors cut their teeth in silent cinema: Hugo Reisenfeld, who included *Sunrise* (F. W. Murnau, 1928) among his score credits, at United Artists; Erno Rapee, a conductor of New York cinemas who scored *The Iron Horse* (John Ford, 1924), at Warner Bros.; Leo Forbstein, who conducted cinema orchestras in Kansas City and Grauman's Egyptian in Hollywood, who followed Rapee at Warner Bros.; and William Axt, who scored *Ben-Hur* (Fred Niblo, 1925) and *Don Juan* (Alan Crosland, 1926), at MGM. Other musicians with experience in silent film crossed over into sound. Carl Stalling, who had been a silent film accompanist in Kansas City, joined the new Disney studio as a composer (although he would soon decamp for the animation unit at Warner Bros.). While some of the earliest employees of studio music departments, such as Steiner, Reisenfeld, and Rapee, came from Europe, it was the second wave of European émigrés in the mid-1930s, fleeing political turmoil in Europe, that would shift the balance in studio music departments from America to Europe.

The craze for popular music sputtered by 1931, however, coinciding with one of the worst years of the Depression. Popular songs no longer filled the soundtrack, and songwriters found themselves unemployed. Many returned to New York. The West Coast offices of music publishing firms trimmed staff and some closed offices entirely. The background score was essentially eliminated and music relegated to the Main Title and End Title. Virtually the only music present in a film had to be performed onscreen and justified by the plot. Explained Max Steiner, "They never used music unless it could be explained by the presence of a source like an orchestra, piano player, phonograph or radio, which was specified in the script."[47] Of fifty-nine staff composers, MGM retained only "a couple"; Fox's music department "shrunk to a mere handful or less," and Paramount, which once had twelve staff composers, was down to three.[48] MGM disbanded its entire orchestra in 1931, and it was far from the only studio to do so. It was no better on the East Coast, where New York musicians battled over "job scarcity" and *Variety* reported that, like Los Angeles, "New York is . . . over-crowded with musicians."[49] Of course, the Depression affected more than musicians in Hollywood: layoffs, reduced paychecks, shrunken production schedules, and threatened shutdowns were widespread. Movie theaters closed and attendance fell precipitously. It would be a few years before studios acknowledged the utility, much less the necessity, of the background score. And until they did, there were a few very lean years for musicians (as well as many others) in Hollywood.

Sound: A New Profession Is Born

The advent of sound, however, created a new set of studio jobs: sound engineers, experts who would oversee the installation, maintenance, and development of recording systems; recording specialists, often engineers, who captured the sound; and a variety of postproduction personnel such as sound mixers, sound effects specialists known as effects men, and sound editors, among others. Many of these new sound workers came from the radio and telephone industries. Albert De Sart, head of the sound department at Paramount, was trained in chemical engineering, had worked for the telephone company, and was a radio engineer during the war. Nathan Levinson, head of sound at Warner Bros., was an electrical engineer and, like De Sart, was a radio engineer during the war. Murray Spivack, on the other hand, an early effects man and later a postproduction mixer who numbered among his credits *King Kong* (Merian C. Cooper and Ernest B. Schoedsack, 1933), had been a percussionist in New York.

Initially, sound was recorded on a single live track and captured simultaneously with the recording of the images. The only way to allow editing within a scene was to film with more than one camera from different angles and different focal distances. Technicians had limited ability to manipulate sound. The volume could be adjusted to minimize distortion, for example, or the amount of electrical current could be regulated before the electrical impulses were sent to the recording devices, located, often, in another building entirely. Prerecorded sound effects and music for subsequent playback on the set during filming resulted in poor sound quality, so, like the dialogue, they were generally recorded as the action was being filmed. In the case of musicals with big production numbers and complex logistics, however, it was often necessary to prerecord music and play it back during filming, even with the diminished sound quality. Otherwise, musicians were either written into a scene and appeared in the film, or were positioned offscreen and recorded along with the action; the latter was the case with the Astaire-Rogers musicals at RKO, which kept orchestras on set (but out of sight) and utilized live recording right up until *Top Hat* (Mark Sandrich, 1935).[50] At Universal, the composer Hans J. Salter remembers the orchestra in a tent in the corner of the soundstage.[51] Effects men had to hide, too, which wasn't always easy. Murray Spivack remembers dragging an automobile motor onto the set to get the sound of a car engine.

Picking up sound often required imaginative solutions. Scenes had to be blocked to best utilize the microphone hidden on the set. One typical solution, favored at Warner Bros., was to outfit a telephone with a microphone and place it in the scene. But these microphones were omnidirectional and picked up every sound within their range indiscriminately, and thus controlling noise on the set became a constant problem. As a reporter from the *Los Angeles Examiner* described her experience visiting a soundstage, "A too-loudly drawn breath, the rustle of a garment, the turning of a book page, a puff on a pipe will sound like a machine-gun attack."[52] Dialogue scenes were recorded in sound rehearsals, test versions designed to spot problems and fix them before the cameras rolled. Norman Foster, then a young actor fresh from Broadway, remembers listening to the playback of a sound rehearsal on the set of *Gentlemen of the Press* (Millard Webb, 1929) only to hear "a noise like a tornado" roaring through it, produced, it was soon ascertained, by the actor Walter Huston "tearing off his little corner of newspaper."[53] The solution: wet the newspaper.

Everything was heavily padded to absorb sound: the walls of the soundstage, the set, the props, even the shoes of the actors. Paramount ordered "bales" of woolen blanket material that they used to canopy the sets. As the industry organ, *Sound Waves*, reported, "Studio officials have found these coverings of heavy cloth excellent assurance that silence will prevail during the making of talking sequences, for all outside noises are absorbed by the heavy woolen material."[54] Actors had to keep movement to a minimum. Doing so while singing proved difficult for some, however: Eleanor Powell stood on a rubber mat because she tapped her feet when she sang; Robert Taylor kept his hands in his pockets to prevent him from snapping his fingers; and Jeanette MacDonald held the back of a chair to keep from swaying in time to the music.[55] Lights were noisy, as were the cameras that were housed in soundproof and immobile booths known as "tanks" or "iceboxes." As late as 1937, sound could be difficult to control. A mysterious tapping, inaudible on the set of *The Good Earth* (Sidney Franklin, 1937), materialized on its soundtrack. Its recording director, Douglas Shearer, explained: "It was traced, and we found a plumber hammering a pipe a quarter of a mile away. The pipe ran under the sound stage."[56] Outdoor and location shooting was a nightmare. The *Los Angeles Times* published a series of cartoons depicting the troubles of location filming with sound (see figure 2). On *Hallelujah!* (King Vidor, 1929), "lookouts were posted to warn director and players on the first approach of airplanes."[57]

A number of developments gradually improved sound recording. The microphone was soon no longer "an impossibly severe and immovable master."[58] Directional mics could isolate and capture a single sound source. Portable booms made mics mobile. "Blimps," portable soundproof housing for the camera, did the same for the camera. Incandescent lighting replaced noisy carbon arc lamps. The Movieola, the standard device for film editing, was adapted for sound-on-film systems in 1930; "blooping" eliminated the pop produced by a film splice running over the sound head of the projector. Improved prerecording and playback allowed singers to prerecord their songs and lip-sync to playback on the set without unduly compromising sound quality. Noise reduction systems were introduced.

Two technological developments in 1929, generally credited to the directors Rouben Mamoulian and King Vidor, were especially important. The introduction of more than one microphone by Mamoulian for one sequence in his 1929

FIGURE 2: A series of cartoons in the *Los Angeles Times* depicts a sound man on location shushing, among other things, a car, a fire truck, a train, and a baby. *Los Angeles Times Sunday Magazine*, December 1, 1929, 5.

film *Applause* opened up the possibility of multiple microphones and multichannel recording. Sound mixers would soon combine and blend multiple sources of sound from their position at a console on the set, initially mixing "in the air," meaning live on the set. Postsynchronization allowed King Vidor to shoot entire sequences on *Hallelujah!* silent, enabling him to exploit the moving camera while waiting until postproduction to synchronize sound effects to previously filmed action. This demonstrated that sound could be divorced from capturing an image. Of course, Walt Disney perfected the synchronization of image and sound more than a year earlier with his first sound cartoon, *Steamboat Willie* (1928); consequently, the term "mickey mousing" came into Hollywood's vocabulary to denote the precise synchronization of music and onscreen action.

These technological developments liberated filmmaking from live sound and facilitated a shift in focus from sound recording to sound rerecording. Both the radio and the record industry were still locked into live performance: radio at this time was largely transmitted live; phonograph recordings had to be made in a single take until after World War II. As Lea Jacobs points out, "Film was effectively the first medium that afforded extended opportunities for the recombination of sounds after the recording stage."[59] Although the process was gradual and transpired at different studios at different times, the technique of rerecording in postproduction (referred to as "dubbing" at that time in the industry) begins to appear in trade journals as early as 1929 and in practice around 1931.[60] Dubbing allowed for sound to be rerecorded after the film had been shot without unduly compromising sound quality. Now problematic sound could be fixed in postproduction so that, for instance, a line of dialogue could be rerecorded in a process known as "looping." Fred Astaire could dub the sound of his taps in postproduction, a painstakingly laborious process but one that produced clean and sharp sound. Most importantly, sound could be manipulated for specific effects. For *King Kong*, Murray Spivack created Kong's "love grunt" by recording his own growl through a megaphone and slowing it down to half speed (thus lowering its register).[61] He created the sound of the elevated train with "a pair of rollerskates on a steel plate . . . and just a couple of little bumps on them."[62] The language of the "animal men," in *Island of Lost Souls* (Erle C. Kenton, 1932), was produced by Loren L. Ryder, the rerecording engineer, by mixing animal and human sounds, playing it backward and then slowing it down.[63] Film historians have estimated that anywhere between 50 and 100 percent of sound in this era was rerecorded.[64]

By this time, studios had begun creating "noise libraries," where the "booming of guns, howling of gales, airplane motors and many other varieties of recorded sounds are [collected] . . . for possible use in motion pictures."[65] MGM's library, the first in existence, was "said to be worth a fortune."[66] Universal's contained "8,000,000 feet of sound track," the equivalent of 1,500 miles.[67] As early as 1931, William De Mille, writing for the Academy of Motion Picture

Arts and Sciences, proclaimed that "the hands of the creative artist have been freed,"[68] but it was closer to 1933 when the technology was in place to allow separate tracks for dialogue, sound effects, and music, recorded at different times and in different places (and often with little or no relationship to onscreen sources), to be mixed in postproduction after the film had been edited. It then took until the late 1930s for these practices to be fully deployed throughout the studio system.

Innovation and improvements in sound recording and rerecording continued throughout the 1930s and 1940s. As Helen Hanson and Steve Neale have demonstrated, "The 'soundscapes' of Hollywood's films were constantly changing as sound personnel sought to provide solutions to problems" and generally to improve the experience of sound.[69] One noteworthy development was the creation of stereophonic sound at Disney for *Fantasia* (1940). Dubbed "Fantasound," the system propelled stereophonic sound through speakers positioned strategically in specially outfitted theaters to surround audiences in sound, not unlike Dolby systems of today, and utilized forerunners of noise reduction systems that were decades away. Less than epic box office returns for *Fantasia*, however, coupled with the expense of outfitting individual theaters, doomed the venture.

Training and retraining the industry for synchronized sound was managed on a variety of fronts. Paramount offered classes on sound to their employees; First National established a "talking school" for their actors,[70] MGM for their cameramen.[71] Private schools and coaches suddenly materialized in Hollywood. Advertisements targeting actors without stage experience began appearing in the trades such as one that promised to teach "Intonation, Transition of Speech, Poise, How to Laugh, Make Your Audience Cry, Repose, English, and Every Essential as Used on the Legitimate Stage. Dancing. Foreign Artists Need our Method. Private Lessons or in Class."[72] So many "Schools of Dramatic Art" and classes in "Voice Culture" came into existence that they merited a separate section in the phone book.

But the best-organized and most successful of these efforts was launched by the workers themselves, who in 1927 founded an organization, the Academy of Motion Picture Arts and Sciences, to advance the industry. From 1928 to 1930, and again in 1936, the Academy School in Sound Fundamentals not only trained sound recordists but also retrained cinematographers, lighting directors, editors, costumers, and set designers to work in the new medium. By 1930, over 900 employees from seventeen different studios had been through the Academy's school.[73] The Academy sponsored lectures, published a *Technical Digest* and *Technical Bulletin*, teamed up with the Society of Motion Picture Engineers (SMPE) to disseminate technical information about sound recording, and produced *Recording Sound for Motion Pictures* (1931), a collection of lectures from the Academy School.

Classical Filmmaking and Sound

Hollywood, like the nation itself, had been hard hit by the Depression. Initially it might have seemed that Hollywood was immune to its effects—1930 was a peak year for attendance—but by 1931, theaters were closing, movie attendance was down, profits plummeted, and the majors were straining under massive debt loads. Beginning in 1933, with Franklin D. Roosevelt now president, newly instituted economic reforms and recovery programs began to provide some relief. Attendance at the movies began to increase, an upward trend that would not peak until 1946. The first signs of economic recovery couldn't have come at a better time for Hollywood, which was at this moment poised on the brink of a major creative leap as a result of advances in sound. What emerged from this convergence of technological development and economic recovery was what David Bordwell, Janet Staiger, and Kristin Thompson have dubbed "classical" filmmaking.[74] Throughout the remainder of the 1930s, Hollywood perfected a combination of technology and aesthetics informed by economics, enacted through style, and shared among workers at the various studios.

Sound—dialogue, sound effects, and music—like other aspects of filmmaking in Hollywood, was produced on an assembly-line model that exploited the individual contributions of a number of different workers, each performing a highly specific task. Hollywood depended upon its legions of behind-the-scenes workers, and without them the finished products that the public consumed would not have been possible. Such a collaborative system allowed for quick, efficient, and standardized production and fostered allegiance to the studio rather than to individual productions. The description of Hollywood as a factory was a feature of much writing about Hollywood as early as the 1920s. The conversion to synchronized sound challenged Hollywood's mode of production but did not subvert it. The system quickly adapted to the needs of sound production, generating standard operating procedures and best practices that responded to changing technologies. And yet, the system depended upon a certain degree of product differentiation for marketability. Indeed, sound would become one of the ways through which a studio could differentiate its product, such as the innovative use of sound in Universal's horror films or the early use of symphonic scoring at RKO. I am interested here in outlining what craftspeople actually did in the practice of sound during this period, whether it be creating, coaching, directing, or delivering dialogue; recording and rerecording sound; or composing a musical score. Of course, the practice of sound differed from studio to studio, from production to production, and from year to year as Hollywood adapted to numerous developments in sound technology. So consider this an overview of a process that was ever changing throughout the period from 1933 to 1946.

Dialogue

Dialogue was the engine of Hollywood's assembly line for sound. Because it was directly tied to narrative exposition, dialogue was privileged in Hollywood's hierarchy of sound, typically the component in the sound mix that drew the audience's attention first and foremost, usually through volume. But the genesis of dialogue was long before. Although it was subject to numerous changes before it was ever uttered by an actor on the soundstage, dialogue was created by the screenwriter. Early sound films were loaded with dialogue to showcase the new medium and screenwriters assumed a more prominent position in the studio hierarchy. In the hyperbole common to the era, "The 'Talkies' have made the writers the King-Pin of creative work."[75] Some studios employed as many as seventy-five writers, necessitating new buildings for them. Victory Pictures, a short-lived B studio, boasted, "over fifty ace scenarists" alone.[76] By 1931, it was reported that 300 "Word-Artists" were working in the studio system.[77]

During the transition years between silent and sound film, dialogue experts were routinely assigned to scripts to write the dialogue. Even Frances Marion, called by the Writers Guild "the most prolific writer in Hollywood history,"[78] turned her scripts over to "a second writer who specialises in writing dialogue."[79] Films of this era often carried separate credits for different writing functions: "screenplay," "dialogue," "additional dialogue," and "story." But as the 1930s wore on, such contributions were increasingly obscured and writing dialogue for another writer's screenplay was increasingly uncredited. In fact, the term "script doctor" was coined in the 1930s to refer to writers, often uncredited playwrights and novelists, who were brought in to fix, polish, or otherwise punch up dialogue, such as, famously, William Faulkner and F. Scott Fitzgerald. In 1941, the Screen Writers Guild regulated the practice, putting in place a series of rules for screen credit, but the practice of script doctoring continues to the present day.

Actors now had to memorize specific lines of dialogue. For those with stage experience, this was not a problem, but for actors who had learned their trade in silent film, memorization, like the dreaded voice test, proved another challenge to conquer. Actors developed strategies for learning lines, trading techniques and sharing secrets in acting handbooks, the trades, and even fan magazines. Paul Muni, known for "deep and intensive study on the part," knew all his lines long before shooting began, while Reginald Owen confessed that he lost "the essence of the screen—life and vitality—through too much rehearsal" and learned his at the last minute.[80] Bette Davis, too, would usually learn her lines the night before: "Then they are fresh in my mind for the day's work. But if I have a difficult scene with many long speeches, I start learning it weeks ahead."[81]

Sound produced the phenomenon of the dialogue coach and the dialogue director. Both were charged with helping actors deliver a performance. The dialogue coach generally worked one-on-one with an actor to realize a performance from a script. As Martin Shingler, one of the few scholars to focus the spotlight on this craft, has convincingly demonstrated, dialogue coaches did more than rehearse line readings. According to Shingler, Bette Davis and her long-time dialogue director (and later director) Irving Rapper "spent considerable time preparing for her roles . . . working closely on the script, developing her characterization, rehearsing her lines, and devising her interpretation."[82]

Dialogue directors were generally in charge of all aspects of dialogue, from preparation to delivery on set; they became so important that they often shared screen credit with the director. In the early years of sound, it was generally thought that it was necessary to have one director "experienced with dialogue—preferably a stage director,"[83] to handle the dialogue (credited as "dialogue director") and a second director experienced in film direction to handle the action (credited as "director"). Directors with both stage and film experience were considered "the happy medium."[84] In fact, many directors lured to Hollywood from Broadway by the advent of sound, such as William Keighley, John Cromwell, George Cukor, and Irving Rapper, found their first jobs as dialogue directors. As the practice of sound film developed in the 1930s and 1940s, these dialogue directors disappeared from the credits but not from the ranks of the creative personnel who helped actors shape their performances.

Sound

By the mid-1930s, collecting, recording, and rerecording sound had evolved into a sophisticated process involving a number of technicians. Although each studio would have a sound chief, typically an engineer, in charge of all sound operations, there was no single person responsible for a film's sound design in its entirety, that is, from preproduction through postproduction. During preproduction—before shooting started—the sound department would produce a sound script, a version of the script with notations for the sound effects necessary for any given scene. From this, an "Effects List," a list of sound effects keyed to individual scenes, would be produced (see figure 3). Most sound effects would come from a studio's noise library, but if an unusual sound couldn't be found there, it would be necessary to find it or create it.

The chief mixer typically supervised the actual recording operations, positioning the microphones, readying the set for sound recording, and controlling the sound equipment during shooting while sitting at a console and listening, through headphones, to the sound being collected. As the arbiter of sound quality, it was the chief mixer who would accept or reject each take. The recording engineer was responsible for operating the machinery necessary for the collection of sound. Sound collection on location posed a few more problems, but numerous technological advances soon made location shooting more viable: wind and rain gags, for instance—wire frameworks covered by silk—were designed to cut down on the sounds of wind and rain.

FINAL SCRIPT

"A L I C E   A D A M S"

May 16, 1935   Prod. #836
                            EFFECTS LIST

1	Street and traffic noise	EXT. BUSINESS STREET	SC 2
2	Car pull in	EXT. HOME DISTRICT	" 3
3	Sound of lawn mower (Sc. 5 to 8)	EXT. SIDEWALK	" 5 to 8
4	Sound of sewing machine on and off scene (Sc. 13 to 16)	INT. ADAMS' HALL & INT. MOTHER'S ROOM	" 13 to 16
5	Sound of water running and rattling of dishes	INT. ADAMS' KITCHEN	" 21
6	Saucer breaks in sink	" " "	" 21
7	Rain	EXT. PARK	" 25
8	Blatant honking of auto horn (OFF)	INT. ADAMS' HALL	" 43
9	Car door bangs with a tinny sound	EXT. ADAMS' HOUSE	" 45
10	RUNNING SHOT of Ford car - Car starts and stops on cues (Sc. 46 to 54)	INT. FORD	" 46 to 54
11	Horn honking on cues (Sc. 46 & 50)	INT. FORD	" 46 & 50
12	Car pull in	EXT. PALMER HOUSE	" 54
13	Two cars pull in - Car pull out	" " "	" 58
14	Crowd babble and laughter (Sc. 61, 63 to 116)	INT. DRAWING ROOM	" 61, 63 to 116
15	Crowd dancing (Sc. 66 to 74, 75 to 77, 80 to 86, 87 to 116)	" " "	" 66 to 74, 75 to 77, 80 to 116
16	Crowd applause (Sc. 73, 77 & 86)	" " "	" 73, 77 & 86
17	Girl sobbing on and off scene (Sc. 118 and 119)	INT. UPPER HALL	" 118 & 119
18	Street and traffic noise to fit picture (Sc. 137 to 152)	EXT. DOWN TOWN STREET & EXT. PARK	" 137 to 152
19	Truck pulls in and out of scene (Sc. 145 and 147)	EXT. NEIGHBORHOOD STREET	" 145 & 147
20	Clock with a quick, high, nervous note chimes ten o'clock	INT. ADAMS LIVING ROOM	" 159
21	Car passes by	EXT. ADAMS' FRONT PORCH	" 164

FIGURE 3: An "Effects List" from *Alice Adams* (George Stevens, 1935). George Stevens Papers, Margaret Herrick Library, Academy of Motion Picture Arts and Sciences

The final steps in the creation of the soundtrack took place in postproduction, but this had to wait until a work print, a provisional edit of the film, was complete and the score had been recorded. An almost entirely different set of personnel, specializing in rerecording techniques, was required here to mix and rerecord the separate and multiple tracks for dialogue, effects, and music for a final composite track. In charge (generally) was the supervising sound editor, who was guided by, among other things, the "Re-recording Cue Sheet," a list of sound effects keyed to lines of dialogue and music. On the dubbing stage, more accurately described as a small theater with a screen at the front and a sound booth at the back, the final rerecording of the film transpired. The director was often there, particularly when decisions about the final mix were necessary. As for producers, even those such as Hal B. Wallis and David O. Selznick, who were hands-on when it came to sound, rarely attended a dubbing session. John Hammell, describing Paramount in the 1940s, remarked, "They were all so busy with grinding out these pictures that they didn't have any time to go to a dubbing session. God, to get Hal Wallis to come up to that stage and hear something was a federal job."[85] Composers were rarely invited to attend.

In the early 1930s, there would generally be a single sound mixer at the dubbing stage who would handle dialogue, sound effects, and music, but soon there were so many tracks (up to twelve in this period) that separate mixers would be assigned to dialogue, effects, and music, although the dialogue mixer generally was the most important, not surprising considering the privileging of dialogue in the studio system. Each would fight for his own track, but dialogue usually won. By the mid-1930s, however, a supervising sound editor was in charge of assembling the various soundtracks into one composite. A final playback would be screened and any changes made before previews. Changes after this stage could be difficult and costly.

Music

The production of the musical score was no less complex. By 1933, studio music departments were beginning to come back to life. As a result of sophisticated sound mixing and editing techniques, a background score including underscoring, or the use of music under dialogue, was now possible. Some visionary producers, such as Merian C. Cooper and David O. Selznick at RKO, were ready to capitalize on orchestral scoring as a way to differentiate their product. Film music historians have tended to privilege Steiner's score for *King Kong* as the seminal moment in the birth of the sound score, the point at which its idiom was determined as Romantic, its form as symphonic, and its mode as original composition by a single composer. Recent scholarship by Nathan Platte and Michael Slowik, however, questions this standard interpretation of Steiner's score, arguing that the development of classical scoring principles was not straightforward and uncomplicated and that the status of *King Kong* as a new model of background scoring was not immediately apparent. Both focus on the success of alternative approaches from less celebrated practitioners such as Nathaniel Finston, who oversaw the production of scores at Paramount and exemplified an alternative model that promoted collective (and uncredited) composition and relied upon preexisting music.[86] In fact, such "scissors-and-paste-pot"[87] scores would remain the operative model at the minor studios where music was often recycled from one film to another. At Universal, Hans J. Salter recalls that he worked, largely uncredited, on every film produced at the studio, along with fellow composer Frank Skinner, well into the 1940s. The prevalence of teams of anonymous composers and recycled music surely contributed to the decision of the Academy of Motion Picture Arts and Sciences to award Oscars for scoring not to the individual composer but to the studio's music director, who often got the sole screen credit during this period. Steiner, whose score for *The Informer* (John Ford, 1935) won the Oscar that year, was able to collect the statue himself only because he happened to be RKO's music director at the time, but it was Leo Forbstein who collected the Oscar for Erich Wolfgang Korngold's score for *Anthony Adverse* (Mervyn LeRoy, 1936). In 1938, the Academy decided to award the Oscar to the individual composer, not the studio's music director, but a film such as *Stagecoach* (John Ford, 1939), an "A" western but scored more along the lines of a "B" oater, sorely tested the new guidelines. Its Academy Award for Music (Scoring) went to four composers who shared screen credit.[88] Even as the classical score, with its focus on individual and original composition, displaced the scissors-and-paste-pot scores, individual composers at major studios might still be aided by additional uncredited composers who would help to finish a score on time or rewrite or compose additional material once the original composer had left the production.

Music departments depended upon a highly specific division of labor and the craftspeople employed there, from the music directors to the composers, on down the line to the songwriters, music editors, arrangers, orchestrators, copyists, librarians, studio musicians, and conductors, who worked, as did all craftspeople in the studio system, on an assembly line of production made even more stressful by the fact that music was at the end of the process. Thus, the music department was under tremendous pressure to finish its job quickly. If the music department couldn't finish its job on schedule, the film could not be released on time. Salter remembers that "they sometimes gave us wrong release dates in order to put pressure on us so we would be ready."[89] A typical timeframe would be four to six weeks, with many films on even more abbreviated schedules. Dimitri Tiomkin remembers working on *Alice in Wonderland* (Norman McLeod, 1933) "20 hours a day for 10 days," a schedule he described as "terrifying, fantastically stupid."[90] Some composers such as Korngold were in a position to demand more time. But no composer ever approached the amount of time that Igor Stravinsky deemed necessary to produce a feature-length film score: one year. Needless to say, Stravinsky never scored a Hollywood film.[91]

Composers did not generally begin composing until the film was in rough cut, a provisional edit of the film. In the studio era, most composers had neither the time, the opportunity, nor the inclination to begin work until this point. Steiner boasted of never reading a script: "I run a mile every time I see one."[92] And Korngold famously composed the Main Title for *King's Row* (Sam Wood, 1942) with no more information on the production than its title; thinking it a swashbuckler, he created a heroic overture with brass fanfare for what he later learned was a psychological drama set in small-town America. (Still, Korngold didn't stop requesting scripts or composing themes before he saw a rough cut, unconventional practices made possible by Korngold's privileged position in the Hollywood system, the result of his international reputation as a composer of opera and concert music.) The music department did plenty of work, however, before the composer began his. There would be budgeting, of course, auxiliary hiring, and often research into period or other preexisting music as well as negotiations for copyright clearances for this music. Any prerecordings for onscreen performances would be made so they could be synched live on the set.

The composer's job typically began with the spotting session, generally a meeting between the film's director and producer, the studio's music director, and the composer to spot the film, that is, to identify likely spots for music. The music editor would then prepare a complete breakdown with detailed timings in both seconds and feet. Some composers began composition from that breakdown: Salter, for instance, asserted that "you could plan your composition just by looking at this timing because it recalled the whole scene for you."[93] Steiner, on the other hand, claimed that when he began work on a film he did "not consider . . . timing. . . . I have the picture run again, reel by reel, to refresh my memory. After that I begin composing," using the breakdown sheet and "fitting my music to the many changes of scene and location."[94] Composers sketched out their music generally on anywhere from two to four staves that were then passed on to an orchestrator or orchestrators. Orchestration was a touchy point among composers, many if not most of whom were capable of orchestrating themselves, many having begun their career as orchestrators. But in Hollywood's highly specialized division of labor, composers were too valuable to be allowed to work at a task that could be accomplished by someone else. To compensate, many composers produced highly detailed sketches with clear delineations for orchestration or, if they were in a position of some prominence in the studio, they developed close relationships with an orchestrator they could depend upon to realize their intentions, such as Steiner with Bernard Kaun or Korngold with Hugo Friedhofer. Bernard Herrmann, however, insisted on doing his own orchestration and did.

Copyists would copy the parts for the individual players in the studio orchestra. At Universal, there were three to four copyists on staff and more hired if the work necessitated it. Copyists also prepared the cue sheet, the final record of musical cues for a film used for copyright purposes, and the conductor copy, which, despite its name, was not always the actual copy of the score used in conducting. Some composers liked to conduct from their sketches instead, but a conductor copy generally served as the copy of record, used for copyright and credit purposes and the one filed in a studio's music library. The music librarian was in charge of collecting and updating music for use in studio productions, cataloguing all the music collected by and housed in the studio, getting the music to the soundstage for recording, and then afterward returning all of it, especially the conductor copy, to the music library. Some of these libraries were massive. Twentieth Century–Fox's had "more than twenty thousand original compositions" alone.[95] But that pales in comparison to Paramount's music library, under long-time head librarian Al Gabor, with its

> standard sheet music dating from 1833 to 1946, of which there are over 10,000 pieces, 15,000 printed stock orchestrations made by members of the staff from standard music, 1,000 books of international sheet music with each book containing about 1,000 compositions relative to opera, operettas, musical comedies, etc. Further, [there were] files containing 40,000 piano parts from standard, released orchestrations, and hundreds of books containing active choral music for use in choir and chorus numbers . . . [and] approximately 40,000 original orchestrations.[96]

Recording the score could be very pressured because it came near the end of the assembly line. Most studios had rebuilt their orchestras beginning in the mid-1930s with some musicians on staff, and others brought in to supplement them on a freelance basis. Twentieth Century–Fox had about a dozen first chairs on staff augmented by dozens of others. Warner Bros.' orchestra had eighteen players on staff and expanded the orchestra to upward of sixty players for their biggest productions. Universal had thirty-six staff players and more when necessary: for *Christmas Holiday* (Robert Siodmak, 1944), a Deanna Durbin picture, there were seventy-eight musicians on the recording stage. This mix of staff players augmented by freelancers would remain the norm until 1944 when the American Federation of Musicians was able to coerce the major studios to hire and retain staff orchestras of anywhere from thirty-five to fifty players.

As was done with dialogue in the early years of sound, test recordings were made of music recording sessions to identify and fix problems before the recording was actually committed to film. Ideally the score would be recorded in a day or two, but they could be long days. Writes one observer, "I have seen O'Keefe [business manager of the music department], along with musical director, orchestra, chorus, arrangers, copyists, etc., on the soundstage at Twentieth Century–Fox as late as six o'clock in the morning after twenty or twenty-two hours' steady work."[97] It was the prerogative of the studio's most prestigious composers to conduct their own scores, but staff composers often didn't have this same privilege.

During a film's preproduction and production stages, the music department was in charge of the score, but after recording the score became the province of the sound department that supervised the final mix on the dubbing stage. Ideally the score was in final form at this stage, although it was not unheard of for changes to be made after previews, necessitating difficult cuts (or expansions) to the score and rewriting and rerecording.

Throughout the scoring process, the composer had little control over the music and was subject to the demands of individual directors, line producers, and production chiefs. With very few exceptions, the studio owned the copyright to all the music produced for its films.[98] The music director functioned as a go-between and generally tried to advocate for the composer, but ultimately power over the score resided with the studio and its minions, not the composer. Tales of musical ignorance on the part of directors and producers are legendary, but it is worth pointing out that some producers knew quite a bit about music or at least had good instincts about it. Nevertheless, an adversarial relationship often developed between the director (and sometimes the producer) and the composer over the music, resulting in battles that the composer usually lost.

Conclusion

In 1946, Hollywood was riding high. The war years had proved a boon for the studios, as the labor troubles and looming government investigations that were beginning to beset the industry during the Depression were eclipsed by the nationwide war effort. Movie attendance was at an all-time high in 1946 and so were profits. Hollywood was getting ready to celebrate the twentieth anniversary of the coming of sound. Warner Bros. was planning a four-month-long celebration "on an international scale, including exhibits, conferences on future developments, and events emphasizing the use of sound film in education and the promotion of international understanding."[99] Other studios would soon join in the "Tribute to Scientific Pioneers of Sound Pictures."[100] Advances were on the horizon that would revolutionize sound production: magnetic tape recording technology and stereophonic and multichannel sound systems. Musical styles such as jazz, pop, rock 'n' roll, and even electronic music would soon be introduced into Hollywood's musical palette. Hollywood was poised to enter a new stage in its development after the war, and sound would be one of the engines driving that change.

3

POSTWAR HOLLYWOOD, 1947–1967 Nathan Platte

Surveying Hollywood's offerings of 1967 put film music critic Page Cook in a foul mood. "Music has all but disappeared from films," he began. "Noise has replaced it. What was once a functioning part of the cinematic art form has deteriorated into an assortment of auditory effects which derive, when they derive from anything beside ineptitude, from the major and minor neuroses of Western Civilization. . . . Hitherto, film music never worked *against* a film, but today's 'scores' definitely do."[1] Music had not truly disappeared, of course, but its sound had changed rapidly over the postwar era, confounding Cook's belief that music "should relate, in its themes and treatment thereof, to locale, time, plot, and characterizations." "The current fashion of imposing *unrelated* sounds on an audience," elaborated Cook, "instead of evoking relevant emotions by means of *related* sounds is a reversion to the uncouth and even to the barbaric."[2]

Delineating "related" from "unrelated" is a subjective task, and it is here that Cook's argument devolves into a tirade. For Cook, "unrelated" evidently meant music that eschewed the symphony orchestra, the default ensemble for underscore from the late silent era through the studio era. By the late 1960s, however, there were many exceptions to this norm. "Slapping 'hard rock' onto a sound track is a truckling to the ignorances of the nihilists among today's young," Cook averred, adding: "In consequence, non-composers, astonished to find so lucrative a market for non-music, do not hesitate to collect fat checks for putting together the idiocies of 'pot' music, freak-out blues, and (now old hat) cool jazz."[3] Indeed, three of the five films nominated by the Academy for Best Picture of 1967 had dispensed with or marginalized orchestral underscoring, featuring instead songs by Simon and Garfunkel (Mike Nichols's *The Graduate*),[4] Earl Scruggs's banjo (Arthur Penn's *Bonnie and Clyde*), and a combo assembled by Quincy Jones including blues guitar, electric bass, cimbalom, mouth percussion, and jazz flute (Norman Jewison's *In the Heat of the Night*). But whereas Cook feared for the future that these sounds portended, this chapter considers the historical context from which these diverse soundscapes blossomed. How exactly did changes in technology, marketing, and aesthetics transform the music and sound of postwar Hollywood cinema to such a radical degree?

Cook's polemic that film music had become noise is a helpful place to begin, as one of the central preoccupations of postwar Hollywood would in fact be the material, "noisy" qualities of sound and music, manifested in film after film through readily distinctive audio effects, timbres, acoustics, and musical styles. This heightened attention to sound quality and timbre was not happenstance. Rather, it arose from two interrelated developments in the postwar era. The first concerned the broad adoption of magnetic tape, a technology that reconfigured sound recording and editing for broadcast and recorded media. The second stemmed from the rapid diversification of the American media soundscape, abetted by a postwar boom in regional radio stations, television shows, and record albums. Americans could now experience—and experiment with—an astonishing range of musical genres available within their own homes. The consequence of this embarrassment of riches was that mainstream approaches to popular music and film scoring ceded ground to new musical styles and idiosyncratic, conspicuously non-mainstream sounds, now readily accessible on the radio and television. For this reason much contemporary discourse on Hollywood's new postwar sounds emphasizes musical content, as the following pages attest. The enhanced clarity of magnetic recording, however, also fostered broader appreciation for the artistry in sounds beyond music, a development the Academy finally recognized in 1963 with a "Sound Effects" award.[5] But in order to contextualize these tectonic cultural shifts alongside Cook's frustrations in the late 1960s, it is best to rewind the clock about twenty years, to Academy Awards night on March 13, 1947—just before magnetic tape had taken Hollywood, but at a time when some of these interests were nonetheless emerging.

The big winner that night was *The Best Years of Our Lives* (William Wyler, 1946), which received ten nominations and nine awards, including Best Picture and Best Score. *Best Years* was also the year's highest-grossing production, a telling tribute to a film that tackled a difficult theme: the wounds and anxieties that three returning veterans and their communities bore in the indefinite aftermath of World War II. Although the film was not without scenes of great sentiment, neither did its happy-ending reunions eclipse unresolved social tensions and fears. As Fred, a recently divorced veteran, embraces Peggy, his new, empathetic partner, he murmurs: "It may take us years to get anywhere. We'll have no money, no decent place to live. We'll have to work, get kicked around." This grim line, delivered as the film's stars gaze into each other's eyes and the film's guiding theme swells triumphantly, is *Best Year*'s last. It is a memorably ambivalent ending to a film that the film historian Barry Langford describes as "pregnant with possibilities of a new direction for postwar American cinema."[6] If Fred's line anticipates the challenges Hollywood and its audiences faced in the coming years, so too did Hugo Friedhofer's music presage changing attitudes toward film sound and musical style in American film.

Hugo Friedhofer's presence at the Award podium was itself emblematic of change and also continuity. On the one hand, Friedhofer was steeped in the norms of classic Hollywood underscore, a style he had helped fashion while working as an orchestrator and assistant composer for Max Steiner, Erich Wolfgang Korngold, and Alfred Newman during the 1930s and 1940s. With *Best Years*, however, he was hailed in articles by Frederick Sternfeld and Louis Applebaum for boldly breaking from the mainstream embodied by his colleagues. "The lush strains of 19th-century Romanticism, so often imposed on a helpless audience—however far removed the actual situation from the emotionalism and exhibitionism of that noble period—are happily absent," wrote Sternfeld.[7] Applebaum praised the score's opening theme for its "simplicity [and] straightforward, warm harmonization."[8] Sternfeld found that the theme, "reminiscent of both [Paul] Hindemith and [Aaron] Copland, stays refreshingly clear of the overly lush chromaticism so abundant in lesser scores. . . . By his economy Friedhofer insures that the chromaticism used in a few tense scenes is really effective."[9] Both writers also praised Friedhofer's stylistic versatility, observing that the score incorporated elements of children's song, jazz (in the manner of a "saucy, Gershwinesque strain"), "folksy" passages, and even a "tongue-in-cheek" incorporation of the melody "Home, Sweet Home."[10] Summing up, Applebaum applauded "Friedhofer's clear orchestral thinking, his appreciation and understanding of the orchestra's resources, his sensitive feeling for tone color, and his good taste."[11]

These articles, both published in 1947, neatly encapsulate two emergent trends in postwar film. First, they conceptualized Friedhofer's music within the film and beyond it. For Sternfeld, this meant including numerous annotated music examples and a page of full score to demonstrate compositional strategies that function independently from the film's narrative. Applebaum pointed to the music's relative inaccessibility apart from the film: "It is sad that present utilization of film music material does not allow for any kind of distribution of the music itself. True, in rare cases, excerpts from film scores are recorded on commercial discs . . . but those interested in [this] score have recourse only to reviews such as this one. The only alternative is to go repeatedly to see the film in order to become more familiar with its music."[12] Public interest in film music apart from films themselves would continue to grow over the postwar era.[13]

Second, although Sternfeld and Applebaum devote substantial attention to Friedhofer's development of recurring themes, it is the timbral palette of *Best Years* as rendered through melodic, harmonic, and textural means that charmed them: its "economy," "simplicity," and "straightforward" qualities, which remain "refreshingly clear of the overly lush."[14] Sternfeld also observed that music, dialogue, and sound effects worked in tandem in *Best Years* to achieve maximum expressive effect through minimal means. (*Best Years*' sound director and industry leader, Gordon Sawyer, had also received an Oscar nomination for Best Sound.)[15] In a scene in which an inebriated veteran disposes army boots from a high apartment window, Sternfeld observes that the humor of the moment arises from sparse but carefully timed sound and musical effects: "Just as camera and sound track rely on only a few elements [namely, the delayed yet gratifying thud of the boots hitting the ground], so the composer, weaving a brittle and transparent fabric, proceeds swiftly and sparingly."[16] By discussing music in relation to other soundtrack elements, Sternfeld illuminated both the musicality of sound effects as well as the sonic qualities of music. An even more remarkable blending of music and sound effect occurs earlier in the film as the three veterans ride home in a bomber. Friedhofer's music, heard for the first time since the opening titles, emerges from the throbbing rumble of the bomber. Rerecorded engine noise serves here as a pedal tone to melodic material.[17] In the years that followed, these themes—a growing appetite for new music styles, increased demand for film music apart from films, and greater emphasis on tone color (musical and otherwise)—would come to characterize postwar trends, abetted in large part by significant changes in production methods and technology.

The alignment of commercial and critical success in *The Best Years of Our Lives* was especially affirming given that 1946 broke all previous records in annual box office receipts ($1.692 billion) and weekly attendance (90 million).[18] But in subsequent years it became clear that this was a peak rather than a step to greater heights. The box office record would remain unbroken until the mid-1970s; the attendance record held for two years and then fell 30 million over the next two. Receipts also tumbled steadily downward to $903 million before beginning a slow rebound in 1963. The reasons for this plunge are many; they are also well rehearsed in histories of the era. As Peter Lev notes in his history of 1950s cinema, television kept ever more people at home: Americans bought more than five million new sets every year from 1950 to 1959.[19] In 1948, the Supreme Court declared that studios' ownership of theater chains represented an illegal trust; by 1950 all studios were required to divest their theaters, a move that slashed revenues, reduced control over exhibitors, and placed greater financial risk on each individual film.[20] Broad social shifts in postwar America also affected Hollywood financially. Hollywood lost more moviegoers to childrearing and leisure activities, including golfing and out-of-town vacations, which were newly accessible to Americans enjoying greater amounts of disposable income and time.[21] The Cold War, the civil rights movement, the rise of youth culture, and second-wave feminism affected film content, filmmakers, and moviegoing practices in complex and deeply felt ways.

Looking at Hollywood's ledger alone, it is easy to draw pessimistic conclusions from this volatile era. In contrast, rapidly changing fiscal and social circumstances prompted industry responses that were at times boldly experimental and collectively diverse. In 1954 Barbara Berch Jamison captured this zeitgeist in a *New York Times Magazine* feature entitled "And Now Super-Colossal Headaches": "Nothing—not Valentino or sound, the gangster cycle, depression or war—has had such an impact on Hollywood as the twelve months just passed. They have seethed with the varied crises of television competition, closing theatres, growing unemployment, Cinerama, 3-D, widescreen, stereophonic sound, CinemaScope, public apathy—and yet, some of the most phenomenal box-office grosses in film history."[22] This upheaval reverberates audibly in the sounds of films themselves. Studio attempts to overshadow television with heightened spectacle brought forth larger orchestras heard in stereophonic sound. Filmmakers—many enjoying greater independence from the studio system—looked beyond the symphonic style entirely to jazz, electronic, and popular music.

Even studios' downsizing of music departments in the 1950s had complex ramifications. Dismissals hurt long-established composers like Max Steiner, whose contract at Warner Bros. ended in 1953. Miklós Rózsa observed that the loss of studio talent also affected those who stayed: "There was a deadly atmosphere at MGM at this time—a smell of disease and decay and disintegration. People were fired left and right, budgets slashed."[23] When Rózsa's contract expired in 1962, the composer of *Ben-Hur* (William Wyler, 1959) departed without fanfare: "I was glad to go; it wasn't the MGM of the old days. I left without a word of thanks or a goodbye from anybody. My only contact with [MGM] after that was when they asked for the repayment of two weeks' salary, as I had had my two weeks' holiday without completing a year. This after fourteen years without a free Sunday!"[24] Fewer contracts, however, made it easier for filmmakers to recruit new musical talent: some of these musicians, like Leonard Rosenman and Quincy Jones, scored dozens of films. Others, like Leonard Bernstein (*On the Waterfront*, Elia Kazan, 1954) and Simon and Garfunkel (*The Graduate*), made distinctive contributions without ever joining the Hollywood enclave. Some composers whose Hollywood careers had begun in the 1930s and early 1940s—Franz Waxman, Dimitri Tiomkin, Bernard Herrmann—not only continued but reached greater heights as public awareness of film composers' work grew through the proliferation of commercially released movie music albums. Revenues from such albums ultimately transformed music's role in the craft and business of Hollywood film.

The shedding of studio jobs also gave sound personnel more independence, both contractually and aesthetically. As the cinema historian Paul Monaco notes, by the 1960s "more artistic decisions were being made by individual directors and editors in direct consultation with sound technicians," thereby allowing "the development of a creative environment that encouraged experimentation."[25] Underwriting all these changes to the soundtrack was Hollywood's postwar adoption of magnetic tape, which affected not just film but nearly all facets of broadcast and recorded media in postwar America. In the hands of editors, composers, and hobbyists, magnetic tape nurtured what Matthew Malsky has characterized as a "newly developing relationship that people had with their sonic surroundings."[26]

What's That Sound?

At the end of World War II, engineers and scientists from Allied countries descended upon German plants and labs, seeking technological information that might be of military, industrial, or scientific value. One finding included a series of advances German engineers had made in magnetic tape recording. The scientific foundations for magnetic recording technology dated back to the nineteenth century, but magnetic recorders from the early 1900s used steel wire and failed to find a viable market, although later generations of magnetic wire recorders were used by the military during World War II.[27] German engineers made a number of advances before and during the war, including the substitution for heavy steel wire of lightweight tape coated with iron oxide particles. By taking and developing these technologies further, American companies like Ampex Electric Corporation and Minnesota Mining and Manufacturing Company (3M) found numerous applications and markets for the magnetic tape technology, ranging from radio (Bing Crosby was an enthusiastic and earlier adopter who used the tape to record his radio shows for later broadcasting) to aerospace and rocket telemetry.[28]

In some ways magnetic tape was like film: it could be cut, spliced, looped, and run backward. But magnetic recording offered several advantages over the optical sound recording methods used in film production up to that time, including greater audio fidelity, immediate playback (optical film had to be developed and printed in a lab before playing), more flexibility in editing, reusable tape, and increasingly smaller recording units.[29] Magnetic recording simplified both production and postproduction. Units could be transported with relative ease for on-location shooting. Magnetic tape also made automatic dialogue replacement (ADR), the process by which distorted lines of dialogue are corrected by inserting a new recording of the line either on the set or after, simpler than ever before.[30] In postproduction, orchestral music no longer had to be mixed from multiple microphones *during* the recording, a painstaking process that sometimes involved moving microphones as musicians played: "I wore gum-soled shoes," recalled Warner Bros. music recorder and mixer Arthur Piantadosi, "so very quietly I went all around to different microphones, waited until the designated bar [of music], and moved the microphone."[31] In contrast, multichannel magnetic recording captured a single performance on multiple tracks, each with a different audio perspective. These in turn could be duplicated, manipulated, and mixed after the musicians had gone home.[32] The subsequent and most important advantage for studio administrators, then, was that magnetic recording could save considerable expense and time.

Not everyone, of course, welcomed the technology. Sound editors accustomed to "seeing" sound in the ghostly black-and-white formations in optical soundtracks were annoyed that magnetic tape gave no visual cues to aid with cutting. Magnetic tape also initially lacked films' sprockets and could stretch, creating synchronization issues. But these problems were easily overcome by technological adjustments and time. Loren Ryder, a sound engineer at Paramount and member of the Academy's Basic Sound Committee, played a key role in promulgating the technology in Hollywood in the late 1940s.[33] Not only did he lead by example, converting Paramount's recording, editing, and mixing facilities to magnetic tape by 1950 (and winning a special Oscar for his efforts), but he also established Ryder Sound, a company that rented the latest magnetic recording equipment to soundmen at other studios.[34]

For those who worked in music and sound, magnetic recording technology offered new creative opportunities. As the historian of film sound Rick Altman notes, "magnetic recording divorced the sound track still further from the image and from the image's optical technology. Now, any number of sound sources could easily be separately recorded, mixed, and remixed independently of the image."[35] Not surprisingly, magnetic recording and mixing proved a boon for Foley effects: sound effects rendered and mixed by specialists during postproduction. For Alfred Hitchcock's *Rear Window* (1954), Harry Lindgren and John Cope assembled multiple effects tracks from magnetic and optical sources, drawing from recordings made in Greenwich Village, the film's setting, and library sound effects. Although the film was released in mono, Cope and Lindgren's sonic layers create the impression of sounds emanating from disparate acoustic spaces, each echoing differently across the apartment courtyard, where the entire film is set. As one critic noted, the sounds alone evoked a "disquieting murmur and a sense of realism that brings the film's cunning war between conjecture and common sense very close to the audience."[36] Loren Ryder, sound supervisor for the production, received an Oscar on behalf of the sound team for Best Sound Recording.

The creative possibilities of magnetic recording and mixing extended far beyond film and the layering of recorded sounds. Experimental artists like John Cage and Pierre Schaeffer, for example, treated magnetic tape as a raw material for artistic composition. For the avant-garde musical work *Williams Mix* (1952), Cage and several collaborators rendered an elaborate sonic tapestry comprising six hundred taped radio segments that play in dense polyphony over four and a half minutes.[37] (Branded *musique concrète by* Schaeffer in 1948, these tape-based artworks drew heavily from film editing and montage techniques.) *Williams Mix* was part of Cage's "Music for Magnetic Tape" project, and he hired electronic music specialists Louis and Bebe Barron to help. The couple's work was distinguished by their technique: splicing and layering recordings of unstable electronic circuits. The Barrons' experimental soundscapes enjoyed mass audience exposure when they were hired to provide space-age sound effects for MGM's *Forbidden Planet* (Fred Wilcox, 1956), an uncharacteristically expensive sci-fi film shot in CinemaScope. The Barrons assembled a sonic accompaniment for the entire film, obviating the need for a separate score. The undulating roars, plunks, and bloops served as both sound effects and musical commentary, although the distinction between the two is often deliberately ambiguous.[38]

If *Forbidden Planet* represented a relatively rare case of avant-garde tape techniques affecting Hollywood practice, magnetic recording also begot new practices in record label studios that also affected methods in Hollywood. Whereas filmmakers used optical recording before shifting to magnetic, record labels into the 1940s recorded musical performances direct-to-disc, a method that placed considerable pressure on musicians to render an as-perfect-as-possible performance. As sound historian David Morton Jr. notes, "There was no editing or rerecording possible in the making of a phonograph record except under extraordinary circumstances."[39] Magnetic tape exploded that expectation. Engineers could now tape for hours and then construct, as Mark Katz relates, "'performances' that could never have existed."[40] At times this simply meant splicing multiple takes to create the impression of a flawlessly executed performance. Engineers and musicians could also exploit magnetic tape to create effects that would be otherwise impossible beyond the studio. Surveying recording studio trends of the 1950s, musicologist Albin Zak notes: "Records, often the results of elaborate feats of construction, increasingly gave the impression of unique sonic artifacts, with exaggerated reverb, overdubbed performances, sound effects, and instrumental balances controlled electronically by recording engineers. With its unabashed mingling of music making and electronic legerdemain, record making was becoming, on a smaller scale, like making movies."[41]

Indeed, optical recording technology used by the studios had long allowed certain manipulations that could not be rendered in direct-to-disc recording, including splicing, running a track backward (as had been done since the 1930s for sound effects), or certain reverb effects. But magnetic recording made the process simpler. With immediate playback it was quicker and cheaper to experiment, which is exactly what sound editors did, borrowing ideas from record labels just as record labels had done with film. For *In Cold Blood* (1967), mixer Arthur

Piantadosi played Quincy Jones's score backward on the film's soundtrack, pleasing director Richard Brooks, who had already rejected Jones's music in its "frontward" version.[42] With multiple magnetic tracks, editors could also render dramatic stereo effects. These might be relatively subtle. In *The Cobweb* (Vincente Minnelli, 1955), for example, Leonard Rosenman passes chromatic lines across different sections of the orchestra such that the dissonant sounds seem to slither outward from the center of the screen, reflecting spatially the psychological claustrophobia of the film's mentally unstable characters. At the other end of the spectrum are the bizarre sound effects that ricochet about in the 3-D *House of Wax* (Andre de Toth, 1953), prompting the film reviewer Bosley Crowther to object: "The major causes for anxiety presented by this film are in . . . the intolerable artlessness of its sound. It is thrown and howled at the audience as though the only purpose was to overwhelm . . . with an excess of brutal stimuli. . . . The noisy sound of footsteps clattering in the back of the theatre a moment after an actor has appeared to rush forward from the screen is completely illogical and unnerving. It sounds like a riot outside."[43]

Stereophonic Spectacles

Although magnetic recording revolutionized production and postproduction sound practices, its impact in theaters was muffled by exhibitors' reluctance to update sound systems, despite assurances in the trade press that magnetic playback "eliminates sound distortion, foreign noises, and scratchiness."[44] In most cases studios had to convert their magnetically recorded soundtracks to a monaural, optical soundtrack for playback in theaters.

Magnetic soundtracks on theatrical prints did make tentative inroads in the mid-1950s. Establishing this foothold in exhibition was made possible only after bundling magnetic sound with more easily perceived enhancements. Throughout the mid-1950s, filmmakers experimented with a variety of new visual formats—3-D, Cinerama, CinemaScope, VistaVision, Todd-AO, and Panavision, among others—all intended to transform the moviegoing experience through spatially enhanced spectacle far beyond the pale of television. These novel processes not only featured expanded screen dimensions but also immersed listeners in magnetic stereophonic sound, a feature facilitated by the magnetic recording and mixing on multiple channels. Stereo in the cinema had been tried before with "Fantasound," an optical stereo format designed specially for Disney's *Fantasia* (1940), but expense and technical complexity had discouraged widespread adoption of the system. Rather than a standalone novelty, magnetic stereo sound worked in tandem with other enhancements, rendering a triple threat of "glorious Technicolor, breathtaking CinemaScope, and stereophonic sound," as celebrated and cheerfully mocked in Cole Porter's song from *Silk Stockings*

(Rouben Mamoulian, 1957). Porter's lyrics were not terribly far from actual ad copy ballyhooing CinemaScope's sonic virtues. An advertisement for *Beneath the 12-Mile Reef* (Robert D. Webb, 1953) read: "The marvel of CinemaScope's stereophonic sound engulfs you in excitement you've never known as the CinemaScope anamorphic lens captures a spectacular undersea kingdom."[45]

This binding of new sights and sounds was repeatedly emphasized through demonstration films that featured large performing ensembles that could impress audiences through visual size and aural weight. In *This Is Cinerama* (Michael Todd et al., 1952), a mixed choir enters from both sides of the screen while singing "A Mighty Fortress Is Our God." This simple maneuver links a crescendo in dynamics—the result of more singers entering the range of the microphones— with the filling of a refreshingly unfamiliar sonic space defined by Cinerama's new multichannel system. After the film's intermission, audiences were invited to contemplate the soundtrack's new spatiality in isolation. Over a darkened screen, a narrator solemnly intones: "For a few moments now we're going to give you a demonstration of our stereophonic sound. Sound, this time, without picture. For Cinerama is not only an innovation as far as projection and camera work is concerned, but . . . it is accompanied by a whole new sound system."[46] Over thrumming orchestral music,[47] the narrator provides a brief tour of the orchestra's sections and instruments, all the while emphasizing sonic spectacle: "Please note the enormous power without distortion, when the full orchestra plays. . . . Listen to the woodwinds climbing up higher and higher until they reach the star performers of the orchestra, the violins . . . the celesta . . . the contrabassoon . . . the heavenly harp. . . . Now, all together, listen to the tremendous power!"

Other studios pursued similar strategies, albeit with images. When Twentieth Century–Fox demonstrated its CinemaScope technology at the Roxy Theater in late April 1953, Crowther remarked approvingly that "the stereophonic sound was most effectively demonstrated in a scene of a rehearsal of the Fox symphony orchestra, under the direction of Alfred Newman, wherein the sound came naturally and clearly from the sections of the orchestra where it was produced."[48] In subsequent CinemaScope features, both Twentieth Century–Fox and MGM included additional performances by their studio orchestras. These mini-concerts served multiple purposes. In addition to recalling the silent-era practice of beginning films with an orchestral overture, they also demonstrated the stereophonic technology and reminded audiences of the spatial configuration of the instrument sections, information that was key to appreciating the stereo mixing of the orchestra that continued once the feature began, with violins placed in the stereo field on stage left, woodwinds center, and brass and low strings on stage right.[49]

Much like the transition to sound in the late 1920s, the new magnetic stereophonic technologies evolved quickly across and within individual formats. The gargantuan Cinerama, for example, used three projectors, three adjoined screens, and eight playback speakers: five behind the screens and three behind

FIGURE 4: An advertisement for film stock touts magnetic, stereophonic sound featured in CinemaScope productions. *Broadcasting*, November 9, 1953, 81.

the audience.[50] Most studios, however, sought to patent less elaborate technology that might better attract exhibitors and production units. Twentieth Century–Fox's more widely adopted CinemaScope format used a single projector and curved screen (see figure 4). Its original playback system employed three speakers behind the screen and a fourth behind the audience. Not all CinemaScope films had equal sound values, however; they changed depending on the year and studio. Indeed, as the physical width of the sound strip on CinemaScope filmstock changed, it ultimately reduced the aspect ratio of the image from a 2.66:1 ratio down to 2.35:1.[51]

Similarly, stereophonic playback in films did not advance steadily from lesser to greater quality but instead tacked between the competing priorities of exhibitors and studios. Twentieth Century–Fox, for example, required exhibitors booking CinemaScope features to install the curved CinemaScope screen and a sound system compatible with CinemaScope's four-channel magnetic soundtrack. Balking at the expensive costs of the sound system (and the discovery that the magnetic heads in the projector wore out quickly), exhibitors questioned whether audiences would really miss stereophonic sound when enthralled by glorious Technicolor and breathtaking CinemaScope. "When we opened with the first showing of a CinemaScope picture with stereophonic sound," wrote one exhibitor, "the manager appeared on the stage, before the presentation of the picture, and spoke to the audience, explaining the advantages of stereophonic sound. In spite of this, at the break of the show, while we had plenty of comment about the size and quality of the picture, no mention was made about the sound."[52]

Competition among studios generated additional pressure. Almost as soon as MGM licensed the CinemaScope technology from Twentieth Century–Fox it began using Perspecta Sound, a format that imitated stereo effects with an optical—not magnetic—track. Instead of sending independent signals to each speaker, Perspecta used sub-audible tones embedded in the optical soundtrack to indicate variable volumes for the right, center, and left speakers. By turning up one speaker and lowering another, Perspecta Sound could give the impression of sounds issuing from different spaces even though they originated from the same monaural track. For this reason, Perspecta was more effective with discrete sound events, like lines of dialogue, than sustained sounds, like underscore.

Perspecta Sound offered two considerable advantages to exhibitors. First, as an optical track it did not require special magnetic heads for reading the soundtrack. Second, Perspecta Sound was compatible with both stereo and the conventional monaural systems. Exhibitors reluctant to upgrade their sound systems could still show CinemaScope features. Perspecta also freed up filmmakers, who no longer had to record in stereo on the set, as was initially done with Fox's CinemaScope features. As Jay Beck explains, "Because the system was designed to re-channel the information on a monophonic soundtrack into a stereophonic presentation, the 'effect' of multichannel sound needed to be considered only in the very last phase of soundtrack construction: the mix."[53] To its critics Perspecta marked a retreat from new standards of sonic excellence, but many considered these losses negligible.[54] Indeed, Perspecta would become the sound format of all MGM films and Paramount's widescreen VistaVision features, forcing Twentieth Century–Fox to relent on its demand that exhibitors use their proprietary magnetic stereophonic system.[55] Exhibitors could now choose between magnetic or optical as well as stereo or mono (see figure 5). The end result was that moviegoers experienced radically different sound for the same film depending on whether they attended a road show (a reserved-seating screening held in a large theater

FIGURE 5: Twentieth Century–Fox capitulates to exhibitors by allowing them to select CinemaScope prints with stereo, monaural, magnetic, or optical sound. *Variety*, May 12, 1954, 10–11.

before the film entered general release) or listened through a single speaker at a drive-in. An MGM ad aimed at exhibitors speaks to the tensions that filmmakers and exhibitors faced over sound:

> Up to this time MGM CinemaScope productions have been available solely to those theatres which had installed stereophonic equipment suitable for magnetic sound tracks. . . . Many theatres have voiced the opinion that motion pictures distributing companies should furnish their CinemaScope productions to the many thousands of theatres which are not yet prepared to expand their sound facilities. [Therefore] all MGM pictures, in whatever dimension, will be released with Perspecta sound tracks permitting exhibitors to employ either stereophonic sound or single channel sound.[56]

After this concession, the tone becomes truculent:

> The exhibition without stereophonic sound of CinemaScope or other MGM pictures would eliminate an effect essential to their full enjoyment.
> We cannot urge exhibitors strongly enough to install stereophonic devices.
> To ignore the advantages of new sound techniques is a disservice to the public and obstruction to the great future of motion pictures. We are on the threshold of tremendous achievement and an improvement in presentation techniques. . . .

It would be sad indeed if exhibitors were induced into a lethargy and not inspired to take advantage of the wonderful opportunities presented by the inventions and achievements of great technicians working in the Studios.

Furthermore, we believe that the theatres which are equipped with stereophonic sound devices will have a great box-office advantage over those theatres not so equipped, and that the movie-going public, which has already put its stamp of approval on CinemaScope with stereophonic sound will further demonstrate its acceptance by preferring to attend those theatres properly equipped.[57]

Since losing their theater chains, studios no longer possessed the same control over exhibitors' practices, as this passive-aggressive manifesto betrays. And so filmmakers found themselves in a situation reminiscent of the silent era, when the quality of a film's sound rested in the hands of individual exhibitors. MGM's announcement even echoes rhetoric of the nickelodeon era, when writers like Louis Reeves Harrison had badgered exhibitors to invest more money in music, as "better music means better patronage and more of it."[58]

Whereas no one objected to improved music in a nickelodeon, however, film critics did not uniformly endorse stereophonic sound. As Jay Beck and John Belton observe in their work on the evolution of film sound, some took issue with "traveling dialogue," in which a character's voice moves across speaker channels, either because the character is moving or the camera angle has changed.[59] Crowther spoke at length on the issue in the aptly entitled "Sound and (or) Fury," acknowledging that "although the exhibitors' anxiety is mainly over the costs, the question [of stereophonic sound] is one for contemplation by the creative artist too."[60] After viewing the crucifixion scene from *The Robe* (Henry Koster, 1953) in both stereo and mono at a private screening, Crowther concluded that the scene "did not impress this observer with any overwhelming advantage in the stereophonic device. As a matter of fact, the single-outlet system was more effective. The explanation is simple. In using the stereophonic device to have voices seem to emerge from the screen approximately where the speaking character is . . . becomes an obvious mechanical contrivance."[61]

Contrivances, however, were not necessarily bad for business or art. Sound and color had once been contrivances too. Like Technicolor in the 1930s and 1940s, magnetic stereophonic sound came to mark select films as especially prestigious endeavors. Indeed, mixing a multichannel soundtrack required extensive planning and intense effort that undermined the cost- and time-saving advantages of magnetic recording. For Stanley Kubrick's *Spartacus* (1960), sound director Don Rogers recalled laboring for nine months "to place the sound of every actor, every sound effect, every footstep, every bang, and every crash exactly where it was on the screen."[62] Through the late 1950s and 1960s, magnetic stereophonic sound became the expected acoustic for sprawling historical dramas and musicals, including *Ben-Hur* (1959), *Exodus* (Otto Preminger, 1960), *Cleopatra* (Joseph L. Mankiewicz, 1963), *The Fall of the Roman Empire* (Anthony Mann, 1964), *Doctor Zhivago* (David Lean, 1965), *The Sound of Music* (Robert Wise, 1965), and *The Sand Pebbles* (Robert Wise, 1966). Even with these films, only audiences at properly equipped locations—typically road show screenings and first-run houses—would experience the sound stereophonically. Beginning in 1958, however, stereophonic film sound could be enjoyed in a more intimate setting, albeit without the film itself: with soundtrack albums played on home stereos.

Movie Music Albums and Stylistic Divergences: Film Music's New Frontiers

The concept of the commercial movie music album (commonly yet confusingly referred to as "soundtracks") predated the war, but these early phonograph recordings, featuring vocal performances and background music from films, were novel commodities. Only a handful of filmmakers bothered with them, notably David O. Selznick, who used albums to promote *Spellbound* (Alfred Hitchcock, 1945), *Duel in the Sun* (King Vidor, 1946), and *The Paradine Case* (Alfred Hitchcock, 1947). Most film releases, as Applebaum had observed with *The Best Years of Our Lives*, were not accompanied by corresponding music albums. After the war, however, more filmmakers incorporated albums into publicity campaigns, with radio exposure and record sales serving to boost ticket sales. As Jeff Smith relates in *The Sounds of Commerce: Marketing Popular Film Music*, studios' realization that soundtrack albums could be an important source of revenue prompted the majors to purchase or start record labels in the late 1950s.[63] No longer did albums serve only to publicize a film: now films served to publicize albums, film composers, and other musicians who covered film themes.[64] In 1957 journalist Joel Friedman remarked that "there . . . appears to be some confusion as to who is sitting in the driver's seat, the film company or the diskery, in bargaining for a release. . . . In an effort to tie up loose ends that might prevent successful bidding, the major [record labels] are now signing as many film names as they can, within reason, including film stars, composers, conductors and background music cleffers [composers]."[65] Once record companies began releasing stereo LPs in 1958, it became possible to enjoy music from a film in a better quality presentation than the local theater could offer. Much like the magnetic recording technology, which had "divorced"[66] film sound from the optical technology, so film soundtrack albums abetted an appreciation of film music (and, less frequently, dialogue and effects) that did not necessarily require an experience with the film itself. As Smith has shown, movie music albums did not strive to replicate the soundscape of the film so much as provide an autonomous musical experience for the album purchaser—one that often contained music and performances not featured in the film.[67] This disconnect between commodities fed a growing public interest in film music and composers, but it also introduced new pressures within the industry that film musicians did not always welcome.

Elmer Bernstein's career trajectory vividly exemplifies this bind. Bernstein initially benefitted from the soundtrack boom after his jazz-infused title theme from *The Man with the Golden Arm* (Otto Preminger, 1955) became a national hit. In late March 1956, multiple covers of the theme vied against one another on *Billboard*'s "Coming Up Strong" list and received notice in "The Week's Best Buys."[68] The album's success brought Bernstein more record contract offers. Reported *Billboard*: "Decca signed Elmer Bernstein, ad infinitum, all with a cautious eye toward landing the eventual album rights to a film property."[69] Such arrangements further enhanced Bernstein's prominence in the industry, fashioning him into something of a star. Bernstein's subsequent contract to Dot Records in the late 1950s, for example, included not only standard soundtrack albums of his film scores but also compilations of film themes by various composers, all conducted by Bernstein. The Dot release of *Bernstein: Backgrounds for Brando* (1958) articulated Bernstein's star status by drawing heavy-handed parallels to Marlon Brando. On the back of the record jacket, pictures of Brando from various roles run down the left side, balanced on the right by a single picture of Bernstein, who is described in the picture caption as "versatile and youthful." Liner notes extend the Brando-Bernstein resemblances: "This distinguished actor has inspired a program of wide-ranging music, and it is superbly performed here by a musician of wide-ranging talents."[70]

However much these products augmented Bernstein's value for studios and record labels (see figure 6), he soon became an outspoken critic of trends the soundtrack industry helped inculcate, namely the prioritization of catchy melodies that might sell as singles covered by multiple recording artists. "Elmer Bernstein Warns of Hazards in Trying to Write Pic Tunes as Pop Hits," read one *Variety* headline from 1965: "Pressure comes from producers for hits, he explained, because such tunes are great ads for pix. Also they pay off in money and prestige for cleffer. But this concentration on hits too often can result in a bad score, Bernstein emphasized."[71] By 1967 Bernstein had become still gloomier on the topic: "The present state of film scoring is reverting back to the early days of sound films when composers just strung series of well-known tunes together."[72] Here the journalist could not help but observe some irony: "The success of such film songs as [Dimitri Tiomkin's] *High Noon* [Fred Zinnemann, 1952] and *Man with the Golden Arm* . . . spurred the pursuit of hit title songs for every picture. . . . Bernstein, incidentally, wrote *Man with the Golden Arm*, but said that music was an integral part of the film action and was not pasted on as an afterthought."[73]

FIGURE 6: Jay Rothman's portrait of Elmer Bernstein allowed fans to put a face to the name. The portrait adorned album jackets and ads. *Variety*, August 1, 1962, 41.

Bernstein's gripe that film scoring had become less about film and more about record sales reflected not just anxiety over filmmakers' commercial proclivities—hardly a new phenomenon—but rather concerns that musical taste in Hollywood was favoring pop-oriented sounds at the expense of symphonic scores. Pointing to a growing number of underemployed yet previously celebrated film composers, Bernstein observed: "These men have mastered the highly complex art of scoring. They know how to serve the needs of the film. But many producers are not using them because they want pop songs." Although Bernstein did not specify names, the fiasco involving Bernard Herrmann and Alfred Hitchcock over *Torn Curtain* (1966) was probably on Bernstein's mind. After working with Hitchcock on nine films over twelve years, Herrmann had been fired for ignoring the studio's request to furnish a catchy main theme.[74] Yet while such incidents supported Bernstein's point, they also reflected a much broader and pervasive musical drift that involved not just Hollywood, but also popular culture in postwar America.

American experiences with radio, for one, had changed after the war. A surge in record releases and regional radio broadcasting licenses combined with a new willingness on the part of stations to feature albums instead of live performers produced, in the words of Albin Zak, a "dynamic effervescence":

> With at least a hundred records released each week, there was a vast pool to draw from, with musical styles and idioms to appeal to nearly every taste. There was, of course, the great pop mainstream. But there were also record labels specializing in gospel music, Yiddish music, Mexican music, blues, hillbilly, polka, and more. . . . The radio dial provided access to an abundance of cultural expression that made the airwaves a pluralistic cornucopia. . . . The radio could take a listener to musical worlds of wholly unfamiliar yet fascinating sounds, jostling one another as they perched side by side on the dial.[75]

Another dial—that of the television—also offered an outlet for sampling disparate sonic styles with remarkable ease. With so much stylistic variety immediately accessible in American homes, it is not surprising that filmmakers and film musicians also explored stylistic options beyond the symphonic underscore mainstream. As Zak acknowledges, similar trends were underfoot among pop musicians in the early 1950s: "In the place of the big bands that had accompanied so many pop singers of the 1930s and 1940s, ad hoc groups began appearing on records, one-off ensembles put together in a recording studio for a particular session or even a single song."[76] Vocalists backed by big bands, of course, did not entirely disappear from the pop landscape, and neither did symphonic underscore from Hollywood film. But both were joined by a diverse array of stylistic alternatives, producing what film music historians have characterized as a musical "divergence"[77] embracing jazz (Johnny Mandel's score for *I Want to Live!* [Robert Wise, 1958]), electronic music (*Forbidden Planet*), idiosyncratic ensembles (an unaccompanied, wordless chorus replaces the orchestra in David Snell's score for *Lady in the Lake* [Robert Montgomery, 1947]), atonal and nonfunctional harmonic writing (*The Cobweb*), and various popular styles, including rock 'n' roll ("Rock Around the Clock" in *Blackboard Jungle* [Richard Brooks, 1955]). Just as the postwar fascination with magnetic recording had produced new means for arranging and conceptualizing sound in film and records, so too did the introduction of widely divergent musical styles, ensembles, and instruments into Hollywood film direct attention to timbre and the sonic qualities of the recording itself.[78]

An early example is the solo zither score from *The Third Man* (1949), composed and performed by Anton Karas, a musician with no previous experience in films. *The Third Man* was a European coproduction between Alexander Korda and David O. Selznick. The decision to have a zither-only score was reportedly serendipitous: British director Carol Reed heard Karas at a party for production members in Vienna and ultimately had the musician score the film.[79] But the novelty of the sound and an aggressive publicity campaign in the United States by Selznick's production company sparked a wildfire. In "Coast in Big Dither over Popularity of the Zither," Charles Emge reported that "with the picture not due for nationwide U.S. release until [April], Selznick's publicity department is worrying—but not too much—for fear the widespread popularity of numerous versions of *The Third Man Theme* recorded by U.S. firms may have gotten to this country just a bit too far ahead of the picture."[80] Karas's contribution, however, was not welcomed by all. Anticipating Elmer Bernstein's objections by fifteen years, critic Lawrence Morton argued passionately that Karas's success reflected "the public's insatiable taste for the trite" but not a victory for film music.[81] Emge also noted that movie musicians were wary of its popular success:

> It's not surprising that Hollywood's high priced fabricators of film scores and the high salaried staff orchestra men who record them are figuring on the possible economic effects of this *Third Man* music with narrowed eyes and furrowed brows. The significant slant is that this zitherist not only provided the film with all the music a good movie could possibly require, he also supplied an exploitation feature that beats anything our local press agents have been able to produce to date from a music angle.[82]

Such complaints, however, carried little weight with filmmakers and record labels monitoring popular buzz and album sales. While fears that zitherists might overrun Hollywood proved unfounded, the popular interest, commercial success, and critical backlash of *The Third Man* score encapsulated the possibilities and anxieties of the postwar era's musical divergence.

In 1955, MGM music director Johnny Green observed that even the sound of standard symphonic scores had changed noticeably in Hollywood, a sentiment that echoed Sternfeld's praise for Friedhofer's *Best Years* score:

> Green . . . feels that the term of opprobrium—"Hollywood Sound"— will no longer exist in describing film music. The lush over-writing and schmaltzy scores usually identified with Hollywood pix, he feels, are on their way out and will be replaced by a more individual approach. . . . Even the old-line composers, such as Bernard Herrmann and Franz

Waxman, according to Green, are changing their styles, the result being
that the veterans and the newcomers, encouraged by producers, . . . are
introducing "a sparse and linear" type of music.[83]

Seven years later, André Previn acknowledged in a *Variety* interview that creative
options available to film composers had expanded well beyond Green's imagining: "More leeway is being given the composer in terms of size and conception of
a score and there's more of a chance to be inventive."[84] For Previn this involved
developing radically different sounds for each production. In *The Four Horsemen
of the Apocalypse* (Vincente Minnelli, 1962) he provided "fulsome" symphonic
writing, but elsewhere he opted for non-symphonic idioms, including jazz in
films like *The Subterraneans* (Ranald MacDougall, 1960) and a piano-only score
for *Long Day's Journey into Night* (Sidney Lumet, 1962).

By the late 1950s, there was yet another reason for filmmakers and composers
to forgo the traditional symphony orchestra: what had begun as a studio orchestra
boom in the 1940s went bust in the late 1950s. Beginning in 1944, the American
Federation of Musicians succeeded in negotiating annual contracts that forced
major studios to keep orchestras of thirty-five to fifty musicians on the payroll,
whether they worked or not. (Previously studios had kept a smaller number of
principal players on contract and hired additional musicians when needed.)
Although this arrangement initially fit the predominant trend of scoring films
for full orchestra, the financial model became unsustainable after studios began
releasing fewer films each year in the 1950s. In November 1953, a *Down Beat* cor-
respondent noted that the dip in recording work also set Hollywood musicians
on edge, pushing some to find work elsewhere:

Not since the deep dark days of the depression have our staff orksters
[orchestras] been so severely shaken by the grim specter of insecurity.
Many of them have been sitting at home for weeks and even months
during the last year, drawing their checks as usual, by mail, while their
employers struggled over whether to try 3-D or CinemaScope or to go
back into the cloak and suit business. The musicians . . . know it just can't
last. . . . Television, which had little to offer musicians in its early stages,
is beginning to lure some top-drawer musical talent away from the film
studios.[85]

Five months later RKO disbanded its orchestra, negotiating an alternative deal
with the musicians union that promised to budget $10,000 for musicians' salaries
on each production.[86] In 1958, an American Federation of Musicians strike on
Hollywood studios ended badly when the studios made alternative arrangements
with a new labor group, Musicians Guild of America (MGA). Musicians would
be paid more per hour, but only on an as-needed basis. No longer would studios

keep full orchestras under contract.[87] Now the size of the accompanying ensemble for a given film reflected not only an aesthetic decision on the part of the composer and director, but also a budget decision made by the studio.

In *Pictures at a Revolution: Five Movies and the Birth of the New Hollywood*, Mark Harris scrutinizes each of the five films nominated for Best Picture in 1967, arguing that, rather than presenting a "five-snapshot collage of the American psyche as reflected in its popular culture," the nominees—*Bonnie and Clyde*, *Doctor Dolittle* (Richard Fleischer), *The Graduate*, *Guess Who's Coming to Dinner* (Stanley Kramer), and *In the Heat of the Night*—instead "illuminated . . . the movie industry's anxiety and bewilderment at a paroxysmal point in its own history."[88] Such a summation fits well with Page Cook's baffling "film music as noise" outburst, which was directed at some of these very films. Indeed, most bore little resemblance in sound to films of the 1930s and 1940s that had been made on studio lots, scored by studio composers, and recorded onto optical track with studio orchestras. The institutional structures that supported such a production model had atrophied during the postwar era.

More positively, this turn had created space and demand for new approaches, ideas, and individuals. The result was much more complicated than simply "out with the old and in with the new." Even after studios disbanded their orchestras in the late 1950s, for example, composers continued to furnish symphonic scores for generously budgeted productions, in part because demand for symphonic soundtrack albums like *Exodus*, *Lawrence of Arabia* (David Lean, 1962), and *Ben-Hur*, which received not one but three soundtrack releases, ensured compensating revenues. More traditionally oriented symphonic scores of the late 1950s and 1960s also exhibited on their own terms novel and unusual timbres. The Academy Award–nominated score for the three-hour historic epic *The Sand Pebbles*, a film about a U.S. gunboat navigating uncertain waters in 1920s China, is one case in point. Composed by the thirty-seven-year-old Jerry Goldsmith, who had only six years previously shifted from television to film, the music is performed by an enormous orchestra augmented with nontraditional instruments, including angklungs, a gamelan, crotales, Chinese temple bells, wood drums, cimbalom, and a harpsichord.[89] The sounds of these instruments emphasize the exoticized locale, but are still further defamiliarized through the magnetic, stereophonic techniques. As the credits begin, Goldsmith, his orchestrator David Tamkin, and recordists Murray Spivack and Douglas Williams create an unsettling effect as symphonic and non-symphonic instruments enter sequentially—violins, temple bells, cimbalom, wood drums, cellos—each entrance calling into question the identity of the full ensemble. Although the instruments sound together, they are separated spatially, each occupying a distinct space in the stereo field, an effect that draws attention to the magnetic stereophonic sound system but also reflects the film's Eastern-Western cultural tensions. In the film's road show souvenir program Goldsmith's aesthetic is outlined in terms that neatly reflect postwar priorities: "He likes to employ unusual instruments and unusual combinations of more conventional instruments. When possible, Goldsmith provides the unexpected 'sound'—that is, music which first might be judged inappropriate for a scene but which actually helps the sequences make a greater dramatic impact."[90]

Exploring "inappropriate" yet dramatically potent sounds was also the aim of another recent arrival who had established his career as jazz performer, arranger, bandleader, and record producer: Quincy Jones. Jones's film career had taken off in the mid-1960s, and in 1967 he wrote music for *In the Heat of the Night*, which won Best Picture, and *In Cold Blood*, for which he received his first nomination for Best Score, becoming the second African American composer after Duke Ellington to receive the recognition. Both efforts not only reflect Jones's "great flexibility and openness to experimentation,"[91] but also represent a high-water mark for aesthetic and technological trends of the postwar era. For *In Cold Blood*, Jones composed a score specifically crafted for the high-profile jazz musicians he had gathered. But the resulting score could hardly be described as "only" jazz, as Jones had taken steps to break the stylistic expectations of even that broadly defined genre. When asked about the strange sound effects heard throughout the score, including a buzzing, woozy timbre, Jones responded:

> That weird effect in the title track isn't an electronic instrument; it's just Frank Rosolino playing his trombone with a wire buzz-mute. But we did use all kinds of electronic and human noises. One was a moog-synthesizer, a strange device that can simulate just about any sound on earth—or off—including space-age effects. We had an electronic clavichord, played by Dave Grusin. The percussion sounds—man, we did everything! Shelly Manne slapping his knees, Louis Bellson imitating wire brushes with his mouth, me doing bottle-pops with my cheeks, Emil Richards mumbling . . . [92]

Strangest of all was Jones's decision to accompany the initial scenes of the Clutter family—the film's tragic victims—with warm, placid textures for strings and woodwinds. Never before has "conventional" orchestral underscore sounded so disconcertingly out of place; what in more conventional circumstances might have been ignored is transformed by Jones into something foreign and vaguely foreboding. Jones's experience with record production also meant that he was especially sensitive to the aural possibilities of magnetic recording and the limitations of theater sound systems. Reflecting back on *In Cold Blood* four decades later, Jones recalled:

> One of the frustrations I found in writing music for film was that you couldn't always get the music to the screen. Optical sound couldn't handle the music. We'd record on magnetic tape and [onscreen] the bottom

end just wasn't there. *In Cold Blood* had a very low score, with cellos and basses and one of the first synthesizers on a soundtrack. [Director] Richard Brooks knew about my concerns, so he went with an RCA engineer to adjust all of the speakers in all of the 65 first-run theaters . . . so that the music would be right.[93]

Not surprisingly, Jones's experiments were singled out in Page Cook's "Film Music as Noise" diatribe, where he claimed that *In Cold Blood* was a "conscienceless" blend of "mocking mush" and "primitive jazz."[94] What Cook found objectionable, however, was precisely what audiences, filmmakers, and other critics detected as especially exciting: Jones's stylistic versatility was itself virtuosic, and his tactile conception of sound was accessible yet astonishingly original. In one of the film's few lighthearted scenes, the two murderers assist a boy gathering glass bottles along the roadside. Jones's upbeat cue includes drumming on glass bottles, a musicalized transformation of the clinking glass sound effects on the soundtrack.

For *In the Heat of the Night*, Jones once again constructed the film's sound around specific musicians, including jazz flutist Roland Kirk, who simultaneously plays and shouts into his instrument. (Jones claimed that Kirk's style conveyed a sense of anger and loneliness necessary for the film.)[95] Like Jerry Goldsmith on *The Sand Pebbles*, Jones partly drew inspiration from the film's setting, pairing the Deep South locale with blues harmonies and gestures. But even more than the *In Cold Blood* score, the music defies stylistic categories: distorted bass, banjo, aggressive mouth percussion, twanging cimbalom, jazz flute, murmuring low strings, and bellowing French horns share the same soundtrack, drawing from not just blues, but also jazz, rock, and symphonic idioms. In addition to co-writing a title song for the credit sequence (performed by Ray Charles), Jones also co-wrote the film's pop songs, many heard on radios and jukeboxes in the film. The songs themselves traverse various genres, including R&B, rockabilly, and rock 'n' roll. The songs' dual function as both aural props and commentary on narrative situations reflect the emerging trend of the compilation score, in which songs rather than instrumental music frequently serve as underscore in films like *The Graduate*, *Easy Rider* (Dennis Hopper, 1969), *The Last Picture Show* (Peter Bogdanovich, 1971), and *American Graffiti* (George Lucas, 1973).[96] *In the Heat of the Night* also won an Oscar for Best Sound and another nomination for Best Sound Effects; there are many instances in which sound effects by James Richard and Jones's music shrewdly elide, whether through the realistically tinny sound of Jones's songs on a portable radio or the habitual gum-chewing of the town's sheriff, Gillespie (Rod Steiger), its speed and slushy timbre transfigured in score into deft mouth percussion performed by Don Elliott.

Like *The Best Years of Our Lives*, *In the Heat of the Night* confronted a timely social problem. While passing through a southern town, Virgil Tibbs, an African

American police detective (Sidney Poitier), is first accused of a murder and then asked to solve it. By film's end, Tibbs and Gillespie, the town's white sheriff, have become friends. Awarded the Academy Award for Best Picture mere days after the memorial service for Martin Luther King Jr., the film did not—could not—resolve the pervasive racism it depicted. Listening to the sounds of *In the Heat of the Night* today, however, it is hard not to be swayed by the infectious enthusiasm of Jones's eclectic, multicultural sounds. They exemplify the postwar era's trajectory of stylistic divergence to an extreme degree while also articulating the film's themes of racial tension and reconciliation. Applauding Jones's recent achievements on *In Cold Blood* and *In the Heat of the Night*, jazz critic Leonard Feather asked Jones to comment on the current state of music in Hollywood. Pondering the same "noisy" soundscape that Page Cook had dismissed, Jones offered a different outlook. The "bold, original" efforts of new composers like "Johnny" Williams, Neal Hefti, Lalo Schifrin, and Benny Golson boded well to Jones. "It's a brave new world," he added, "and I sure dig being a part of it."[97]

Cook's pessimism and Jones's optimism presented opposing sides of the same coin: an acknowledgment that aesthetic and commercial pressures in the late 1960s favored a more conspicuous soundtrack in which music and sound effects vied for audiences' attention through ever bolder gestures. In musical terms, this trend registered through the growing popularity of compilation scores, which emphasized stylistic heterogeneity through selections of preexistent music that reflected "the gradual incorporation of rock, funk, soul, and country and western styles into film composition."[98] Compilation scores also placed greater control of the soundtrack in the hands of the filmmakers, whose idiosyncratic preferences articulated musical sensibilities independent of any particular composer.[99] If a surge in preexistent music in films drew audiences' notice, so too did filmmakers' penchant for sound that diverged, in the words of James Monaco, "from an aesthetic of naturalism toward a more artificially crafted and manipulated motion-picture sound design." The trend granted Foley artists more opportunities to contribute elaborate aural effects, prompting the Academy to add a new sound effects category in 1963 (Walter G. Elliott won for his work in Stanley Kramer's *It's a Mad, Mad, Mad, Mad World*). Although magnetic, stereophonic rerecording techniques in Hollywood continued to outstrip the playback capabilities of most theaters, public appreciation of stereo sound grew as more individuals experienced its expressive potential through classical, popular, and movie music albums played on home hi-fi systems. A solution to theaters' increasingly dated sound systems finally emerged in the late 1960s, although the technology was not introduced commercially until the mid-1970s. Much as magnetic tape had revolutionized film sound production in the postwar era, so Ray Dolby's noise-reduction and stereo technologies would give filmmakers, sound designers, and composers of the Auteur Renaissance an entirely new palette of sonic possibilities.

4

THE AUTEUR RENAISSANCE, 1968–1980   Jeff Smith

The late sixties and early seventies were an important transitional era in Hollywood's history. A wave of mergers and acquisitions produced a new managerial class in Hollywood, replacing much of the remaining old guard from the studio system's Golden Age. The elimination of the Production Code Administration created a new spirit of frankness in the dramatic treatment of violence, sexuality, and adult themes. And despite *The Sound of Music*'s (Robert Wise, 1965) record-setting take for domestic box office revenues, the sixties saw the epic failure of several big-budget spectacles, a situation that portended an increasingly volatile marketplace.

Economic uncertainty eventually subsided, though, toward the end of the seventies, gradually stabilizing thanks to new opportunities for ancillary revenues and robust new strategies for managing risk. More important, as the "movie brats" came of age, directors such as George Lucas, Francis Ford Coppola, Martin Scorsese, and Steven Spielberg established themselves as the leaders of a new generation of Hollywood powerbrokers. Indeed, the Auteur Renaissance, also known as the Hollywood Renaissance, is now viewed as a kind of lost Eden, a time when studio executives took unusual artistic risks and American filmmakers challenged audiences with complex characters, novel storytelling techniques, and a seriousness of purpose more commonly associated with their European counterparts. Ranging from gritty portraits of urban crime to incisive character studies to revitalized treatments of traditional genres, films like *The French Connection* (William Friedkin, 1971), *The Godfather* (Francis Ford Coppola, 1972), *Cabaret* (Bob Fosse, 1972), *Jaws* (Steven Spielberg, 1975), *Taxi Driver* (Martin Scorsese, 1976), and *Annie Hall* (Woody Allen, 1978) were among the most popular and critically acclaimed titles in Hollywood's history.

The Hollywood Renaissance also proved to be an important, if somewhat atypical, period for the history of film sound. The gradual breakdown of the studio system opened up new points of entry into the industry and new possibilities for creative exploration. Moreover, although the previous generation's innovations were driven mostly by changes in visual technology, technological change during the Hollywood Renaissance occurred more autonomously. In the case of film sound, much of this was driven by the rapid adoption and diffusion of transistorized, solid-state equipment in the music industry, which by 1970 had become an important rival to Hollywood in the competition for American consumers' leisure dollars. In what follows, I examine these changes in the aesthetics of film sound by teasing out their relationship to larger industrial and technological pressures. This chapter also considers the contributions of the era's most important sound designers, who helped film audiences hear the world anew as they pushed the boundaries regarding the ways that ambient noise and even the human voice could be recorded, mixed, and electronically processed. In doing so, these sound "auteurs" made the soundtrack a more layered, more textured, and more visceral component of the overall cinematic experience.

The Hollywood Renaissance

By the end of the 1960s, Hollywood started to realize some of the pitfalls of its earlier business strategies. Although the "make them bigger" philosophy yielded some huge hits, like *The Ten Commandments* (Cecil B. DeMille, 1956) and *Ben-Hur* (William Wyler, 1959), a string of big-budget bombs, including *Cleopatra* (Joseph Mankiewicz, 1963), *Doctor Dolittle* (Richard Fleischer, 1967), and *Tora! Tora! Tora!* (Richard Fleischer, Kinji Fukasaku, and Toshio Masuda, 1970), placed one of the major studios—Twentieth Century–Fox—on the verge of bankruptcy. Even seemingly surefire projects fizzled. Coming off the huge success of *The Sound of Music,* Julie Andrews and director Robert Wise reteamed for *Star!* (Robert Wise, 1968), a three-hour biopic about Gertrude Lawrence, an early Broadway great. The film's budget was almost twice that of its predecessor, but *Star!* returned only about $4 million, a pittance compared to *Music*'s $163 million gross.

By the mid-sixties, Hollywood found itself struggling to find an audience, largely because of its inability to keep pace with larger social and cultural changes. Many of Hollywood's "old lions," like John Ford, Howard Hawks, and Vincente

Minnelli, were nearing the end of their careers. Other seasoned craftsmen, like Robert Stevenson and George Seaton, soldiered on, occasionally turning out hits like *The Love Bug* (Stevenson, 1968) and *Airport* (Seaton, 1970) that recalled the old-fashioned entertainments of a bygone age. In a particularly telling anecdote, Peter Biskind describes a scene in which a limousine picks up director Norman Taurog to take him to the set of *Double Trouble* (Taurog, 1966), the latest in a series of nondescript Elvis Presley musicals. The sixty-six-year-old was losing his eyesight and therefore physically incapable of driving.[1] The fact that a major studio would entrust a film to a director so visually impaired attests to the degree to which Hollywood kept one foot firmly planted in its illustrious but rapidly vanishing past.

In searching for talent more attuned to the emerging counterculture, studios turned to a younger generation of directors. Some, such as Arthur Penn, John Frankenheimer, Paul Mazursky, Arthur Hiller, and Steven Spielberg, emerged from the ranks of television production. Others, like Martin Scorsese, Francis Ford Coppola, and George Lucas, were culled from the film programs that were popping up at major universities. Still others, like Woody Allen, Peter Bogdanovich, and Mike Nichols, broke into directing from related fields, such as stand-up comedy, film journalism, and Broadway theater. These filmmakers, who are often grouped together under the term "Hollywood Renaissance," have wildly different styles, but their combination of irreverence and thematic depth helped these directors connect with an audience dissatisfied by Hollywood's usual bromides and happy endings.

Yet the Hollywood Renaissance's critical acclaim and its aura of sophistication would mean little if its films failed at the box office. Instead, as studio executives quickly realized, many of these directors provided huge box office returns on rather modest investments. *Love Story* (Arthur Hiller, 1970), for example, cost a little more than $2 million to produce, but earned back more than $100 million at the box office. Coppola's *The Godfather* made more than $130 million on its negative cost of approximately $6 million. Even Spielberg's *Jaws,* a film often cited as the prototype of the modern blockbuster, cost a relatively modest $8 million to produce. *Jaws* nearly earned that back in its opening weekend, and went on to add another $190 million to its total. Of course, it didn't hurt that each of these films was based on a best-selling book. Yet, in recognizing the importance of presold literary properties, Hollywood executives also realized that the glossy spectacle associated with older hits was neither necessary nor desirable.

The seeming schizophrenia created by Hollywood's mixture of old-fashioned showmanship and new aesthetic sensibilities is beautifully captured in Mark Harris's *Pictures at a Revolution,* a book that charts the fortunes of the five Best Picture nominees for the 1968 Academy Awards.[2] Two of the five nominees seemed reminiscent of the kinds of projects that were popular during the fifties. Stanley Kramer's *Guess Who's Coming to Dinner* (1967) starred Spencer Tracy and

Katharine Hepburn in their last film together. The film not only stirred echoes of their previous collaborations, but also recalled earnest postwar "soapboxers" like *Pinky* (Elia Kazan, 1949) and *No Way Out* (Joseph Mankiewicz, 1950). *Doctor Dolittle* attempted to recapture the glitz of the road-show musical, but the troubled production ended up being precisely the kind of bloated, big-budget bomb that the industry now sought to avoid.

At the other end of the spectrum were *Bonnie and Clyde* (Arthur Penn, 1967) and *The Graduate* (Mike Nichols, 1967), two projects that anticipated Hollywood's future direction in the seventies. The former achieved notoriety for its violence, its frank handling of sexual themes, and its cheeky treatment of gangster film conventions. The latter rather effectively used its protagonist's ambivalence and confusion about his future to expose the hypocrisy and spiritual emptiness of his parents' generation. Interestingly, both films also tweaked the use of particular sound techniques in ways that anticipated the kinds of formal innovations seen in the seventies. As Jay Beck points out, *Bonnie and Clyde* heightened the impact of its sound effects not only to intensify moments of explosive violence, but also to sharpen the film's sudden tonal shifts from farce to tragedy and back again.[3] *The Graduate* used radical disjunctions of image and sound to underline the main character's sense of cultural dislocation.

The eventual Best Picture winner, *In the Heat of the Night* (Norman Jewison, 1967), fell squarely between these two extremes. The film shrewdly tapped into the era's civil rights zeitgeist by embroidering its old-fashioned "whodunit" plot with scenes exploring the divisiveness of racial prejudice in the South. The film's frank depiction of racial conflict broke certain representational taboos for the period. As Mark Harris reports, when local plantation owner Eric Endicott slapped Philadelphia homicide detective Virgil Tibbs (Sidney Poitier) for his impertinence, Tibbs slapped him back, a gesture that frequently drew gasps from movie theater audiences.[4]

Changes in Film Sound Technologies

The sense of a generational sea change described by Biskind and Harris is also evident in sound recording practices of the period. For years, Hollywood sound personnel opposed the use of magnetic sound recording and playback technologies, even though the latter had demonstrably better fidelity than the optical sound systems then predominant. In 1969, these advantages led the Sound Committee of the Society of Motion Picture and Television Engineers (SMPTE) to recommend the adoption of four-track magnetic striping on 35mm prints as the industry standard. In a telling addendum, the *Journal of the SMPTE* reported that, among its sixty-five active research projects, "there is currently no study of optical stereo within the Sound Committee."[5]

John Belton has rightly described the innovation of magnetic sound in the 1950s as a "frozen revolution," one that collapsed under the weight of both cost and established practice.[6] By the early sixties, magnetic sound was reserved for large-gauge systems, like 70mm film, a format frequently used for road show exhibitions featuring multichannel stereo mixes. Although magnetic sound for 35mm film never caught on, magnetic tape did make important inroads as a medium for sound capture. The development of transistors for audio equipment led to the introduction of new lightweight, portable recorders that used quarter-inch magnetic tape. Perfectone, Stellavox, and Nagra each produced their own models weighing less than twenty pounds. But Nagra quickly established itself as the industry standard in the United States, largely because it had been engineered to meet the standards of motion picture recording.[7] In an interview published in 1994, production sound mixer Les Lazarowitz explained why the Nagra became a mainstay for film work: "When you go out to work on a movie, you want something that is dependable, reliable, and is going to do the job for you. You don't want to worry about it—you have enough to worry about. Your bottom line is that all of your effort is ending up on a seven-dollar piece of ¼ inch tape."[8]

Besides its dependability, Nagra's lightweight design made it an ideal recording device for location shoots. Before the Nagra, location shoots required sound trucks that carried about eight to ten tons of batteries, amplifiers, and synchronizing generators. Nagras eliminated the need for trucks, relying instead on a Neopilot system that placed two very narrow sync recorders in a push-pull arrangement down the center of the audio track.[9] The portability of the Nagra meant that filmmakers in studios could work with smaller sound crews. As *Variety* reported in 1967, the typical four-man sound crew consisted of a recorder, a mixer, a boom operator, and a cable man. With the switch to quarter-inch tape, however, the recorder was left with little to do since the mixer could quite easily thread the Nagra or insert a tape cartridge. The craft unions loudly objected to the mixer's usurpation of the recorder's duties since they had a strong incentive to preserve the jobs of their members. Columbia Pictures developed a workaround that satisfied union demands by allowing the recorders to load enough tape on a machine for an entire day's shoot and then unload it when production for the day had wrapped. The recorder, though, then remained in the studio's sound shop while the rest of the crew handled the logistics of actual sound capture.[10]

Despite pushback from unions representing sound technicians, the trend toward three-person or even two-person crews eventually became the norm. In fact, in 1976, *SMPTE Journal* reported that a single individual could now perform all the functions done previously by a four-person team.[11] All that was needed was a fishpole microphone and a one-pound recording device mounted atop a five-pound mixing unit equipped with automatic level control.[12]

Meanwhile, as the studios themselves sought to shed overhead and labor costs, they increasingly began to outsource sound production and postproduction services to independently owned facilities. Given the new industry niche occupied by low-budget independent films, these postproduction houses became ever more important. In 1970, the owners of three separate postproduction services— Synchro-Film, Edit-Rite, and Producers Sound Services—banded together to create a single, full-service postproduction facility.[13] With plans to build a new six- to eight-story building and anticipated annual gross revenues of $2 million, the new business venture hoped to capitalize on its earlier success with *Easy Rider* (Dennis Hopper, 1969), which was produced on a budget of $400,000 but grossed more than $60 million worldwide.

Perhaps the most important consequence of the shift to quarter-inch tape as a recording medium was that it lessened the sound team's reliance on studio sound effects libraries. As a 1948 article in *Variety* noted, the studios collectively cataloged and maintained libraries with more than 100,000 different individual sounds. A "Biffs and Bangs" file, for example, might contain an assortment of different fight noises, such as kicks, slaps, punches, and blows. Maintaining such a vast collection of sounds increased efficiencies in the production of soundtracks, since a gunshot sound recorded for one film could be dubbed and reinserted into others.[14]

The use of library sounds was undoubtedly cheaper and more efficient, but it also had a liability. For *The Charge of the Light Brigade* (Michael Curtiz, 1936), Warner Bros. recorded twenty-three new exterior gunshot ricochet sounds for the battle scenes, and then reused them in their productions for the next thirty years. Even with a variety of different options for a single sound effect, the reliance on library effects meant that certain sounds were overused. Indeed, a connoisseur, like sound designer Ben Burtt, could identify the studio that produced a film just by listening to its sound effects without ever needing to glance at the images onscreen.[15]

Although library sounds continued to have an important place in the work of sound effects editors, the ease and portability of the Nagra encouraged a younger generation of sound technicians to experiment with the technology, creating whole new personal libraries of sound effects in the process. Walter Murch, for example, more or less improvised the creation of the jet cycle sounds for *THX 1138* (George Lucas, 1971). Using his Nagra, Murch herded together several female employees at Francis Coppola's American Zoetrope, took them into the company washroom, and asked them to scream as loud as they could. Murch overmodulated the recording of these screaming voices so that they distorted. This created a combination of low frequency pulsing and a high-pitched element that sounded like the oscillation of a motor. Murch then added a Doppler shift to the recording and the sound of the jet cycles was born (see figure 7).[16]

Although the trend toward portable, lightweight devices was an important development for sound recorders and mixers, perhaps a more important shift took place in the implementation of noise reduction technology for both the

FIGURE 7: Sound designer Walter Murch created the sound of jet cycles for *THX 1138* (George Lucas, 1971) by recording and then manipulating the shrieks and cries of a small group of female employees at American Zoetrope.

production and exhibition sectors of the industry. Noise reduction, in and of itself, was not a new idea. In fact, as early as 1941, Bell Telephone Laboratories (BTL) had developed the basic principles used in later noise reduction technologies.[17] Hollywood studios, however, did not adopt BTL's noise reduction system, even though some of its techniques were incorporated into the Fantasound system created for Walt Disney's *Fantasia* (Walt Disney, 1940).

By the early seventies, several factors encouraged filmmakers to reassess their earlier resistance to noise reduction technologies. For one thing, advances in the magnetic recording devices and microphones used in production allowed for the capture of a much larger frequency range, especially for sounds above 10 kHz. The use of loudspeakers for playback in theaters, though, employed the Academy curve adopted in 1948 to minimize high-frequency hiss as well as noise caused by dirt and scratches on release prints. With a roll off of sounds above 4 kHz, the Academy curve created a huge mismatch between the frequency ranges that were now possible in production versus those possible in exhibition.

Another factor that encouraged the implementation of noise reduction technologies was the development of solid-state electronic components for audio. As diodes and transistors gradually replaced vacuum tube technology, modular, solid-state devices were created that could be inserted easily into the recording or playback chain. Such devices enabled theater owners to improve their sound systems without having to replace existing components or do extensive rewiring. Toward the end of 1972, the *Journal of the SMPTE* recommended the implementation of noise reduction circuitry as a simple, practical means of upgrading sound reproduction at a relatively reasonable cost for exhibitors.[18]

At the start of the seventies, the company best positioned to capitalize on this desire for improved playback in theaters was Dolby. As Jay Beck notes, Ray Dolby founded the Dolby Laboratories in 1965 with the aim of creating a "workable solution to the problem of tape noise."[19] Drawing on the same principles used by BTL for its "compander," Dolby's A-type noise reduction employed filters to stratify the audio signal's frequency range into four separate bands: (1) below 80 Hz, (2) from 80 to 3,000 Hz, (3) from 3 kHz to 9 kHz, and (4) above 9 kHz. Dolby's combination of filters, compressors, and limiters enabled the compression of the signal as a whole while adding for an appropriate gain in amplitude and a boost in the signal's high frequencies during recording. During playback, the process was reversed, yielding an increase in dynamic range of up to 10 dB.[20] As Ioan Allen, a Dolby engineer, explained, "The system works only on the quietest signals during the compression and expansion process," leaving the largest part of the signal's dynamics unchanged, "thus avoiding transient overshoots and consequent risk of clipping of the recording or transmission medium."[21]

Initially, Dolby focused on marketing his system to the music industry, which many believed was more technologically advanced than the typical studio sound department. Decca Records became an early adopter, acquiring nine Dolby type-A units in 1965 and releasing the first album produced with noise reduction technology in November 1966—a recording of Gustav Mahler's Second Symphony conducted by Georg Solti. After gaining a foothold in the music recording business, Dolby then turned his attention to the consumer market, licensing its type-B noise reduction system to KLH Corporation for use in the manufacture of a quarter-inch magnetic tape recorder.[22]

By 1970, Dolby Laboratories had shifted its attention to film, recognizing that its demands were quite different from that of the music industry. As the decade began, multichannel, magnetic soundtracks represented the state of the art for high fidelity film sound. Yet Dolby understood that the restriction of this technology to road show houses also left a huge part of the exhibition market untapped. The key to this segment was its reliance on optical sound for playback. More important, any gain in the quality of sound in either production or postproduction could not be fully realized without comparable improvements to theater sound reproduction.

Touting the success of noise reduction in music recording and playback, Dolby initially entered the film business by implementing its type-A system on film scoring stages in the United Kingdom. Dolby processes were successfully employed in the production of magnetic master tapes for *Oliver!* (Carol Reed, 1968) and *Ryan's Daughter* (David Lean, 1970).[23] Yet the real breakthrough for noise reduction in film sound came in 1971 when director Stanley Kubrick incorporated Dolby's system for all the postproduction sound on *A Clockwork Orange* (1971).[24]

Regrettably, though, the company quickly realized that these benefits ultimately were lost when that audio information was transferred to an optical soundtrack.[25] Without a transmission medium as good as a magnetic master, all efforts to improve the quality of sound in theaters would prove fruitless. Thus, in

November 1970, Dolby used Delbert Mann's telefilm of *Jane Eyre* as an opportunity to test its noise reduction processes on the type of optical soundtracks that were standard for 35mm release prints. After comparing reels that featured noise reduction encoding to reels processed normally, Dolby's engineers surmised that the difference was "not startling."[26] The experiment led Dolby engineers to conclude that the problem was not the presence of noise in and of itself, but was based on both the inherent limitations of optical sound as a transmission medium and the frequency response constraints associated with the Academy curve.

In an effort to address these problems, Dolby introduced its Model 364 sound unit in February 1972 as a device specifically designed to decode optical soundtracks recorded with type-A noise reduction.[27] The device more or less languished until Dolby representatives gave public demonstrations of its noise reduction and equalization techniques to industry personnel in London and Hollywood. Soon after, Dolby introduced its Model CP100 cinema processor, described by the *Journal of the SMPTE* as a "compact unit" that "contains all the necessary noise reduction, equalization and control circuitry (with the exception of power amplifiers) to play back conventional optical tracks, Dolby-encoded mono and stereo optical soundtracks, and conventional magnetic stripe soundtracks."[28] By 1975, Ioan Allen boasted that the company's mono packages had been installed in about four hundred theaters and that eleven films, mixed at four different studios, had been released with Dolby-encoded variable area optical soundtracks.

Of all the directors who gained prominence in the Hollywood Renaissance period, Robert Altman may have been the one who benefited the most from Dolby's innovation of noise reduction technology. In a 1978 piece published in *Film Comment,* entertainment journalist Charles Schreger asserted that Altman had "found a vital ally in Ray Dolby," and further claimed that the director's 1975 masterpiece, *Nashville* (1975), "could not have been made without Dolby."[29] Due to its elimination of background noise and its improved frequency response, Dolby enabled Altman to layer sounds atop one another, creating a polyphonic weave striking in its density and complexity.

Altman is chiefly known for his rather startling use of overlapping dialogue. In and of itself, overlapping dialogue was hardly new. In fact, it was fairly common in newspaper films and screwball comedies, genres that often featured quick-witted, fast-talking characters. Altman, though, pushed the boundaries of this technique in ways that no other director had. Striving for a new kind of aural realism, he often recorded several voices together in an effort to capture something of the actual buzz and din of groups engaged in conversation. In doing so, he evoked the cocktail party effect in which listeners pick out the frequency of a single speaking voice from the chatter of other discussants.[30]

In theory, Altman's films increase viewers' cognitive load to the extent that they have to pick out these bits of dialogue from a tangled skein of other voices.

Yet even though his approach roughens our perception, most spectators have little difficulty in following the plots of his films, since they get the gist of the dialogue even if they do not catch every word that is spoken. Moreover, as Mark Minett points out, Altman often artfully used mixing techniques and natural conversational pauses to highlight the most narratively salient moments of dialogue.[31]

Although he experimented with overlapping dialogue in some of his earlier films, Altman's breakthrough came with *M*A*S*H* (1970), a surprise hit that updated the classical Hollywood service comedy with irreverent humor and a surprising sexual frankness. He showcased the technique in several scenes set inside the camp's mess tent and its operating room. In a vivid demonstration of the cocktail party effect, we listen to several doctors speak at once as they direct their staff, crack jokes, and make inappropriate overtures to their nurses.

A key to Altman's technique involved the use of wireless radio mikes. This enabled him to capture several voices simultaneously during production. On *M*A*S*H*, however, all these inputs from the microphones were still fed into a single recording device, which limited the sound team's ability to do much with it in postproduction. As Altman's production sound mixer, Jim Webb, recalled, "If you walk into a bar, you hear eight conversations; there's no sane way to do this except on multitrack. In fact, he tried to shoot *McCabe and Mrs. Miller* (Altman, 1971) that way. The production sound mixer made a valiant effort but it didn't really produce what Altman wanted."[32]

Working with Webb, audio engineer Jack Cashin, and rerecording mixer Richard Portman, Altman later experimented with the use of multitrack recording for production sound on *California Split* (Altman, 1974). Cashin contrived an eight-track portable recorder and powered it with a twelve-volt car battery. Cashin's improvised device enabled Webb to record as many as seven different microphone inputs on separate tracks with the remaining channel serving as a control track. Webb and Cashin also created a console for the multitrack recorder, which allowed for input levels to be monitored for each individual channel. Then during postproduction, Portman could combine these sounds in any possible relationship, pulling any interesting bit of dialogue out of the mix as a whole. Because the film was a modest character study of two gamblers, Webb usually only miked two or three actors at a time, using the remaining channels for live music or even groups of people improvising unscripted conversations.

Using *California Split* as a kind of trial run, Altman and Webb raised the stakes on *Nashville,* a kaleidoscopic portrait of the country music industry and American politics. For this film, Altman typically miked six or seven actors at a time (see figure 8). An example of this occurs in the scene where actress Julie Christie, playing herself, pays a visit to Haven Hamilton's table. As Haven exchanges pleasantries with Christie and her publicist, Altman's trademark use of overlapping dialogue also allows us to hear Delbert and John discuss Christie's

FIGURE 8: Julie Christie's cameo in *Nashville* (Robert Altman, 1975) creates a brief bit of hubbub among a group of characters attending a club performance by Vassar Clement. Altman renders their reaction to Christie's unexpected appearance as two over-lapped conversations. For such scenes, Altman's sound team used wireless radio mikes and a multitrack recorder to capture the voices of six or seven different actors at a time.

film work, including her breakthrough performance in *Doctor Zhivago* (David Lean, 1965). He pushed the premises of multitrack production sound even further on *A Wedding* (Altman, 1978). Whereas *Nashville* purported to have twenty-four significant characters, *A Wedding* featured forty. Using two eight-track record-ers and two full sound crews, Webb miked and recorded as many as fourteen different actors at a time. With so much material to work with, Portman often sifted through as many as twenty-five different dialogue tracks for a single reel. Much of Portman's time was spent smoothing cuts from one track to another and building it all into a coherent passage of time.[33] The final effect was of a thick murmur of conversation with brief isolated comments from the crowd cutting through the background atmosphere.

Film Music during the Hollywood Renaissance

The classical Hollywood score remained an important stylistic option through-out the sixties and seventies. *Airport*'s languid, lyrical love theme and brassy, rhythmic main title—written by Alfred Newman, one of the "old lions" of the studio era—show that the big symphonic sound of Hollywood's Golden Age per-sisted, even though the industry sought younger audiences and opened its doors to a new generation of directors. This classical strain also appears in Miklós Rózsa's score for *The Private Life of Sherlock Holmes* (Billy Wilder, 1970), which adapted the composer's violin concerto to the big screen.

The style, though, was hardly confined to the late work of studio-era compos-ers. It also informed the work of a younger cohort who grew up steeped in the Hollywood tradition. Ernest Gold, who began writing film music in the 1950s, continued his long association with director Stanley Kramer by crafting a fairly traditional score for *The Secret of Santa Vittoria* (Kramer, 1969). Like its classical predecessors, Gold's music adds local color and character to the story of an Italian village seeking to conceal a million bottles of wine from a Nazi occupation force. Similarly, Marvin Hamlisch's theme song and score for the period romance *The Way We Were* (Sydney Pollack, 1974) underline its bittersweet tone.

Classical scoring techniques were also invigorated by an infusion of talent from abroad. French composer Michel Legrand's melancholy theme for *Summer of '42* (Robert Mulligan, 1971) added nostalgic sweep to a coming of age film. Nino Rota's music for *The Godfather* added emotional heft and ethnic colorations to Francis Ford Coppola's revisionist mafia epic. British composer Richard Rodney Bennett infused Sidney Lumet's whodunit *Murder on the Orient Express* (1974) with an appropriate aura of mystery while simultaneously evoking memories of 1930s detective films.

Moreover, just as they did in the fifties, composers also continued to incorporate jazz elements into their film scores. For example, Jerry Goldsmith's haunting trumpet melody for *Chinatown* (Roman Polanski, 1974) recalled the memorable collaboration between Miles Davis and Gil Evans on albums like *Miles Ahead* (1957) and *Sketches of Spain* (1960). Marvin Hamlisch's arrangements of Scott Joplin rags added a jaunty note to Best Picture winner *The Sting* (George Roy Hill, 1973). Other composers, however, updated the jazz idiom in film by drawing upon new sounds popularized by fusion artists, such as Chick Corea, Herbie Hancock, and Weather Report. This fusion influence can be heard in Earth Wind & Fire's score for the Blaxploitation classic *Sweet Sweetback's Baadasssss Song* (Melvin Van Peebles, 1971), in Lalo Schifrin's scores for cop films like *Bullitt* (Peter Yates, 1968) and *Dirty Harry* (Don Siegel, 1971), and in the scores written by Quincy Jones for a trio of caper films: *The Split* (Gordon Flemyng, 1968), *The Anderson Tapes* (Sidney Lumet, 1971), and *The Hot Rock* (Peter Yates, 1972).

All of these examples show composers either continuing or updating style topics that were well established within previous generations of Hollywood practice. Others, however, pushed against these norms, considerably enlarging the stylistic palette available to film composers. One strand of this expansion involves the incorporation of high modernist techniques, like twelve-tone serialism. Jerry Goldsmith's score for the science fiction classic *Planet of the Apes* (Franklin Schaffner, 1968), for example, combined atonal musical structures with unusual chamber orchestrations. Goldsmith's score featured several atypical wind and percussion instruments, such as a bass slide whistle, conch shells, a ram's horn, a Brazilian culka, and even tuned stainless steel bowls.[34] John Williams's score for Robert Altman's psychodrama *Images* (1972) proved equally audacious. It showcased the work of Japanese percussionist Stomu Yamashta and contained several cues that take shape as atonal, aleatoric bursts of sound. Yamashta performed his parts on metal and glass sculptures, but Williams fleshed out these sonic textures with the addition of Inca flutes, Kabuki percussion, bells, wood chimes, and human grunts.[35] Similarly, Henry Mancini explored the possibilities of microtonal inflections in his music for the thrillers *Wait Until Dark* (Terence Young, 1967) and *The Night Visitor* (Laslo Benedik, 1971). For these scores, Mancini utilized two pianos tuned a quartertone apart. By playing alternating chords in succession, the music added an appropriate feeling of menace and paranoia to these films about psychological torment.

At the opposite end of the spectrum, several of the "movie brats" utilized various pop and rock idioms to connect with the youth audience that emerged as Hollywood's most important demographic. As Julie Hubbert notes, some members of the Hollywood Renaissance directors developed a fictional correlate to documentary's *cinéma vérité* aesthetic by using source music as a way of fleshing out their films' social milieus.[36] In *The Last Picture Show* (Peter Bogdanovich, 1971), for example, a mélange of fifties pop songs and Hank Williams classics captured the emotional experience of growing up in a small, dying Texas town. Similarly, in *Mean Streets* (Martin Scorsese, 1973), the use of classic rock songs by Johnny Ace, the Ronettes, the Miracles, the Rolling Stones, and Eric Clapton neatly underlined the mix of love, sin, and machismo displayed by Charlie and Johnny Boy as small-time toughs in New York's Little Italy.

In other films, though, directors used pop and rock songs in ways that more closely paralleled the functions of classical Hollywood scores. In these instances, the songs are nondiegetic and are used to underscore character traits, to reinforce aspects of a film's setting, or to enhance a film's sense of formal unity. In *Easy Rider*, for example, Steppenwolf's recording of "Born to Be Wild" contributed a sense of pace and excitement to shots of the film's heroes—Wyatt and Billy—as they roll through America's highways. The song also reinforced an important aspect of their characterization, namely their desire to live outside the structures and constraints of normal society. In *Super Fly* (Gordon Parks Jr., 1972), Curtis Mayfield's title song added a dose of sexiness and even a certain vulnerability to Priest, the hard-bitten drug dealer who serves as the film's ostensible hero. That being said, however, as Christopher Sieving notes, other songs in the film, like "Pusherman" and "Freddie's Dead," acted as a kind of internal critique, questioning the visual register's tendency to romanticize the criminal life and reminding viewers that the character's actions lead to violence and the destruction of community.[37]

All these songs contributed to the narrative meanings of the films in which they appeared. Yet the music of popular recording artists also helped to manage the economic risks of production by adding a potential stream of ancillary revenues to a film's bottom line. For some films, the music revenues provided by popular theme songs and soundtrack albums helped to offset potential losses for underperforming titles. *Shaft* (Gordon Parks, 1971), for example, earned a relatively modest $12 million return on its $1 million budget, but Isaac Hayes's famous theme song and soundtrack album sold extremely well, topping

Billboard's sales charts and eventually earning Gold Record certifications in the mid-1990s. Similarly, the soundtrack for *FM* (John A. Alonzo, 1978) went platinum on the strength of its roster of marquee artists, such as Steely Dan, Linda Ronstadt, Jimmy Buffett, and the Steve Miller Band. The film, though, returned less than $3 million in rentals, greatly disappointing its distributor, Universal.

In other cases, however, the success of both a film and a related music property could reinforce each other's popularity at the box office and on record charts. *The Graduate*, for example, grossed about $100 million worldwide, sold more than two million copies of its soundtrack, and spawned a #1 single in Simon and Garfunkel's "Mrs. Robinson." Moreover, like its predecessor, the "coming of age" classic *American Graffiti* (George Lucas, 1973) also illustrated the potential benefits of such cross-promotional strategies. The film grossed about $140 million worldwide and its soundtrack was certified gold just four months after its debut. Even more impressively, *American Graffiti*'s soundtrack showed the kind of long-tail potential that such products can have in the marketplace as the album went on to sell an additional 1.5 million copies over the course of the next two decades.

The Robert Stigwood Organization pushed these cross-promotional campaigns to new heights with the release of *Saturday Night Fever* (John Badham, 1977). Stigwood had been a successful music promoter, manager, and label executive before establishing a branch of his company devoted to film production. After achieving a modest success with a film version of the Who's rock opera *Tommy* (Ken Russell, 1975), Stigwood developed a marketing plan for *Saturday Night Fever* that built upon a prerelease strategy that already had demonstrated its value with Barbra Streisand's *A Star Is Born* (Frank Pierson, 1976). Beginning in September, RSO Records president Al Coury released a string of chart-topping singles from the film soundtrack: "How Deep Is Your Love," "If I Can't Have You," "Stayin' Alive," and "Night Fever." The releases were staggered to maximize exposure for the film and album. After one song reached the end of its chart run, another was released to replace it. Coury also featured all four of the singles in a trailer for the film that was distributed to theaters about a month before *Saturday Night Fever*'s December release. The trailer functioned simultaneously as an ad for the film, as an ad for the album, and as promotion for each of the four songs pegged to the overall marketing plan.

Coury's cross-promotional campaign left an impressive legacy of chart and box office success. The four singles were each certified gold, with two of them—"Stayin' Alive" and "Night Fever"—reaching platinum status. (Indeed, the three Bee Gees' singles together sold more than 6.6 million units.) Sales of *Saturday Night Fever*'s soundtrack album were even more impressive, with domestic sales topping the 15 million mark. Of course, none of these sales figures would be terribly meaningful if the film bombed at the box office. It didn't. *Saturday Night Fever* grossed more than $94 million in domestic box office and another $143 million in foreign sales. After *Saturday Night Fever*'s success, the industry developed greater self-awareness about the kinds of things that were needed for successful film and music cross-promotions. As *Billboard* magazine noted, the basic ingredients for an effective campaign included "Commercially viable music. Timing. Film cooperation on advance planning and tie-ins. Music that's integral to the movie. A hit movie. A hit single. A big-name recording star. A big-name composer."[38]

The latter part of the seventies also saw the emergence of hybrid scores that intermingled popular songs with background music cues. *National Lampoon's Animal House* (John Landis, 1978) became a prototype of this approach, mixing Elmer Bernstein's Elgar-ish orchestral cues with new songs written for the film by Stephen Bishop and period classics, such as "Shout," "Louie, Louie," "Shama Lama Ding Dong," and "Wonderful World." *American Gigolo* (Paul Schrader, 1980) similarly combined an electronic score by Giorgio Moroder with new songs by Blondie, John Hiatt, and Smokey Robinson and the Miracles. The mixing of songs and scores remained a common tactic for Hollywood films well into the new millennium.

Without question, though, the most important film composer to emerge in the Hollywood Renaissance period was John Williams.[39] Williams collaborated with many of the era's key directors, including Robert Altman, Steven Spielberg, and George Lucas. More than that, however, Williams also revived the fortunes of the classical Hollywood score, an idiom that began to seem increasingly anachronistic after the infusion of modernist styles and pop sounds described earlier.

At the start of the Renaissance period, John Williams was "Johnny Williams," a composer who mixed scoring duties in film and television and who initially seemed to be a jack-of-all-trades. His early assignments included *Valley of the Dolls* (Mark Robson, 1967), a trash-fest adapted from Jacqueline Susann's pulpy bestseller; *The Reivers* (Mark Rydell, 1969), a picaresque adaptation of William Faulkner's novel; and *The Long Goodbye* (Robert Altman, 1973), Altman's jokey screen version of Raymond Chandler's detective novel. Williams made his mark, though, on a string of disaster films scored in the early seventies. He did the music for *The Poseidon Adventure* (Ronald Neame, 1972), *Earthquake* (Mark Robson, 1974), and *The Towering Inferno* (John Guillermin, 1974) in relatively quick succession, earning Oscar nominations for the first and last of these titles. Shortly thereafter, he consolidated his reputation with *Jaws*. The score's famous two-note motif, written for the low bass register, and its Stravinskian harmonies and primitivist rhythms all suggested the primal threat embodied in the film's monstrous great white shark.

If *Jaws* brought Williams to the attention of movie fans, his music for George Lucas's *Star Wars* trilogy made him a household name. In developing the concept of Williams's score, Lucas asked the composer to write in the style of Erich Wolfgang Korngold, a figure who helped to define the sound of Hollywood's Golden Age. Additionally, Lucas also created an extensive temp track—that is, music temporarily slugged into the film to aid picture editors during postproduction—and its mix of pieces by nineteenth- and twentieth-century concert music composers, such as Gustav Holst, Sergei Prokofiev, Antonín Dvořák, and William Walton, provided Williams a stylistic template from which to work.[40] The fact that he imitated these sources has led some scholars to argue that the score is a derivative pastiche of the classical Hollywood model. Yet such criticism overlooks the degree to which Williams adeptly synthesizes these disparate elements into a mellifluous whole. His "Main Title" for *Star Wars* (George Lucas, 1977) is a case in point. The trumpet fanfare that serves as the film's main theme is a thinly disguised reworking of Korngold's own "Main Title" for *King's Row* (Sam Wood, 1942). But, as James Buhler points out, Williams also incorporates a rhythmic counter figure that is itself inspired by Holst's "Mars, Bringer of War," the first piece in the British composer's orchestral suite *The Planets*.[41] Williams's combination of these elements adds a dash of excitement and energy that invigorates his brass fanfare in a manner that is quite unlike Korngold's stately original.

In fashioning his score, Williams employed the leitmotif principles that became common during the classical Hollywood era. Williams not only composed evocative musical themes for the film's principal characters—Luke Skywalker, Princess Leia, and Obi Wan-Kenobi—but also wrote indelible motifs for Darth Vader, the Death Star, the Jawas, and the Tusken Raiders. Like Korngold, he showed an unusual flair for orchestration, often passing these themes to different solo instruments or sections of the orchestra in a manner that displayed the composer's mastery of tone color.

Star Wars' soundtrack album also proved to be as big a hit on record charts as it was at the box office, selling more than four million copies. In a moment of sublime absurdity, recording engineer Grover Hensley reported that while he was doing the Village People disco classic *Can't Stop the Music* (Nancy Walker, 1978), he was visited by the film's executive music supervisor, who said bluntly, "I want *Star Wars!*" Hensley's reply, predictably, was to ask how the film's musical team was going to get a *Star Wars*–type orchestral sound out of a five- or six-man rock band.[42] In retrospect, the music supervisor's suggestion seems ridiculous, but it attests to the massive popularity and influence of Williams's score. Williams followed up *Star Wars* with similarly styled scores for *Close Encounters of the Third Kind* (Steven Spielberg, 1977) and *Superman* (Richard Donner, 1978). By the start of the 1980s, Williams had established himself as Hollywood's chief practitioner of neoclassical film music, a position that remained unchallenged for many decades to come.

Sound Designers in the Hollywood Renaissance

The Hollywood Renaissance period also saw the emergence of the sound designer as a new craft position that consolidated the techniques of sound recording, editing, and mixing under the aegis of a single, unified aesthetic concept. The term "sound designer" is itself the subject of considerable debate among both practitioners and scholars, both because it encompasses several meanings, depending on who uses it, and because it fails to conform to the parlance used within craft unions and for award designations. The Academy Awards, for example, currently have categories for Best Achievement in Sound Mixing and Best Achievement in Sound Editing. Yet there is no comparable category to recognize the achievements of self-proclaimed sound designers. Because the position seemed to combine the duties of a sound effects man, a rerecording mixer, and a supervising sound editor, it quite consciously blurred the boundaries associated with more traditional designations found within the typical studio sound department. Yet, as Jay Beck observed, it was "nearly impossible for the concept of a sound designer to take root within the fixed hierarchical structure of the Hollywood labor system."[43]

Although sound design work emerged out of this institutional framework, the actual origin of the term "sound designer" is shrouded in a certain amount of uncertainty. According to director Francis Ford Coppola, he and Murch discussed different ways of designating the work the latter was doing on *THX 1138* in order to avoid ruffling the feathers of craft unions:

> We wanted very much to credit Walter for his incredible contribution—not only for *The Rain People,* but for all the films he was doing. But because he wasn't in the union, the union forbade him getting the credit as sound editor—so Walter said, Well, since they won't give me that, will they let me be called the "sound designer"? We said, We'll try it—you can be the sound designer. . . . I always thought it was ironic that "Sound Designer" became this Tiffany title, yet it was created for that reason. We did it to dodge the union constriction.[44]

Coppola's account highlights some of the factors that favored the sound designer's rise during the Hollywood Renaissance. Yet there are some reasons to view it with skepticism. First and foremost, the credit that Murch actually received on *THX 1138* was for "sound montages," a term that seems equally nebulous but that is most certainly distinct from "sound design." Second, Murch did not take a "sound design" credit on one of Coppola's films until *Apocalypse Now* (Coppola, 1979), thereby raising a question about why Murch waited nearly a decade before finally adopting the "Tiffany title" proposed earlier. Lastly, as Jay Beck and Vanessa Theme Ament note in the next chapter, sound technician Frank Serafine described his work creating custom sound effects for *Star Trek: The Motion Picture* (Robert Wise, 1979) as "sound design," a development suggesting that another meaning of the term circulated around the time of *Apocalypse Now*'s release. Still, one cannot rule out the possibility that Coppola and Murch "spitballed" the idea of using "sound design" as a credit on *THX 1138,* long before Murch finally received it for his work on Coppola's troubled Vietnam War epic.

Yet even though the first credit for "sound design" did not appear until late in the Hollywood Renaissance period, there seems to be little question that several individuals performed the functions in production and postproduction that later became associated with the term. Indeed, by the mid-seventies, people like Walter Murch, Ben Burtt, and Alan Splet all came to embody this new breed of sound technician.[45] Chafing against Hollywood's craft restrictions, these individuals revolutionized the aesthetics of film sound by fusing its different elements together in service to the era's unique blending of genre conventions and art cinema storytelling techniques.[46] Based in the San Francisco Bay Area, Murch, Burtt, and Splet flourished within this new position, not only because they were geographically removed from Hollywood as the center of the industry's labor market, but also because the smaller scale of the films they worked on helped shield them from studio scrutiny. They also benefited from the support of a group of emerging auteurs that included Francis Ford Coppola, George Lucas, Philip Kaufman, Carroll Ballard, and David Lynch. By conceptualizing the soundtrack's role in collaboration with a film's director, the sound designer bridged the gap between production and postproduction, thereby enabling film audiences to hear films in an entirely new way. In what follows, I consider the individual careers of Murch, Burtt, and Splet in order to illustrate their important contributions to the history of Hollywood sound production.

Walter Murch

For Walter Murch, the opportunity to contribute to the emerging Auteur Renaissance came about largely as a matter of happenstance. After editing an educational film and freelancing at a commercial production house, Murch was asked to do the sound effects work and final sound mix for Coppola's 1969 road film *The Rain People.* Coppola was starting a new production company, and the assignment offered Murch a chance to get in on the ground floor of the new enterprise.

Early on, Murch established his reputation by rather ingeniously crafting low-tech solutions to the problem of creating high-tech sounds. To give the human voices in *THX 1138* a slightly robotic, computerized quality, Murch took his clean recordings of the voices and broadcast them into the cosmos with a ham radio. Then, after he received the same signal back, he used a Nagra to capture the retransmitted voices. As he noted, this gave the voices a wonderful "sideband" quality that was very much in keeping with George Lucas's vision in the film of a "used future."[47]

For *American Graffiti,* the challenge involved creating a realistic sonic palette that captured the changing audio perspective of the film's characters as they cruised around the town in their automobiles. During postproduction, Murch and director George Lucas produced a two-hour fake radio show complete with music, advertisements, phone requests, and Wolfman Jack's disk jockey patter. Murch and Lucas then played back the recorded radio show in the backyard of a house in Mill Valley, California, and rerecorded it using a separate Nagra. During playback, Murch varied the angle of the original recording's loudspeaker as well as the angle of the microphone on the second Nagra. In doing so, he created a variety of different secondary and tertiary reflections of the sound, making it clearer at one moment and then muddied and nearly inaudible the next. Murch and Lucas rerecorded the entire program twice, giving Murch not only the clean original track, but also two different variants of his "worldized" rerecording. During mixing, he could shift instantaneously from the relatively direct, unmediated sound of the radio inside a car to that same sound as it bounces off the town's buildings and pavements.[48]

The capstone of Murch's early career, however, was Coppola's *The Conversation* (1974), a film for which he not only did sound recording and mixing, but also served as the picture editor. Although *The Conversation* is remembered as a rather potent Nixon-era conspiracy thriller, it also did for sound recording what Michelangelo Antonioni had done for photography in *Blow-Up* (1965)—that is, it reflexively explored cinema as a medium that many believe captures important aspects of our lived reality. Much more than Murch's other projects, *The Conversation* is centrally about the meaning of sound. The film tells the story of Harry Caul, a surveillance expert hired to record the lunchtime conversation of Mark and Ann, a young couple involved in an extramarital affair. In the film's most famous sequence, Coppola and Murch self-consciously showcase the soundman's tools of the trade as he shows Caul trying out a variety of filters, equalizers, and other gadgets in an effort to isolate the sound of the couple's voices from the background noise of Union Square. Using these filters, Caul hears Mark whisper to Ann: "He'd kill us if he got the chance." Caul fears that Ann's jealous husband will harm the couple, but, even with all his tools, he misinterprets the meaning of Mark's phrase, a mistake that leads to an unfortunate and tragic outcome.

Ben Burtt

As was true for Murch, Ben Burtt's resourcefulness and his ability to fashion evocative sound effects established him as one of the era's leading sound designers. Also, like Murch, Burtt initially gained notoriety in science fiction films, but he later revealed his mastery of editing sound effects across a number of other genres, such as the combat film, the adventure thriller, the fantasy film, and the documentary.[49] His breakthrough came when producer Gary Kurtz hired him to create sound effects for *Star Wars*. In an unusual move, Kurtz and director George Lucas brought Burtt onto the *Star Wars* team about six months before the film went into production. Burtt used this time to build a library of effects for the various high-tech machines and extraterrestrial creatures that appeared in the film, often manipulating everyday sounds to rather startling effect. For example, to create the Wookie language spoken by Chewbacca, Burtt mixed walrus calls with other animal sounds. For the laser blasts used in many of the fights between the Rebel Alliance and Imperial Storm Troopers, Burtt tapped metal objects (a hammer, Burtt's wedding ring) against a radio tower's guy wire. Additionally, in crafting the hum of *Star Wars'* light sabers, he mixed the sounds of old movie projectors with the buzz made when one passes a microphone over a television set.[50] All in all, Burtt created 250 new sounds for *Star Wars*. For the sequel, *The Empire Strikes Back* (Irvin Kershner, 1980), he developed more than a thousand new sounds. Echoing Murch, he noted years later, "Science fiction films had generally been associated with electronic noises. We wanted real motor sounds, rusty, clanky things, to create the sense of a used world."[51]

The major exception to this rule of thumb also proved to be Burtt's supreme achievement in *Star Wars,* namely the various tweets, beeps, and burbles made by the robot R2D2. In developing R2D2's range of vocalizations, Burtt found inspiration in earlier movie creatures, such as King Kong and Cheetah from the Tarzan series, who managed to be expressive and convey intelligence without having to say actual words. According to Burtt, after several months of trial and error, R2D2's sounds "ended up being a combination of my voice performing funny little baby-like sounds and at the same time doing some electronics on a keyboard."[52] Along with actors Mark Hamill and Harrison Ford, the astro-mech droid became one of the film's breakout stars and remains an icon of the *Star Wars* universe.

Alan Splet

The third figure in the great triumvirate of seventies sound designers was Alan Splet, who inventively used ambient sounds to create some of the most evocative soundscapes in the history of American cinema. He was especially skilled at using environmental sounds to add atmosphere and mood to a film's setting, establishing a style that Ric Gentry has described as a kind of "audio expressionism."[53] Splet also benefited by chance from the fact that the first two feature films he worked on—*Eraserhead* (David Lynch, 1977) and *The Black Stallion* (Carroll Ballard, 1979)—featured long stretches with very little dialogue, a circumstance that placed his unique talents front and center on the soundtrack.

Working with his spouse and professional partner, Ann Kroeber, Splet strove to capture the sounds of the "insides of things."[54] On *Eraserhead,* for example, he placed a microphone inside an old metal heater. Lynch then blew air into the heater, an effect that captured the movement of air within this hollow resonance. To get another unusual ambient sound, Splet put a microphone inside a five-gallon bottle and then floated it in a bathtub.[55] Later, Kroeber consulted with audio engineer Arnie Lazarus to develop a particular type of contact microphone called a FRAP (Flat Response Audio Pickup).[56] It was small—Kroeber described it as about the size of her little finger—and because of its compactness, Splet could put it in unusual places on objects, something that yielded new ways of hearing them.

Although Splet won an Oscar for his work with Ballard, *Eraserhead* was the film that best illustrated his unique talents. Splet proved to be an ideal partner for Lynch, crafting aural ambiences that gave weight and dimension to the visionary director's haunting postindustrial landscapes. Marketed as a "dream of dark and troubling things," the film's mutant chicken-babies, tapeworms, the dancing Lady in the Radiator, and the horribly scarred and disfigured Man in a Planet all served to motivate Splet's murky mix of electronic buzzes, low-pitched hums, and machine noises. A disquieting combination of absurdism and surrealism, *Eraserhead* quickly developed a cult following, both for its disturbing psychosexual imagery and its feeling of a collective waking nightmare, a sensation greatly enhanced by Splet's acoustic miasma.

Lynch and Splet collaborated on three more projects, including *The Elephant Man* (David Lynch, 1980). Nominated for eight Oscars, the story of John Merrick, a Londoner grotesquely disfigured by congenital disease, briefly brought Lynch into the orbit of mainstream Hollywood. Although *The Elephant Man* is a biopic, Lynch and Splet implode the genre, adding expressionist touches to both its images and its sounds. Shooting in luminous black and white, Lynch used overcranking, step printing, blurred motion, and penetrating camera movements to excavate small beauties hidden beneath the squalor and grotesquerie of Victorian England circa 1890.

Splet's soundtrack not only serves as an objective correlative of Merrick's profound sense of isolation and social unease, but it provides a unique representation of what a typical Londoner might have heard during the period. As Anne Kroeber recalls, "David wanted to recreate the sounds of England back then. He loves industrial sounds: gadgets and gizmos and steam and radiators and mechanical devices."[57] Several of these industrial noises become aural motifs in *The Elephant Man*, including sounds of hissing steam, gaslight flames, and the repetitive rhythmic noise of large machinery. This bed of ambient industrial racket is often set against the film's apparently more organic sounds, such as John Morris's circus-themed score and Merrick's labored, heavy breathing.

This mix of mechanical and animalistic noises is introduced in *The Elephant Man*'s brilliant opening sequence. Following the simple black and white titles of the credit sequence, which are accompanied by Morris's limpid, minor key waltz, the film opens on a close-up of a woman's eyes. The camera then tilts down to a close-up of her mouth. A cut back to a more distant view reveals these to be part of a framed photograph, and Lynch dissolves from this to film footage of the same woman. As the camera tracks in, the image fades to black, accompanied by an ominous sustained low tone and the clanking sound of a machine. A fade-in introduces a long shot of elephants at the circus, framed in profile and backlit so that they appear mostly as silhouettes. The image of elephants is accompanied by a new sound element added to the mix, an airy timbre that resembles the sound of gaslight flames heard later in the film. A double exposure superimposes the previous image of the woman over the elephants, accompanied by the gradual swell of a chord played on a circus organ.

After more shots of the elephants, including a closer view of one with its trunk raised, Lynch cuts to a shot of an elephant's trunk hitting the woman on the shoulder. A match on action shows the woman falling to the ground, screaming and turning her head from side to side. Curiously, though, we never hear her scream. Instead, we hear only the elephant's roaring, a sound filtered to eliminate some of its brassiness, an effect that makes it more muffled and hollow. The last four shots of the sequence alternate between shots of the elephant and shots of the woman as she rolls around. The film footage appears to be optically printed to create its slow-motion effect, a technique that not only preserves the motion blur of the woman's face, but also endows the elephants' movements with a slightly jerky, unnatural quality. The sequence closes with a final image: an expanding cloud of steam accompanied by the cry of a baby mixed with the same sort of airy timbre heard just moments before.

This convoluted opening sequence depicts the story that Bytes, the proprietor of the "Elephant Man," later tells about Merrick's condition as part of his ballyhoo. Legend has it that Merrick was disfigured when a wild elephant struck down his mother during the fourth month of her pregnancy, a circumstance that heightens his sense of inadequacy and his underlying dread of maternal rejection. Although this brief description captures the sequence's denotative elements, Lynch's expressionist treatment of the event carries a clear undertone of sexual violence and unconscious libidinal energies. More important, the blurring and slow motion of the footage allows the camera to linger on the woman's gaping mouth and bared teeth, an expression of both primal fear and aggression. A common visual motif for Lynch, the screaming mouth evokes the same sort of existential angst found in the work of likeminded painters, such as Edvard Munch and Francis Bacon.[58]

Merrick's voice, though, proves to be the film's most important sound insofar as it marks his humanity in opposition to the animal and mechanical noises mentioned above. Two scenes prove to be key here. The first occurs just after Merrick's interview with Mr. Carr Gomm. Merrick is visibly ill at ease. His social anxiety causes Carr Gomm to conclude that he is both mentally and physically challenged. After Dr. Treves and Carr Gomm leave the room, however, Merrick loudly declaims the text of the Twenty-third Psalm. When Merrick reaches a part of the psalm not taught to him by Treves, the doctor realizes belatedly that John not only can read, but also is fully able to communicate. Reciting one of the Bible's most beautiful passages, John's voice—slurred

FIGURE 9: In a film filled with mechanical noises and strange ambiences, the most important marker of John Merrick's humanity is his voice. In the film's most famous scene, Merrick confronts an unruly mob, shouting, "I am not an animal! I am a human being!" (*The Elephant Man*, David Lynch, 1980).

speech and all—reveals the sensitive soul lurking within his ruined and misshapen body.

The second scene takes place just after Merrick escapes from Bytes, aided by a merry band of other circus freaks. After disembarking from the ship that has returned him to England, Merrick is taunted by a trio of obnoxious young boys. In his haste to flee from his tormentors, Merrick inadvertently knocks a little girl to the ground. A crowd gathers in response to the hubbub. Merrick uses their confusion as an opportunity to escape, but he is eventually cornered in the men's toilet. Merrick turns on his pursuers, shouting, "I am not an elephant! I am not an animal! I am a human being" (see figure 9). As in the earlier scene, John's voice functions as an emblem of his personhood, conveying a power and authority that momentarily disarms the mob, stunned into a hushed silence.

As these examples indicate, *The Elephant Man*'s sound design aligns the viewer with Merrick's psychology, which is often expressed as a mixture of humiliation, resignation, and unease. First exploited as a circus freak and then as a medical curiosity, Merrick is all too often the victim of the most venal sorts of human cruelty. To convey his overwhelming sense of dislocation, Lynch and Splet crafted a soundscape filled with subterranean bass textures, ambient hums, vaporous presences, and mechanistic pulsing, an audacious mix that confirmed their status as masters of mood and atmosphere.

Between 1968 and 1980, several changes within the film industry gave rise to important innovations in sound design for films, both at the level of technology and at the level of style. The increased use of quarter-inch magnetic tape as a production sound medium encouraged sound recorders and mixers to move away from their previous reliance on studio effects libraries. The Nagra enabled production sound teams to work cheaply and efficiently on location. More important, the Nagra also emboldened a new breed of "sound designers" to build their own effects libraries, often experimenting with the end results in ways that made them feel fresh and original. Additionally, advances in noise reduction technology enabled filmmakers to pack in more and more auditory information by eliminating ground noise, minimizing distortion, and expanding the range of frequencies at both the low and high ends of the audio spectrum.

By the end of the seventies, however, the cold, hard realities of craft specialization and workflow replaced the spirit of high-flying innovation. In retrospect, it is easier to see that sound designers, like Murch, Burtt, and Splet, enjoyed a creative autonomy largely denied to their counterparts. Working mostly in the San Francisco area, they were protected by their geographical isolation from Hollywood and by the fact that their breakthroughs came from assignments in modestly budgeted features.[59] As the Hollywood Renaissance gave way to the New Hollywood, the shift toward blockbuster productions necessitated the employment of larger sound teams and a consequent reversion to older craft hierarchies and aesthetic principles. Even innovators like Splet functioned more as extremely skilled but unadventurous technicians when assigned to more routine projects like *Weekend at Bernie's* (Ted Kotcheff, 1989) or *Don't Tell Mom the Babysitter's Dead* (Stephen Herek, 1991). Film scholars and fans long have recognized the genius of Murch, Burtt, and Splet, but their innovations now appear more like a blip on the cultural radar than a sustained reimagining of the soundtrack's aesthetic possibilities. As we see in subsequent chapters, Hollywood would wait at least another decade for a period that would show a similar level of creative ferment. Only this time the sound would be packaged as a streaming binary code of zeroes and ones.

5

THE NEW HOLLYWOOD, 1981-1999

Jay Beck with Vanessa Theme Ament

Following a longstanding tradition that privileged dialogue editing and mixing over other sounds in the picture, the majority of the Hollywood films from the 1960s and 1970s relied on the spoken word as their primary narrative motor. An overarching drive for narrative comprehension created a tacit agreement between audiences and filmmakers: everything that the audience is supposed to hear will be heard. As a result, only narratively significant sounds and music could compete with dialogue, relegating additional sound effects and ambiences to lower levels of narrative significance. Divisions of labor within both production and postproduction sound reinforced this hierarchy of sonic signification. In the case of production, the need for clear dialogue tracks often meant abandoning sound perspective, and the exigencies of production schedules made it nearly impossible to record effects and ambiences on location.

In postproduction, the division between sound editors and rerecording mixers was enforced by the unions; dialogue editors, sound effects editors, and music editors generally worked independently. Only the supervising sound editor was able to oversee the assembly of the individual sound elements on the final soundtrack, yet that supervision was limited to postproduction. Because of the separation between the sound recordists' union, International Alliance of Theatrical Stage Employees Local 695, and the sound editors' union, Local 776, there was no official role for an individual to supervise the sound of the film from production through postproduction. It is precisely because of such a tightly structured and regulated system of labor, however, that a number of new sound roles appeared in the 1980s and 1990s. By moving outside of the Hollywood nexus of production, it became possible to expand the responsibilities of sound workers and allow more experimentation in the production and postproduction phases. New roles such as the sound designers, sound effects creators, and Foley artists were indications of the growing significance of film sound in the history of American cinema.

The 1980s and Sound Design

Although the term sound designer is fraught with numerous interpretations, it is possible to identify a distinct strain of sound authorship in its history. Today, sound design summons up the creation of new sounds, the engineering of sound-scapes, the building of acoustic architecture, and the construction of realism through assemblage. From its inception, the role of sound designer encompassed the idea that a single person could control the overall sound of a film by virtue of the technological advances developed since the late 1970s. An examination of sound designers from the 1980s and 1990s demonstrates how the loosening labor structure of the film industry and the decline of the studio system created a space for these "acoustic auteurs" who developed new aesthetic strategies and introduced new technologies to serve their individual needs.

Walter Murch and the Emergence of Sound Design

Starting with his early work on Francis Ford Coppola's films, Walter Murch was regularly consulted during the production and even preproduction phase about the overall sound of the film. For *The Rain People* (1969) he chose the credit "sound montage" to differentiate his work from other sound editors and sound effects editors, and this allowed him to work on both sides of the production process without raising the attention of the sound unions. Due to an employee shortage in the San Francisco area, members of the International Alliance of Theatrical Stage Employees—the union governing sound employees—were authorized to work in any production or postproduction role. Although an individual could have multiple different jobs in production or postproduction, the barrier between the two divisions kept the workforces separated. As a postproduction employee, Murch was entitled to perform any of the tasks involved, including both sound editing and mixing; but on *The Godfather* (Coppola, 1972) he introduced rerecording mixing to his skill set. Despite his active involvement in the entire filmmaking process, Murch chose the screen credit "post production consultant" to prevent the unions from interceding.[1]

Murch's roles reveal a growing conflict between the structure of the labor system and the need for a new role in the creation of the soundtrack. With *Apocalypse Now* (Coppola, 1979) it became difficult to discern the difference between production and postproduction, and Murch started on the film as a film editor in 1977 and moved on to sound work the following year.[2] Coppola tasked him with supervising the creation of the soundtrack as well as constructing a sound technology to realize the film's aesthetic goals. According to Murch:

> When I started the film [Coppola] said he wanted three things. First, he wanted it to be quintaphonic, he wanted the sound to fill the room, to seem to come from all sections of the room which had never been done before in a dramatic film. . . . Second, he wanted it to be authentic, by which he meant the weaponry had to sound like it sounded in Vietnam. . . . The final thing he wanted was the film soundtrack to partake of the psychedelic haze in which the war had been fought, not only in terms of the music . . . but in general, kind of far-out juxtaposition of imagery and sound; for the soundtrack not to be just a literal imitation of what you saw on the screen but at times to depart from it.[3]

What Murch envisioned was not just a strategy for sound use in the film, but a total approach that combined the development and deployment of sounds as well as the modification of the 70mm Dolby Stereo format to accommodate a split-surround mix.[4] To best exemplify his efforts, he chose the title "sound

FIGURE 10: Francis Ford Coppola wanted the juxtaposition between sounds and images to evoke "the psychedelic haze in which the war had been fought" (*Apocalypse Now*, Francis Ford Coppola, 1979).

designer" to foreground the actual design and spatial deployment of *Apocalypse Now*'s soundscape (see figure 10).

Murch's attention to how the film's sound created a "conceptual resonance" with the story is at the heart of his sound design.[5] More than the construction of specific sounds, the sound designer's job was to use the soundtrack to articulate the director's vision. This meant that each film placed a unique demand upon the sound designer, who had to develop a sound strategy that best served the film while suppressing elements or techniques that might allude to his or her authorial presence. When one listens to Murch's soundtracks for Coppola or Lucas, the diversity of approaches is astonishing. It is precisely this "inaudibility" of the sound designer that was crucial for the success of Walter Murch's soundtracks.

Frank Serafine and Sound Effects Construction

The manipulation of sound and the construction of custom sound effects are best exemplified in the work of Frank Serafine. When he started creating sound effects for motion pictures, Serafine was a twenty-six-year-old synthesizer whiz-kid specializing in what he called "electronic sound synthesis."[6] He began calling his custom sound effects for *Star Trek: The Motion Picture* (Robert Wise, 1979) "sound design," a move that caused much consternation among sound technicians. Although his electronic sounds met the demands of the movie, his operating procedure was far from Murch's conceptual resonance. Serafine's overt emphasis on technology represents sound design on its most literal level: the design and construction of custom sounds for films. In the case of *Star Trek*, the goal was to create a unique signature that matched the state-of-the-art visual effects. To achieve this, Serafine used synthesizers to develop a variety of custom sound effects unlike the well-worn library of stock science-fiction sound effects.

This embrace of new technology was the main characteristic of a second approach to sound design. Serafine came to film sound from the music industry and brought several techniques to bear on sound effects creation. In addition to his regular use of synthesizers, Serafine also took advantage of multitrack tape recorders to work apart from the other sound technicians and editors on the picture. In doing so his work represented a further fragmentation of an already highly compartmentalized process. Operating outside of the regular labor hierarchy, Serafine and fellow sound synthesist Alan Howarth were "hired guns" for sound effects creation, and it is not surprising that they soon started branding themselves as "sound designers."

In 1982, Serafine was recruited to create new sound effects for the Disney production *Tron* (Steven Lisberger), the first feature film to make extensive use of computer-generated imagery. In a brief article in *Back Stage*, Serafine was identified as "an electronic film scoring and sound effects generating artist" who provided "sound design and effects generation" for *Tron*.[7] This semantic split in his job description is significant, and it was replicated in his own article for *American Cinematographer* later that year, "Sound Effects Design and Synthesis for *TRON*."[8] Serafine's concept of electronic sound synthesis was more in line with traditional sound effects construction, although the use of "sound design" to describe the process capitalized on its growing appeal. In effect Serafine was performing the job of a sound effects editor, in both the creation and synchronization of sounds to images, and much of the technology that he utilized would eventually make its way into sound postproduction. The difference was that Serafine's work did not embrace an overall sound aesthetic for the picture, since he rarely interacted with the other sound editors, nor was he involved during the rerecording process.

Taking credit as sound designer diluted the work of the rest of the sound team and inappropriately elevated Serafine to the author of the film's sound. Randy Thom expressed unease with the way that the sound designer credit separated the work of sound effects synthesists such as Frank Serafine from the work of sound editors in the past. "If creating a spaceship sound by using digital processing constitutes sound design, then creating a spaceship sound by altering speed and equalization in the analog domain (as was done many times in the 1950s) was surely sound design as well. Should you get the credit 'sound designer' if you only create three or four sound effects in a two-hour film? Probably not."[9] The distinction between sound effects creation and sound design is best exemplified by supervising sound editor Mark Mangini: "One must remember that sound design is, first and foremost, a forum of ideas, not technology."[10] Mangini's observation points to how the original concept of sound design was debased by ersatz sound effects designers. In the work of Ben Burtt and Alan Splet, however, Murch's idea of sound design carried on.

Ben Burtt and the Philosophy of the Soundtrack

After catching the break of a lifetime when fellow USC alum George Lucas asked him to create some original sounds for a science fiction feature he was planning, Ben Burtt worked closely with Lucas on the first *Star Wars* trilogy, *More American Graffiti* (B.W.L. Norton, 1979), and the *Indiana Jones* films, designing sounds and an overall sonic palette for each film. Taking the credit of sound designer, Burtt humbly includes himself as part of a movement that reshaped film sound:

> It would be pretentious to say that I was part of a movement, but I guess it's partly true. It wasn't a conscious thing. I was at a certain place at a certain time. I had the good fortune to be asked to design sounds for [*Star Wars*] in which the producer, Gary Kurtz, and the director, George Lucas, were very interested in innovative sound. They didn't just want to go to the libraries and pull out previously used material.

They were interested in original ideas, so I was given the task of inventing a lot of sounds.[11]

This contrasted with the longstanding job of the sound editor to cut in sounds
from a stock library of effects. According to Steve Barnett, the sound editor's job
of cutting "effects called for by action on screen—sounds that fall in the 'See a
dog, Hear a dog' category—or off-screen effects called for by the script, are what
is required to make a movie's soundtrack believable on the most basic level."[12]
Always wary of this literalism in sound effects work, Burtt set forth to sculpt
sounds to match what he thought objects *should* sound like. More than simply
finding suitable sounds, Burtt's sought a stylistic consistency:

In my first discussion with George [Lucas] about the film, he said—and
I concurred with him—that we wanted an "organic," as opposed to electronic and artificial, soundtrack. Since we were going to design a visual
world that had rust and dents and dirt, we wanted a sound world which
had squeaks and motors that may not be smooth-sounding or quiet.
Therefore we wanted to draw upon raw materials from the real world:
real motors, real squeaky door, real animal sounds, real insects; this sort
of thing.[13]

Reflecting on his work, Burtt was succinct, saying, "My function was sound
design," and the purpose of that role was "to create a sound effects track that
would work dramatically with the images."[14] One of the powerful ironies of
Burtt's role as a sound designer, or for anyone using the term as their official
credit on a film, is that the position was not recognized by either the sound union
or the Academy of Motion Picture Arts and Sciences. In fact, when *Star Wars*
won the Academy Award for Best Sound, Burtt was not included because Academy rules recognized production sound mixers and rerecording mixers only.[15]
Nevertheless, the Academy did present him with a "Special Achievement Award
for Sound Effects" to acknowledge his substantial and innovative contribution to
the film. This is because the work of sound editors was routinely ignored by the
Academy until the early 1980s. Walter Murch shared the 1980 Academy Award
for Best Sound on *Apocalypse Now* only because he was credited as rerecording
mixer, not because of his credit as sound designer. That same year the Academy
issued another "Special Achievement Award for Sound Editing" to Alan Splet
for his contributions to *The Black Stallion* (Carroll Ballard, 1979). It wasn't until
after the Academy gave Ben Burtt a second "Special Achievement Award" for
sound effects editing on *Raiders of the Lost Ark* (Steven Spielberg, 1981) that they
decided to recognize sound editing officially by creating a new annual award. In
1983, "Sound Effects Editing" became its own category, won by Charles Campbell and Ben Burtt for *E.T. The Extra-Terrestrial* (Steven Spielberg, 1983).

Burtt's involvement during all phases of a film's production was central to his work as a sound designer. By collaborating with the director from the start of pre-production and creating a sense of stylistic unity in constructing sound effects, Burtt transcended the normal function of a sound effects editor. Like Murch's conceptual resonance, Burtt's sound design also included a higher function: the unification of film sound with the needs and demands of the story. According to Burtt: "Being a sound designer is not a new task, just a new name for the job which includes sound recording, sound editing, and sound mixing—a job tradi-tionally done by at least three distinct people. . . . I find that I have been pretty much unique to my experience, and other sound designers haven't really been given those opportunities too often."[16] The unique quality of Burtt's and Murch's experiences was a byproduct of three factors: the sense of freedom and experi-mentation fostered in the 1970s after the breakdown of the studio sound shops, the close relationship between the sound designer and the director, and the abil-ity to work on both production and postproduction without union interference. Very few individuals were privileged enough to work under similar conditions, and with the acceptance of Dolby Stereo as an industry standard in the 1980s, much of the freedom of experimentation was undermined by a subservience to strictly regulated mixing practices. This rise and fall of the role of sound designer can be traced through the career of Alan Splet.

Alan Splet's "Audio Expressionism"

Whereas Burtt placed a priority on the creation and development of specific signature effects in his films, Splet mastered the fine art of ambience. Through-out his career, Splet understood the dramatic importance of how background sounds and acoustic atmospheres affect audience interpretations. Unlike Burtt or Murch, Splet had neither a film school education nor prior experience within the studio system. Instead, he started working at Calvin-Defrenes, an industrial film company in Philadelphia, where his job included recording sounds and editing stock music. It was there that he met director David Lynch, who was looking for sound effects for his film *The Grandmother* (1970); Lynch and Splet would go on to work together on four feature films over the next decade, shaping and crafting some of the most unusual soundtracks of the period.

Following an approach similar to Burtt's in sound effects construction, Splet was hired by Lynch before production began to start creating sound effects; yet unlike Burtt, Splet specialized in a form of "audio expressionism" that augmented the visual materials while heightening the film's dramatic impact.[17] Preferring to regard himself as the "focal point" for ideas about sound, Splet was more cau-tious in his consideration of his role, and he expressed some early reservations about using the title of sound designer: "That term is misleading, at least for me. It suggests someone who goes into a room and sits down and thinks and lays out a track, as maybe a composer would lay out a musical score, so that it remains only for some key people to come along, paint by the numbers, and fill in the spaces."[18] Instead of taking the credit of sound designer in the 1980s, Splet oscillated between sound designer and supervising sound editor on his films. Unlike Murch or Burtt, Splet was less involved in the final mixing process than the construction of a sound field in which his sound effects would operate. In this regard, he straddled the fine line between Murch's concept of sound design and sound effects creation. Instead, Splet added his own unique approach to sound design by crafting some of the richest and most expressive ambiences in his work.

For Splet, the creation of strong ambient sounds was as important as making hard effects. Because his earliest work was on films that had little to no dialogue or relied on voiceover narration, it became increasingly important for the sound to carry a large portion of narrative weight. To achieve this, Splet worked closely with his directors to match the films' sounds to the story material. He spent a large amount of time recording ambient sounds in remote locations to ensure that there would be no interference from passing airplane jet engines,[19] and for *The Mosquito Coast* (Peter Weir, 1986) he gathered insect and bird sounds from dozens of disparate sources to build up the effect for a South American jungle.[20] According to Splet, his approach was different from Burtt's direct linkage of characters and sound effects: "I tend to amplify what you see on the screen to heighten the picture by sort of interpreting what's there. The sound may or may not correspond with the visible movements of things on the screen. Instead, it adds to it to create a mood, an atmosphere."[21] This approach proved to be very fruitful in Splet's early career with Bay Area directors Carroll Ballard and Philip Kaufman. Expanding the San Francisco aesthetic pioneered by Lucas and Coppola, both directors believed in recording original sound effects rather than relying on stock libraries. In his close relationship with Ballard, Kaufman, and Lynch, Splet cultivated a new approach to sound design that placed equal importance on the development of atmospheres as well as sound effects.

Continuing the process that developed on their prior films, Lynch and Splet spent two weeks discussing their conception of the worlds represented in *Dune* (1984) and the sounds of outer space. They approached the film as a joint artistic venture, where Lynch discussed the image and Splet discussed the aural concepts.[22] Lynch, an acutely sound conscious director, understood how sound could aid the storytelling process: "Film is picture and sound, and so the trick is finding the right sound to make that mood go hand in hand with the picture. Only a couple of sounds are right when millions and millions are wrong."[23] Splet's contribution, as Ric Gentry explained, began by "recording and creating effects far in advance of the first exposed frame of film. Eighty percent of the sounds for *Dune*, besides the music [according to Splet], were *made*."[24]

To achieve the original sounds needed for the futuristic devices and planetary atmospheres, Splet and his wife, sound editor and production mixer Ann Kroeber, spent the time when Lynch was shooting principal photography in Mexico gathering a range of industrial sounds that were mixed and processed to create the Harkonnen world of Gedei Prime. Splet preferred this method: "I like to go out and get new material. On *Dune*, I used far less of the library than I had before. . . . You can't find sounds that correlate with things in the film because they aren't there."[25] This method of sound collection and alteration is different from the creation of sounds with synthesizers. As with the organic origins of the sounds recorded by Burtt for the *Star Wars* films, Splet also preferred "working with natural sounds and then changing them, as opposed to synthesizing things electronically."[26]

Unlike the sound synthesists, Splet did not prioritize technology over technique, and his collaborations with Lynch represent the pinnacle of sound as an equal partner in the narrative process. In part this is due to Lynch's understanding of how sound can work. As rerecording mixer John Ross noted, "[David's] definitely not a 'See a dog, hear a dog' kind of guy. He's more, 'See a dog and possibly imagine what the dog is thinking.'"[27] The fusion of sound design with storytelling is best heard in the disturbing ambiences in *Blue Velvet* (1986). The film, centered on the exploits of young Jeffrey Beaumont, pulls back the veneer of his small town of Lumberton to reveal the rot lying beneath. This is hinted at during a bravado introductory sequence where the camera plies along white picket fences and red roses, set to the strains of Bobby Vinton's "Blue Velvet," before settling on Jeffrey's father watering the lawn. This idyllic scene cuts to the water spigot and the sound of an unnerving vibration and gurgling, which, in turn, is followed by Mr. Beaumont grabbing his neck and falling to the ground from a stroke. As he lies immobile, the camera follows the arc of the water, cuts to a close-up view of the lawn, and plunges into the humus to reveal scores of insects beneath. This action is accompanied by a mutating soundtrack where the sinister rattle and gurgle of the hose overtakes the music's limpid strains, and the brittle scuttling and crunching of the bugs envelops the soundscape (see figure 11).

FIGURE 11: David Lynch and Alan Splet used specially designed sound effects and sinister ambiences to reveal the dark side of the idyllic town of Lumberton (*Blue Velvet*, David Lynch, 1986).

Splet mastered the fine art of creating sounds that subjectively match the moods being expressed in Lynch's films, and, as in the example above, transitioned between two divergent acoustic realms. According to Frank Spotnitz: "Jeffrey's Lumberton is filled with the sounds of trees rustling, the chirp of crickets and birds singing. But as he enters the apartment building where Dorothy lives, the sound track suddenly becomes industrial, echoey, with the faint sound of a steam engine in the background. There's no literal representation of the sources of these sounds in the film; Splet simply uses them to underscore the mood director David Lynch is seeking to create."[28] As Splet noted, "There's a point where you can talk about things logically and then, after that, you have to leave the world of logic."[29]

In the later phase of his career, from 1988 through his death in December 1994, Splet began working within the Hollywood system on a number of films that limited his creativity and restricted his input to the overall sound of the films. "I've gone back to using 'supervising editor,'" he said in 1989, "because so much of the job has to do with things other than just coming up with sound effects."[30] On *Dirty Rotten Scoundrels* (Frank Oz, 1988), *Weekend at Bernie's* (Ted Kotcheff, 1989), and *Don't Tell Mom the Babysitter's Dead* (Stephen Herek, 1991), Splet was unable to assert the level of control he had practiced with Lynch or the Bay Area directors. As a supervising sound editor, he was brought into the projects in a late phase of postproduction and was unable to spend time discussing the films with the directors.[31] Although the San Francisco directors valued the position of a sound designer, it still remained anathema to Hollywood. Moreover, due to a multitude of sound effects creators billing themselves as sound designers, Splet's work as a true sound designer was devalued.

Although Splet's career can be read as a descent from his exemplary work with Lynch into the mediocrity of the Hollywood system, he finished his career with the stunning sound design of Carroll Ballard's *Wind* (1992). As an object lesson, Splet's career history represents the devaluation of the concept of sound design. Hollywood resisted the idea of a sound designer overseeing the entire construction of a film's soundtrack because it interfered with union regulations and the strict separation of labor. Moreover, it was indicative of Hollywood's longstanding resistance to rethinking labor roles and the individuals involved in the process. The fragmentation of studio sound shops into specialized independent sound houses further fractured the process of soundtrack construction. With each element of postproduction sound being shopped out, in the 1980s and early 1990s, many soundtracks suffered from a lack of stylistic unity. The move to sound effects creation in lieu of studio design provided a sense of increased originality in soundtrack construction, but at the price of losing unity of the sound aesthetics and conceptual resonance with the narrative.

Only on rare occasions, generally when there was an intimate working relationship between a director and a supervising sound editor, as with Ben Burtt/

Steven Spielberg, Randy Thom/Robert Zemeckis, or Larry Blake/Steven Soderbergh,[32] did it become possible for Walter Murch's goal of sound design to exist.
Although he refuses the sound designer credit, Larry Blake expressed his opinion
quite clearly: "I consider that sound design, real sound design, is the pinnacle
of the film sound art."[33] Perhaps the most important change involved in sound
practices in the 1980s and 1990s was that filmmakers and audiences began to
take film sound more seriously. Instead of the perennial notion of sound being
secondary in the storytelling process, sound design demonstrated how sound
needs to be an equal partner in the audio-visual world. Randy Thom summa-
rized these changes best:

> What does it mean to take sound seriously? Most importantly, it means
> being interested in exploring the storytelling capacity of sound, from
> the writing of the script through production and post-production. It
> means more than simply recording sound effects on location, but also
> considering the ways those sounds can be used to make the characters
> and locations in the film more compelling. It means searching for con-
> nections that sound can make between places, characters, and moments
> within the film, and between the film and the culture at large.[34]

The Soundtrack: New Sounds, New Methods

Although the 1970s were marked by major changes in the music industries
and the rise of rock-oriented radio, musical transitions in Hollywood occurred
much more slowly. By the end of the decade a cadre of familiar composers, most
of whom entered the industry in the 1960s, held sway. John Williams, Jerry
Goldsmith, Alfred Newman, John Barry, Georges Delerue, Ennio Morricone,
Alex North, Lalo Schifrin, and Maurice Jarre each were responsible for multiple Academy Award nominations during the decade, and they all displayed
a preference for orchestral scores. On the surface it appeared as though the
motion picture score had not changed since the studio era, but on closer examination several emerging trends can be observed. First, during the late 1960s,
several new composers entered the field from jazz (Quincy Jones, Dave Grusin,
Herbie Hancock), bringing with them new tonalities and compositional strategies. Others, such as Walter Carlos and Jack Nitzsche, brought experimental
instrumentation and recording techniques from classical and rock music,
respectively. Second, concurrent with these changes, Hollywood embraced the
compilation score and the use of popular music on soundtracks. By 1980 a sea
change struck Hollywood as new composers coming from the popular music
industry and the rise of the compilation score challenged the prominence of
the orchestral score.

The Synthesizer Score and New Composers

Synthesizers and their musical predecessors were used on film soundtracks since the 1950s, though few scores relied on them solely. Walter Carlos's score for *A Clockwork Orange* (Stanley Kubrick, 1971) and Gil Mellé's for *The Andromeda Strain* (Robert Wise, 1971) heralded the synthesizer's move from featured instrument to starring role. According to *American Film*'s Terry Atkinson, "In a master's hands, a synthesizer can produce memorable film scores, like those for *Sorcerer* and *Thief* by the German band Tangerine Dream and for *Midnight Express, American Gigolo, Foxes*, and *Cat People* by Giorgio Moroder. But the highest kudos have gone to the 'synth track' of *Chariots of Fire*, an unlikely candidate for an electronic score."[35] Indeed, the synthesizer score struck a chord with theatergoers already familiar with the instrument's use in both disco and new wave music. This was not surprising, given that Tangerine Dream and fellow *kosmische* artists Can provided music for some of the earliest films in the German New Wave, and Moroder and Vangelis were established recording artists before they embarked on soundtrack work.

The newness of the sound also evoked connections to certain genres, which helped the initial surge of synthesizer scores in the 1970s, but limited its acceptance in the 1980s. The connection of the synthesizer to genre films was forged through its ability to evoke the futuristic sounds germane to science fiction, and the association of its unfamiliar electronic textures with supernatural occurrences in horror films. As *New York Times* movie critic Janet Maslin complained, "Already you can hear synthesizer effects too much in horror movies, where they capitalize on those sounds and repeat them over and over without developing them. That nervous-pulse synthesizer sound is just numbing after a while."[36] By 1980 it became possible to wrest the synthesizer from these generic associations after Giorgio Moroder won an Academy Award for his original score for *Midnight Express* (Alan Parker, 1978) and audiences heard synthesizer scores from a variety of genres. Moroder explained his concern: "I hate those sounds which are typical synthesizer—all that *oing-boing* that a lot of rock bands use. . . . It's especially harmful to a score. You have to balance the sound so that it's not too much like an obvious synthesizer and not too much like just another instrument. It should be unexaggerated, subtle, and as natural as possible."[37] By the time of the critical and commercial success of Vangelis's score for *Chariots of Fire* (Hugh Hudson, 1981), the synthesizer had become a scoring instrument of choice.

The Instrumental Rock Score

An advantage of synthesized scores was that they cost far less than symphonic scores. Moreover, they were more viable commercially, and soundtrack albums from *Midnight Express, American Gigolo* (Paul Schrader, 1980), *Cat People* (Paul Schrader, 1982), *Thief* (Michael Mann, 1982), *Chariots of Fire*, and *Merry*

Christmas, Mr. Lawrence (Nagisa Ôshima, 1983) all achieved best-selling chart positions in the United States and the United Kingdom. The crossover of synthesizer artists to soundtrack composers in the 1980s was mirrored by a similar vogue for rock and new wave performers. Some of the early rock scores from Brian May of Queen (*Flash Gordon* [Mike Hodges, 1980], *Highlander* [Russell Mulcahy, 1986]) or Jimmy Page of Led Zeppelin (*Death Wish II* and *Death Wish 3* [Michael Winner, 1982 and 1985]) were valued for their ability to raise adrenaline levels in action films.

In contrast, a series of rock composers from the 1970s started plying their craft with more traditional film scores in the 1980s. Guitarist Ry Cooder got his start as a session musician in the 1960s before recording a series of thematic albums exploring American roots, blues, jazz, ragtime, and vaudeville music. Adept in a broad range of idioms, Cooder seamlessly transitioned into scoring with rootsy southwest themes for *Southern Comfort* (Walter Hill, 1981), *The Border* (Tony Richardson, 1982), and *Paris, Texas* (Wim Wenders, 1984). Similarly, pianist and singer Randy Newman, who started as a songwriter and arranger in the early 1970s, found commercial success with a string of esoteric solo albums in the latter half of the decade. After dabbling with scoring Norman Lear's *Cold Turkey* in 1971, Newman returned in 1981 with his Academy Award–nominated score for Miloš Forman's *Ragtime* and followed it with a second nomination for his score for *The Natural* (Barry Levinson, 1984).

In the United Kingdom, the music and film industries were closer than in the United States, and the crossover between rock artists and score composition began in the late 1960s with soundtracks from Donovan (*Poor Cow* [Ken Loach, 1967], *Brother Sun Sister Moon* [Franco Zeffirelli, 1972]), Pink Floyd (*More* and *La vallée* [Barbet Schroeder, 1969 and 1972]), and Alan Price (*O Lucky Man!* [Lindsay Anderson, 1973]). Mark Knopfler, guitarist and lead vocalist for Dire Straits, provided a trio of guitar-based instrumental scores for Scottish filmmaker Bill Forsyth before his breakthrough Hollywood score for *The Princess Bride* (Rob Reiner, 1987). Chart-topping group The Police were recruited to contribute several songs to *Brimstone and Treacle* (Richard Loncraine, 1982), and the following year their drummer Stewart Copeland composed a stunning rock/musique concrète score for Coppola's *Rumble Fish* (1983) that blurred the line between music and sound effects. Although none of these soundtrack albums were as successful as the synthesizer score for *Chariots of Fire*, they showed the efficacy of rock composers and created a market for other artists to transition into scoring. Subsequently, the mid-1980s witnessed scores from popular new wave artists Eurythmics (*1984* [Michael Radford, 1984]), Thomas Dolby (*Gothic* [Ken Russell, 1986]), and David Byrne (*Married to the Mob* [Jonathan Demme, 1988]).

But the two most significant composers coming from rock followed very different paths in the 1980s. Hans Zimmer started his career writing jingles for music production company Air-Edel while supplying keyboards for groups The

Buggles, The Damned, Ultravox off-shoot Helden, and Shriekback. Through his connection with composer Stanley Myers, Zimmer collaborated on score material for *Moonlighting* (Jerzy Skolimowski, 1982) and *Eureka* (Nicholas Roeg, 1983) before branching out on his own with *Insignificance* (Roeg, 1985) and *My Beautiful Laundrette* (Stephen Frears, 1985).[38] While his background as a synthesizer player helped Zimmer enter the field, he quickly adapted his compositional strategies to better suit the needs of the films. "Filmmakers create these little autonomous worlds. They might be imaginary worlds, but they have to adhere to a logic. I don't like the idea of the score being this objective thing that sits on top of the movie. It needs to come from inside, and seep into the pores of all the buildings, not just the characters."[39] His subsequent scores during the 1980s for *Rain Man* (Barry Levinson, 1988), *Driving Miss Daisy* (Bruce Beresford, 1989), and *Black Rain* (Ridley Scott, 1989) display the versatility of his style, which was modified to suit the idiom of each film. In 1989, Zimmer started Media Ventures with music producer Jay Rifkin as a one-stop location for film music. Media Ventures was responsible for a string of hit soundtrack recordings in the 1990s, and Zimmer has become virtually synonymous with blockbuster spectacles such as the *Dark Knight* trilogy in the 2000s.

In contrast, Danny Elfman seemed an unlikely candidate to become a major composer of motion picture scores. As front man for Los Angeles–based cabaret rockers Oingo Boingo, Elfman recorded a few modestly successful synth-driven pop albums before being asked by director Tim Burton to provide music for *Pee-wee's Big Adventure* (1985). Elfman was selected because Oingo Boingo's idiosyncratic sound matched the highly stylized look and tone of Burton's film, yet the score avoided the synth-rock sound that defined his band. "There really wasn't much electronics. I try to minimize the amount of synthesizers used because synthesizers are too slow in trying to achieve sounds while the whole orchestra's waiting, and you're under enormous pressure."[40] Although he composed his music on synthesizers, Elfman relied on fellow Boingo alum Steve Bartek to transcribe and orchestrate it. Elfman followed a more traditional approach to developing themes and leitmotifs for characters, explaining that "even as a rock and roll artist, I came out of musical theater, and so those roots were helpful. . . . I've listened, probably, in my lifetime to more Kurt Weill than I have Rolling Stones."[41]

Unlike Zimmer's, Elfman's early scores were instantly recognizable and often stood out. Julie Hubbert writes: "Where the classical model made room for non-thematic underscoring, what [Aaron] Copland called 'neutral' music, Elfman's orchestral model is hyperthematized. He uses themes to underscore narrative action, but he 'sound tracks' them by simultaneously conceiving of them as marketable tracks on a record or CD. In *Batman* (Tim Burton, 1989), he engineered the main characters' themes, with the help of film executives, to be as commodifiable as a pop song."[42] Because of his background in commercial music, Elfman

understood the value of the soundtrack album in the compact disc era, and composers such as Elfman and Zimmer rapidly became stars in their own right. As
such, film producers were more cognizant of the crossover potential behind movie
music and combined underscored passages with sequences featuring recognizable
pop songs. As Stephen Holden noted about *Batman*, "The film's noisy soundtrack
presents a pitched battle between two strains of music that have accompanied
movies since the dawn of the sound era: one derived from high culture, the other
from pop. The majority of the film's score is loud, post-Wagnerian action music
composed by Danny Elfman. Sly, subterranean funk songs by Prince make up
the rest."[43] Consequently, the film was represented by two separate albums: Elfman's motion picture score and Prince's vocal songs, only some of which were
used in the film. A similar conflict arose on *Dick Tracy* (Warren Beatty, 1990)
where Elfman had to accommodate Madonna's vocal music. This resulted in
separate record releases for Elfman's score, Madonna's music compiled on her
I'm Breathless album, and a third album of period-style pop songs written by
Andy Paley.

Synergy and the Compilation Score

Soon Hollywood began marketing compilation scores as soundtrack albums.
Following the model of several hit soundtracks from the 1970s, specifically RSO's
Saturday Night Fever (John Badham, 1977) and *Grease* (Randal Kleiser, 1978),
"film companies saw what it could do for their films in terms of promotion to
have songs you could put on a sound track album," noted Becky Shargo. "You got
all this air play, all this free advertising. And in turn the record companies saw
how the film company's marketing campaign could help promote their record."[44]
This corporate synergy between the film and music industries started off shaky,
but the placement of popular songs into films soon became the norm in the 1980s
and 1990s. As Jeff Rona explained, "Film music budgets are often broken into two
parts, one for the score and the other for the licensing of songs. For a song to be
acquired for a film, the producers must approach the song's publishers and negotiate a deal. When you start talking about putting songs on a film's soundtrack
album, things can get quite political."[45]

Although compilation soundtrack recordings were not always hits, they
provided important exposure and worked as an alternate form of publicity.
Even though the programmatic use of popular songs in films often met the
cross-promotional needs of the producers rather than the thematic demands
of the film, several films from the early 1980s started to use popular music
thematically. As Russ Regan, senior vice president for pop music at PolyGram,
observed, "Underscoring used to be the key goal for music in films. It had to be
subliminal to the screen action. The new generation of film makers aren't intim-
idated by music. They realize that pop can enhance a film rather than threaten

it."[46] Although few soundtrack albums had substantial success in the wake of the RSO hits, *Urban Cowboy* (James Bridges, 1980) earned $42 million at the box office in 1980 and had a triple platinum soundtrack with seven different singles released and a $1 million marketing campaign.[47] The potential out-of-the-park success of compilation scores was enough of an enticement for producers to seek out partnerships with record companies and for music specialists to negotiate the clearance rights for musical use. Originally, these "music coordinators" functioned as liaisons between the music and film industries, and before long studios were hiring former music industry veterans to run their pop music divisions.[48]

By 1984 a series of hit films and soundtrack albums proved the effectiveness of cross-promotional synergy and launched the role of the music supervisor. The surprise success of *Flashdance* (Adrian Lyne, 1983) was directly attributed to Michael Sembello's "Maniac" and Irene Cara's title song, and how the film internalized the fast cutting and dynamic cinematography from music videos. Its distributor, Paramount, followed the pattern of priming the film by releasing a single from the soundtrack several weeks before its opening backed by a promotional video for "Maniac" that showed no footage of Sembello but was basically "a four-minute musical trailer" for the film.[49] The success of the film and its soundtrack album solidified the strategy, and, according to *Rolling Stone* reporter Marianne Meyer, "1984 dawned with a new equation: Movie + Soundtrack + Video = $$$."[50] The films that made the most effective use of this formula recognized that the pop songs needed to connect to the themes and narrative of the film. Dean Pitchford, a lyricist for *Flashdance*, wrote the screenplay for *Footloose* (Herbert Ross, 1984) knowing that "I wanted the songs to be a subtext for the film."[51] In addition, Pitchford also wrote all the lyrics because, as music supervisor Becky Shargo explained, "We wanted to have a thread tying through all the picture."[52] Shargo, who served as music coordinator for *Urban Cowboy*, negotiated a deal with Columbia Records that asked for a $250,000 advance for the music rights. This let Columbia load the soundtrack with its artists Kenny Loggins, Bonnie Tyler, and Deniece Williams, and the album eventually yielded six Top Forty singles, four of which also reached the Top Ten. Of course this was a feat of shrewd business acumen on Shargo's part, and Pitchford admitted that it took forty-seven separate deals to negotiate the nine songs appearing on the *Footloose* soundtrack.[53]

Fueled by music videos in heavy rotation on MTV, in September 1985 the three top singles on Billboard's Hot 100 chart—John Parr's "St. Elmo's Fire (Man in Motion)," Huey Lewis and the News' "The Power of Love," and Tina Turner's "We Don't Need Another Hero"—all came from films.[54] The music video and MTV had become the main marketing force behind hit songs, and the connection between movies and the music industry was closer than ever before. Music manager Danny Goldberg outlined this trend, observing, "Where the music helps is when you have a hit video. A video that comes out two or four weeks ahead of the film can be a tremendous help to distributors. The videos are perceived as entertainment, not as advertisement, because they're visual, just like the movie they're promoting."[55]

This complex interplay among films, videos, promotional materials, and record releases was navigated and negotiated by the new role of the music supervisor, an individual whose job was to coordinate every element of "playback" in a film. That meant not just selecting music, but negotiating the master recording rights, the mechanical rights, and permissions for every artist included in a film. David T. Friendly observed that by the mid-1980s, "pop sound tracks became a de rigueur component of the modern feature and a stopgap for soaring marketing costs. But a stubborn push and pull between the record labels and the movie studios evolved. Ideally, studios want bankable music and the music videos that spring from them. Record companies want to have their music showcased in hit movies."[56] The music supervisor's role was to work as a partner with the director in developing a strategy that served the needs of the story, the producer, the distributor, and the record companies associated with the film. As a new generation of music supervisors, such as Randall Poster, Bonnie Greenberg, Alex Steyermark, and Danny Bramson, emerged in the 1990s, the role began to rival that of the composer, and their influence continues to be heard in the use of popular music tracks in films, television, and commercials in the 2000s.

Dolby Stereo: A Tale of Two Formats

If one name is deeply associated with the development and implementation of multichannel film sound, it is Dolby. In 1975, Dolby Laboratories introduced the Dolby Stereo Variable Optical format (also called Dolby Stereo or Dolby SVA), which applied Dolby noise reduction to the optical soundtrack on 35mm film and expanded its dynamic range from 30–6,300 Hz to 40–12,500 Hz.[57] The effect was a radical increase in clarity along with a substantial reduction of noise caused by dirt and imperfections on the optical track. In addition, Dolby Laboratories used the space of the monophonic optical soundtrack to include two sound channels—Left-total and Right-total—that were processed by a matrix to produce four channels of sound information—Left, Center, Right, and Surround.[58]

By 1980, over 1,200 theaters in the United States were equipped to play Dolby soundtracks, and within a year the number rose to 2,000. As the decade progressed Dolby Stereo's presence grew exponentially, with over 250 films mixed in Dolby Stereo by 1984 and 6,500 theaters worldwide wired for its playback.[59] Yet the success of Dolby Stereo was not tied exclusively to its 35mm format. Dolby Laboratories also applied their noise reduction process to the six magnetic tracks of 70mm. This provided an extended dynamic range and reduced noise, but it did not change the way that the films were mixed. The 70mm "discrete-six" format included five channels of sound stretched across the screen—Left, Left-Center, Center, Right-Center, Right—with a single surround channel sent to a bank of speakers in the auditorium. Although the 70mm format had been used for road show presentations since the 1950s, the application of Dolby noise reduction gave it new life. Used on a variety of successful films in the late 1970s, Dolby-encoded 70mm rapidly became the gold standard for theatrical sound, and its success facilitated the development of its 35mm sibling.[60]

Dolby Stereo, however, required the use of a matrix to encode four channels of audio onto two optical tracks. This process, while ingenious in design and execution, did come with problems. It was soon discovered that the advantages of optical stereo—being cheap to manufacture and backward compatible with monophonic projection—were counterbalanced by major disadvantages: decreased headroom over mono, limited dynamic range, and playback aberrations such as dialogue "unpredictably 'pulled' to the sides by certain combinations of sounds."[61] In order to mitigate potential problems, Dolby Laboratories developed its own guidelines for postproduction mixing, and every film required a Dolby supervisor to ensure that these standards were met. Despite the most rigorous supervision, sound artifacts would often slip through.

In particular, Dolby Stereo was susceptible to what was called "magic surround" where the decoder accidentally sent certain sounds to the surround channel. Discussing the Dolby Stereo mix for *Return of the Jedi* (Richard Marquand, 1983), Ben Burtt noticed how "in certain crowd scenes we had the Ewoks running around, panned left and right around the front. In the matrix they were bent around into the surrounds, and it was a much more spatial effect than I got in the [70mm prints]. It sounded more realistic, and was an *accident*."[62] Although this effect created the illusion of a three-dimensional acoustic space, it was neither intentional nor could it be controlled by the rerecording mixer.

Because the 35mm Dolby Stereo tracks needed to be mixed carefully to prevent these accidental artifacts, rerecording mixers were encouraged to monitor the final mix through the Dolby matrix to ensure channel and phase relationships. When production timetables were short or budgets tight, 70mm Dolby prints were created by rechanneling the 35mm Left-Center-Right-Surround submix.[63] Even under the best circumstances, filmmakers found themselves limited by the fact that most audiences would hear the 35mm version of the film. As Alan Splet explained about *Dune* in 35mm, it was "a pale facsimile of the 70mm magnetic 6 track."[64]

Despite the potential for ambitious sound mixes, film sound in the 1980s lacked theatrical standardization, and even the most ambitious sound mixes often were not reproduced correctly.[65] An unfortunate side effect was that many of the multichannel film presentations from the early 1980s were conservative in their use of Dolby Stereo, and filmmakers lagged behind in learning how the technology could aid their storytelling.[66] Even with the flagship 70mm format, Larry Blake argued that the limitations placed on it by conservative Dolby mixing strategies held the format in check: "Sound system headroom, theater noise levels, and the intolerance of 'little old ladies' to loud sounds conspire to bring the dynamic range of 70mm mixes closer to those expected of 35mm Dolby Stereo optical."[67] The "quiet revolution" of Dolby Stereo took most of the 1980s for new aesthetic approaches to multichannel sound's storytelling potential to emerge.

Multichannel and Surround Sound

Perhaps the most novel and controversial aspect of Dolby Stereo was how its surround channel enveloped audiences in a 360-degree field of sound. Although the surround channel existed since the multichannel magnetic formats of the 1950s, it was used sparingly and generally for spectacular effects only.[68] Most stereo mixing positioned the sound sources across the space of the screen's main speakers, with nearly all dialogue channeled to the center speaker to ensure intelligibility. These past practices not only carried over into the era of Dolby Stereo, but several were concretized in the rules for mixing matrixed Dolby 35mm.

In order to ensure a level of standardization for their 35mm and 70mm formats, Dolby Laboratories issued the *Dolby Surround Mixing Manual* with an entire section devoted to the do's and don'ts of surround mixing, specifically warning against excessive use of the surround channel: "The key to a good surround mix is subtlety. Don't draw attention to your techniques. . . . Mixes that are surround heavy will distract the viewer from the on-screen action, so do not put too much information in the Surround channel."[69] Because the surround information would be lost if a 35mm Dolby Stereo print was played on a monophonic projector, rerecording mixers were told that the surround channel "should complement, not distract from on-screen action."[70] After his experience with *More American Graffiti*, where the music and effects sent to the surround channel disappeared entirely in some theaters, Ben Burtt adopted a prudent approach to its use on *Return of the Jedi*. "My attitude was: the surrounds don't exist—nothing was ever destined for the surrounds that was considered an essential piece of information."[71]

This conservative approach to surround use changed over the decade, and by the 1990s a new aesthetic replaced old mixing practices. In lieu of the discrete-six 70mm channel arrangement, an alternative configuration of the magnetic tracks made it possible to provide split-surround channels in 70mm. The "split-six" configuration was first introduced in the late 1970s when Walter Murch proposed the idea for *Apocalypse Now*. Murch discovered that although the surround speakers were fed by one channel of sound, they were set up with separate left and right amplification chains. This made it possible to send surround information to the left and right surround speakers, thereby realizing Coppola's desire for "quadraphonic" sound.

Although the split-surround system designed by Murch and Dolby was used on *Apocalypse Now* and *Superman* (Richard Donner, 1978), it was not put

FIGURE 12: Ben Burtt and Gary Summers made use of the split-surround channels of the Dolby 70mm format to extend the directional sound of onscreen events into the offscreen space of the cinema (*Indiana Jones and the Last Crusade*, Steven Spielberg, 1989).

to extensive use until the late 1980s with *Indiana Jones and the Last Crusade* (Steven Spielberg, 1989). Rerecording mixers Ben Burtt and Gary Summers, in consultation with director Spielberg and producer Lucas, decided to revive the split-surround format, using the surround channels to provide enhanced realism as well as greater spectacle. Because the decision was made early in the post-production phase, both the sound team and composer John Williams were able to collaborate on music and sound effects that could help advance the story. As Burtt explained, "We'd laid out in the music spotting sessions what scenes would not have music, so that was a chance to do a lot of [sound] FX by themselves."[72] This balance between sound and music was another stage in the evolution of sound design, and differing strategies were utilized to avoid distracting the audience or drawing attention to the surround speakers. During most scenes with musical underscoring, the music was spread into the left and right surrounds, leaving the center speaker free for dialogue and allowing spot effects to move across the screen space. In scenes without music, the surrounds were generally active with ambient sounds or occasional crowd "walla."[73]

Arguably the most effective uses of split surrounds occur during two main chase sequences, the aerial dogfight and the tank battle, where quick changes in screen direction fragmented the conventions of continuity editing (see figure 12). "I loved doing the gun battle in the canyon because there was no music," Burtt explained, "and with split surrounds the gunshots are moving all around the room, with ricochets going from corner to corner."[74] In both sequences the split-surround speakers gave the sound team a stable sonic field to anchor the action as the screen images cut across various vantage points. The result was that the split surrounds not only reinforced the diegetic realism while offering acoustic spectacle, but provided a form of sonic continuity. A full-field aesthetics of sound emerged in the 1990s as a way to use all the speakers in the theater to create a stable diegetic space. These techniques can be heard in some of the most creative sound work from the early 1990s, especially in *The Hunt for Red October* (John McTiernan, 1990), *The Silence of the Lambs* (Jonathan Demme, 1991), and *Dracula* (Francis Ford Coppola, 1992).[75]

With the development of digital theatrical sound systems, each featuring their own form of multichannel playback with split surrounds, the conservative approach to sound mixing started to change in the 1990s. The availability of the multichannel digital formats led filmmakers to prepare their production audio with split-surround use already in mind. As Sony's Steven B. Cohen noted in 1996, "With front and rear stereo sound sources, you can locate sound anywhere in the theatre."[76] The result was a change from the spatial stability of what Michel Chion has called the "superfield" of Dolby Stereo—where the sound field was used to anchor the screen action[77]—to the shifting spatial mobility of what Mark Kerins has called the "ultrafield" of 5.1 digital surround sound.[78]

The 1990s and the Digital Decade

The adoption of digital technologies and release formats represented a major change in the history of film sound. It is important to note, however, that digital recording technologies were used in the professional and home markets early on, yet they took much longer to be accepted in film sound. Multitrack digital audio recorders and mixers were introduced by the late 1970s, and in 1982 the compact disc brought digital sound to home consumers. Michael Rivlin prophesied the rise of a "digital decade" that would radically change the way that sounds are recorded, stored, edited, and mixed in film, resulting in "rich stereophonic or even quad audio in a movie theater."[79] While Rivlin was correct in noting that audiences developed a taste for high-quality audio in cinemas and filmmakers were developing more sound-oriented films, he would have to wait almost ten years to see this "digital decade" come to fruition.

Multitrack Recording and Mixing

Rivlin asserted that the move away from sprocketed media—the magnetically striped 35mm "mag stock" used to edit and mix audio in film postproduction—to unsprocketed media occurred because of the infusion of multitrack recorders. Sound editing from the 1930s through the 1970s was based on the mechanical linkage between the image and the soundtracks. The growth of computer controlled recording equipment necessitated film's compatibility with video storage formats, and in 1969 the Society for Motion Picture and Television Engineers developed their SMPTE time code to tag video images with a digital data stream to mark hours, minutes, seconds, and frames.[80] When applied to motion picture film, this allowed editors to precisely re-sync sound and image tracks in postproduction and opened the door for computer-aided editing. But before digital editing became available, sound editors used SMPTE time code to synchronize images with sound on multitrack recorders.[81]

The use of multitrack recorders and slaved video images meant that sound editors could record, audition, and mix sounds before the final rerecording mix for a film. Because premixes of particular effects or sequences could be constructed during the editing process, sound effects editors took on a larger role. While this proved advantageous for auditioning effects, there were problems shifting timing in relation to the image track. A benefit of editing on mag stock was that the synchronization between sounds and image could be slipped in time, whereas this was much more difficult with multitrack recorders.[82] This meant that multitrack recorders were an advantage when either the film was picture-locked—meaning that there would be no further edits to the image track, a rare situation in commercial cinema—or when sync was not important. When sync was important, editing was done using mag stock on Moviolas or flatbed editing stations.

Despite this presumed gap between the technology used in film and music recording, several innovative practitioners devised ways to incorporate multitrack recording and mixing into film production. Ben Burtt developed a pragmatic approach that utilized the benefits of each system: "When I edit sound I divide my sound materials ahead of time into what I can do best on film mag and what I can do best on multi-track."[83] By using multitrack recorders to premix their effects, Burtt and like-minded colleagues were breaking down the barrier between sound effects editing and rerecording mixing, something that could happen only in the Bay Area, where the union regulations were more relaxed.

Also working in San Francisco, sound editor and rerecording mixer Leslie Schatz developed a process of using twenty-four-track recorders to edit and mix the entire soundtrack for David Byrne's *True Stories* (1986). Because Byrne, the lead singer and songwriter for Talking Heads, was very familiar with the use of multitrack recording, Schatz decided to approach the construction of the soundtrack "like the making of a record. We added each new track to the monitor mix, so we could hear the sound effects, the ambience tracks and the dialogue coming together as we worked."[84] Schatz's method was a harbinger of the dissolution between the roles of sound editor and rerecording mixer. This breakdown of postproduction audio roles accelerated with the introduction of digital editing and mixing technologies.

Digital Audio Workstations

During the 1980s nearly all sound effects libraries were still stored on quarter-inch tape, and most of the work done in postproduction involved the transfer of dialogue, music, and effects to mag stock for editing. But for sound recordists, editors, and mixers, the holy grail of the recording chain—digital storage and random access—was appearing on the horizon. As a labor-saving measure, many of those working in film sound sought a random-access digital editing and storage system. Not only could it provide a substantial reduction in time, it would also let sound effects editors perform multiple jobs. "With a random-access system," as Larry Blake envisioned it in 1985, "there will be little difference between the hardware used in sound editing and mixing."[85]

The first digital audio workstation (DAW) was developed for George Lucas's Sprocket Systems, a hard drive–based audio editing and mixing system. In addition to having all the advantages of recording and mixing on multitrack recorders, it eliminated the primary disadvantage of synchronization restrictions. The ability to move sounds in relation to a timeline was the prime selling point of any DAW, and it gave them a clear advantage over both sprocketed and unsprocketed analog systems. The problem, however, was that early sound editing systems were restricted by the processing power and storage capacities available as well as by cost. Therefore, shortcomings of the computing systems at the heart of DAWs in the 1980s limited their wholesale adoption until the end of the decade.

By 1990, DAWs proliferated when nonlinear picture editing became possible with the debut of the Avid editing system. Launched as a music editing system in 1989, Digidesign's Sound Tools DAW was rechristened Pro Tools in 1991 as an integrated sound editing system for film and video. Purchased by Avid in 1994, and linked to their video editing software through the OMF file exchange format, Pro Tools eventually became the dominant audio editing platform in the 2000s. Despite its ubiquity today, Pro Tools was used initially for sound effects editing, with dialogue being edited and premixed in Avid. Adding to the hodgepodge of DAW systems, the DAWN workstation from Doremi Labs was an expandable editing station used as "intelligent digital dubbers"[86] for mixing backgrounds and Foley. On *Titanic* (James Cameron, 1997), the grand scale of the film was matched by an equally sizeable soundtrack that was edited entirely digitally—sound effects on Pro Tools, dialogue on AudioFrame, and music on Sonic Solutions—yet the final mix was done on mag stock.[87]

Although digital audio workstations provided the random access of stored sound effects, which greatly aided the speed and efficiency of sound editing, the lack of a dominant platform in the 1990s led to the growth of specialized sound roles and a mushrooming of mix complexity. But along with this change came an increased need for a single "sound mind" to guide the film's soundtrack.[88] For with the gain of greater ease and speed there was also a loss in terms of the built-in rhythms of analog editing and mixing.

The Art of Foley

A counterintuitive aspect of digital sound's expanded dynamic and frequency ranges was that pictures could be quieter as well as louder. Digital recording technology facilitated mixes that emphasized the subtlety and complexity of sound work without sacrificing detail, and the added dynamics meant that audiences were finally able to hear soundtracks the way that sound practitioners designed them. More importantly, it allowed the desire for sound design in the 1980s to be fulfilled. As Leslie Schatz expressed it in 1986, "The alphabet of *sound* is very elementary at this point, but a new language is being developed. *Musique concrète*, sound montage—generally, sounds that depart from slavishly following the image in one way or another—is the direction I believe and hope will evolve in film."[89] In the 1990s it became possible to create quieter pictures that deployed what Jeff Smith calls the "hyperdetail" of Foley work as an essential element in the storytelling process.[90]

Following its codification as a formal postproduction sound practice, but prior to the 1980s, Foley was utilized as a complement to edited sound effects and was relied upon to contribute footstep cues or enhance prop sounds for the characters. Sound editors, including John Post, David Fein, Ken Dufva, and Ross Taylor, and dancers, such as Jerry Trent and Kitty Malone, graduated to Foley "walkers," professionals who performed footstep cues, reproduced dance sounds, added in effects for props, and replaced cloth sounds for characters' clothing, all in sync with the image.[91] Television began to include Foley in the late 1960s and feature film by the late 1970s. Before the end of the 1980s, a new breed of Foley walkers—who were never editors or dancers—became officially known as "Foley artists," a refined designation which acknowledged that they contributed more than just "walking."

Foley for feature films operated differently from television. While the process was the same, films were likely to be shown overseas and dubbed into foreign languages. Therefore, a version with sounds only and no dialogue, known as a "Music and Effects" mix, would be made. This entailed a complete Foley track including footsteps, props, and cloth movement for each scene. Thus, the recorded Foley would have duplicate recordings made for editing purposes, and Foley editors would tighten the sync and ensure that there were no unwanted sounds in the tracks. Foley artists who worked primarily in features were valued more for their creativity and imagination than for their sync.[92]

The role of the Foley artist went through several notable changes from the mid-1980s until the late 1990s, largely due to the introduction of two key factors: the addition of twenty-four-track mixing, which allowed more tracks for layering Foley effects,[93] and the differing vision of some sound editors who saw the potential of the Foley stage as more of a laboratory for designing sounds than as a room for replacing footsteps and prop sounds. These changes led to a new breed of Foley artist—a Foley effects artist—who was called upon to create special sounds that previously had been relegated to a sound effects editor or even a sound librarian, who would search for special ingredients in the sound effects library.[94]

Several supervising sound editors began to visualize the Foley stage as a laboratory to create special sounds. Gordon Ecker Jr. experimented with new recording techniques under the Foley stage's controlled circumstances. For *The Long Riders* (Walter Hill, 1980), Ecker used the ECM 50—a lavalier microphone generally used for voice—to record horse footsteps, boot steps, and gunshot impacts.[95] Charles "Chuck" Campbell, a former actor, envisioned the Foley stage as a performance space and encouraged the artists to consider the narrative when performing the Foley, even allowing Foley artists to design sound effects for *Who Framed Roger Rabbit?* (Robert Zemeckis, 1988). Many of the sounds that contributed to the Academy Award win for Campbell were actually created by John Roesch and Ellen Heuer.[96] This expanded role of the Foley artist was not without its detractors. Transferring the creation of sound effects to the Foley stage was not cost efficient (sound libraries could be used instead), and it trespassed on editorial territory.

The period from 1980 to 2000 was a transformative era for the Foley artist. The change in the required performance duties of Foley—what began by replacing and enhancing what production had not recorded—became by the end of the era an elite category of sound effects. The Foley artist was elevated from a "walker" to a creator of special sound effects design.

Digital Release Formats

As the final element in the chain of digital sound, the development of digital release formats was generally hailed as a revolution in cinema sound. Cinema Digital Sound (CDS), Dolby Digital, Sony Dynamic Digital Sound (SDDS), and Digital Theater Systems' DTS system all marked a major change in sound quality for movie theaters. Each system featured dramatic improvements in dynamic and frequency ranges, and the digital formats received extensive press, making audiences well aware of the developing sound wars at their local theaters. While these digital formats ensured the delivery of high-quality film sound to the average consumer, the irony is that very little changed behind the scenes in sound recording, editing, and mixing. As Walter Murch observed, "There are differences between 70mm magnetic, Dolby Digital, DTS, and SDDS, but they are primarily in the delivery systems. Creatively, the differences are minute, relatively speaking, between any of these systems."[97] Murch's comment is especially telling because all the digital formats based their designs on the five-channel, split-surround 70mm system with low-frequency enhancement that he designed for *Apocalypse Now*.

Viewed from the perspective of 1993, Dolby, Sony, and DTS were pitched in battle to determine whose digital sound system would become the dominant theatrical format. Each system provided stellar sound and all were backward compatible with analog playback, yet what no one could see was that all three would carry on over the next two decades to make "5.1 sound" the norm for home as well as theatrical sound formats. Paradoxically, this was not because of the inherent advantages of any one of the digital formats, but because each one was based on the 70mm split-surround format and preexisting mixing strategies. Overall, the main advantage of the digital systems was that they allowed 35mm film to meet and exceed the sound quality of 70mm, and the standardization of mixing films for six discrete channels freed sound personnel to explore the creative potential of digital sound.

6

THE MODERN ENTERTAINMENT MARKETPLACE, 2000–PRESENT

Mark Kerins

At the dawn of the twenty-first century, the immediate future of film sound seemed somewhat predictable. Despite ongoing shifts in how the film sound industry was organized on a corporate level, actual work practices remained largely unchanged from previous decades and seemed likely to remain so.[1] The 1990s had seen the advent of computer-based scoring, sound editing, and sound mixing, yet long-established workflows and divisions of labor continued to dominate mainstream feature film production. In exhibition, the transition from analog soundtracks to digital ones was essentially complete, with 5.1- or 6.1-channel digital surround soundtracks apparently poised to remain the theatrical exhibition standard for the foreseeable future. And thanks to the DVD format and the explosion of home theater, a future of technological convergence where soundtracks could be reproduced in homes just as they had sounded in theaters appeared tantalizingly close.

In actuality, the film sound industry saw significant changes in the first decade of the new century. This chapter focuses on the root of many of these shifts: the exponentially increasing pace of technological change, both within the film industry and outside it. Specifically, it explores the impact of technology in three different arenas of film sound: behind-the-scenes production processes, theatrical exhibition systems, and sound design aesthetics. In all three, new technologies encouraged different ways of working, reinforced longstanding practices, or even did both simultaneously; together, they forced film sound professionals to adapt established practices based on control and standardization to a new reality of flexibility and adaptation.

Production Processes

Broadly speaking, creating a Hollywood feature film soundtrack involves three distinct categories of work: on-set production recording, audio postproduction (sound design, editing, and mixing), and music. Usually those working in one of these areas have limited or no direct interaction with those in the others, making it worthwhile to examine each independently.

Production recording has changed the least of the three categories since the late 1990s. Organizationally, the labor delineations established decades earlier still remain largely intact: sound is handled by a two-person production mixer/boom operator team, often assisted by a third person dubbed the cable person or utility sound (the traditional term "cable man" having been replaced with gender-neutral options). Technologically, these years saw the completion of the move (begun in the 1990s) from analog to digital recording on-set. By the early 2000s the analog tape Nagra recorders—long the industry's production recording workhorses— had been almost entirely replaced by digital tape recorders such as the Nagra-D and the Digital Audio Tape, or DAT, recorder. This change simplified postproduction media management and transfers by eliminating generation loss–driven degradation and the time-consuming and imperfect process of converting analog media to digital for editing and mixing. But for the sound crews actually working on set, who did not particularly care about the format of their recordings as long as they sounded good, the transition to digital recorders had little direct practical impact as Nagra-D and DAT recorders functioned almost identically to their analog predecessors.

The only major on-set impact of the shift to digital formats was thus a slightly modified equipment setup during the early years of digital recording, when some mixers (who did not yet trust the reliability of the new digital recorders) simultaneously recorded to both analog and digital tape formats. Ironically, only a few years later when these tape-based digital systems were themselves supplanted by file-based hard drive and flash recorders, many of these same cautious mixers again initially recorded to dual formats simultaneously—this time using digital tape as the proven backup. In both cases, the shift in recording formats happened with little notice or discussion outside the ranks of professional sound recordists.

This complete lack of attention to the analog-to-digital transition in recording stands in striking contrast to the public fanfare and concern surrounding digital shooting and digital projection in the early 2000s, but the difference is hardly surprising given that the former shift was invisible to the moviegoing public. One final change worth mentioning regarding production recording is the proliferation of multicam shooting; as scholar Benjamin Wright notes, this led to an increase in the use of wireless radio microphones in place of the preferred boom mics.[2] But aside from this shift in microphone use, the growth of multicam shooting has had little direct impact on the structure or job responsibilities of the production audio team other than making their jobs more difficult.

Audio postproduction, the second broad category of film sound work, has undergone dramatic changes in the 2000s, most tied to the shift from analog to digital workflows. At the start of the new century, the technological situation in the postproduction sound realm largely mirrored that of on-set recording: the move from analog to digital workflows was not quite complete, but would be shortly. As Jay Beck and Vanessa Theme Ament discuss in regard to the New Hollywood, the 1990s brought a major technological upheaval to audio postproduction with the introduction of digital audio workstations (DAWs) as a replacement for magnetic tape-based editing and rerecording. A variety of DAWs (Pro Tools, WaveFrame, Fairlight, etc.) saw use in the 1990s, but DAW adoption was hindered by incompatibilities between the competing formats and fears of investing in a particular system that might not survive.[3] What the industry needed was for one system to emerge as the clear industry standard. By the early 2000s Pro Tools had done just that;[4] with a standard in place, DAW use skyrocketed and DAWs quickly replaced magnetic tape once and for all.

DAWs have several advantages over tape-based systems: aside from the elimination of generation loss, they allow users to easily move sounds around a timeline and to immediately access huge numbers of sounds. They can also play far more tracks simultaneously than tape-based editing systems—as sound editor/designer/mixer Gary Rydstrom (Steven Spielberg's *Jurassic Park* [1993] and *Saving Private Ryan* [1998]; Andrew Stanton and Lee Unkrich's *Finding Nemo* [2003]) succinctly puts it, "That's a major advantage of digital editing: You can hear so many things at once."[5] In the analog era, it was often not until the final mixing stage that all of a film's sound effects, dialogue, and music could be heard together by the director, sound editors, or anyone else. With DAWs, not only can more tracks easily be edited and mixed together, but practically all of a soundtrack's elements can be heard together throughout the post process.

The ability of DAWs to handle large numbers of audio tracks has unsurprisingly resulted in some overly busy and loud soundtracks. As sound designer and editor Glenn Morgan (Chris Kentis's *Open Water* [2003], Don Mancini's *Curse of Chucky* [2013]) explains, "That's the worst disease that a lot of editors and designers have, they just over cut and throw too many colors on the canvas, and then it all turns brown. It is important to be really clean and specific, and not overdo it."[6]

Additionally, the impulse toward more complexity and more volume has been reinforced by contemporary surround-sound formats with ever-increasing numbers of channels, which allow soundtrack designers to simultaneously play lots of sounds in each of several audio channels. As one rerecording mixer laments, "The fact that you are now mixing in 5.1, 6.1, 7.1, . . . I think it was 'let's go as far as we can and hit everybody over the head,' and people equated quality with the excessive SPL [sound pressure level, i.e., loudness]."[7] Morgan is more direct in his assessment: "I find movies are becoming sonically inappropriately loud."[8] This problem is not new to the DAW era, but has become more common thanks to DAWs and more complex surround formats.

Another crucial difference between tape-based and DAW-based audio postproduction is that the latter allows for a nonlinear workflow that, while possible, was time-consuming and inefficient with the former. Traditionally, audio postproduction has been broadly divided between sound editing and sound mixing.[9] Technological limitations kept this distinction in place in the analog era, and it remained largely intact in the early DAW years, when digital systems were used for sound editing but not mixing. As DAWs replaced tape throughout the entire post process, however, this split began to blur. DAWs like Pro Tools make extensive editing, mixing, and even recording capabilities readily available at every stage of postproduction. Sound editors can pan sounds, add reverb, equalize, and compress tracks; rerecording mixers can easily audition new sounds, reedit existing ones, and do anything else editors can. Indeed, by the late 1990s "sound editors had already begun to question the viability of the jurisdictional boundaries between sound editing and re-recording,"[10] and in 1997 rerecording mixers moved from the mixing union into the editing union, reflecting "a concern over postproduction technology and the widespread acceptance of digital audio workstations by editors and re-recording mixers."[11] Although DAWs were not designed specifically to alter conventional workflows or divisions of labor, they made it possible for the previously linear path between sound design, sound editing, and sound mixing to become much more fluid: "It's so morph-like between the mixing consoles and the digital workstations; nowadays you can't tell where one ends and one begins," as Glenn Morgan explains.[12]

For sound editors, the ability to do mixing tasks has been a double-edged sword. DAWs allowed them to combine and play back large numbers of separate sounds at once, but simply hearing how all those sounds were interacting required editors to be able to do some simple mixing, such as adjusting volume levels. Editors quickly found, however, that once they could do these tasks they were expected to do so. Directors and executives, aware of the capabilities of the new systems, understandably were no longer willing to wait until the mixing stage to hear everything in the soundtrack together, as had been the case in the analog tape era. Rather, they wanted to hear, and give feedback on, pseudo-complete versions of their films' soundtracks throughout audio post.

This process did have its benefits, especially improved directorial feedback. As sound designer Erik Aadahl (Ben Affleck's *Argo* [2012], Michael Bay's *Transformers* [2007], Marc Forster's *World War Z* [2013]) explains, "The director keeps hearing it over months and months so by the time you get to the final [mix] they have already heard the whole movie and there are no conceptual rethinks or anything. It's just a lot better."[13] Supervising sound editor Richard King (Christopher Nolan's *The Dark Knight* [2008] and *Inception* [2010], Kenneth Branagh's *Thor* [2011]) echoes Aadahl in describing his work on *Signs* (2002): "The goal was to be very precise because Night [writer and director M. Night Shyamalan] is very precise in his writing and the way he makes his films. I started very early and that was really the first film I really started doing his mixes and sending them to him as I would get a cut scene, a rough cut scene. I would do a mix of that scene you know, and literally work with him on placing a bird in a specific spot or a kind of a cricket. . . . These mixes evolved and evolved and evolved and were kind of the template ultimately for the final mix."[14]

The trade-off for this creative benefit was that time which formerly had been used for spotting, sound design, or editing was now being spent on mixing work—work that was often ultimately unusable. The universal adoption of Pro Tools meant that all session data could be easily transferred between editing stations and the mixing stage, making it practical for sound editors to do some mixing or panning in the editing phase without fear of forestalling other options down the road. As rerecording mixer Marti Humphrey (Takashi Shimizu's *The Grudge* [2004], Sam Raimi's *Drag Me to Hell* [2009], and *Oz the Great and Powerful* [2013]) explains, "The beauty of Pro Tools is that [the editors' sessions] can be played back on our systems, and we could change it. . . . We're not tied into it like the old days where you had to go ahead and make a commitment to your moves and . . . it was unheard of for editors to go ahead and pan things."[15]

Yet final mixes are done on a dubbing stage—at significant expense—for a reason: dubbing stages, unlike editing suites, have the necessary space and acoustics to mimic playback in a theater. As Aadahl points out, some mixing decisions simply cannot be done properly until the rerecording stage: "Mixing in a small room is going to translate very differently to a big theater. . . . Because you are pushing a certain amount of air and there are delays coming from the screen, and you really want to optimize it for the theatrical experience."[16] Mike Knobloch, president of film music for Universal Pictures, similarly notes that mixing decisions made in tiny editing suites do not necessarily work for a theatrical release: "It is not until [filmmakers] get to the dub stage that [they] really do get to sit down in that environment and go 'Okay, let me listen here, I am not just sitting at an Avid where I have one speaker or two speakers. I am in the theater and I've got my whole 5.1 environment.' . . . And you don't really get to explore that until [the] final dub."[17]

Thus, despite sound editors spending increasing amounts of time mixing, much of the work they do cannot be used in the final mix. "Some places will have the editors do pre-panning and stuff like that," explains mixer Humphrey. "But then it becomes a question on the stage of then adjusting it for the environment that we're in, with all the elements in it."[18] Morgan seconds this opinion, pointing out that "there's a lot of premixing done and sometimes it's done well. But I would say about 60 percent of it isn't done as well and some of the mixing time is spent unraveling what someone had done."[19] Indeed, King notes that although his premixing work on *Signs* was useful as a creative guide for the mixers, little of it made it into the soundtrack unchanged: "[My] mixes were kind of the basis at least, of the framework, the sort of blueprint of the mix. . . . We brought in brilliant rerecording mixers who were able to embellish and elaborate upon those mixes."[20]

Despite these problems, the trend toward premixing in editing rooms continues. USC professor and former sound editor Midge Costin (Michael Bay's *Armageddon* [1998], Tony Scott's *Crimson Tide* [1995]) explains, "It's changing. . . . The colleagues that I worked with are definitely now mixing their own stuff, mixing effects down."[21] This is not a choice, though, as much as a necessity due to postproduction schedules tightening since the late 1990s. As sound editor Scott Sanders (Sylvester Stallone's *Rambo* [2008], Jason Reitman's *Juno* [2007] and *Up in the Air* [2009]) puts it: "Those decisions would be made on the stage when films could be there for a month or two, but nowadays . . . it requires us to do much more upfront work."[22] Likewise, Richard King acknowledges, "I still prefer to work with a good mixer. . . . But more and more, there's time constraints that sort of force us into the role of sound designer/co-mixer."[23] And Gary Rydstrom suggests that awareness of shortened mixing schedules makes editors increasingly want to premix their own sounds, in case there is not time on the mix stage to give their work the care it deserves: "I think the trend is that if editors don't think that they're mixers now, they'll *become* mixers, because they'll be mixing for the sake of their editing."[24]

The tightening of mixing schedules is in part another unintended consequence of the flexibility of DAWs: just as editors are now expected to do more mixing, mixers are being asked to spend more of their time editing. Marti Humphrey notes that since the advent of digital consoles he is asked to do more editing on the dubbing stage, a "huge amount."[25] In the analog era the substantial effort and time required to replace a sound on the stage meant this was only done when absolutely necessary. On all-digital mixing stages, in contrast, it only takes a few moments to audition a different sound or take. This has emboldened some directors and producers to treat the mixing stage as another edit room, regularly stopping the mix to try out different takes of a line, or different recordings of a sound effect, or other changes far easier and less expensive to make during sound editing. Sound editors, meanwhile, also contribute to the increase in editing on the mix stage; with DAWs allowing huge numbers of tracks, some editors will include dozens of versions of the same sound in their session. Although the ostensible goal of such an approach is to provide the director options on the stage, the actual result is that the mixer has to spend precious stage time listening to them all and deciding which to use.[26]

It is not just the mixing phase of audio postproduction where schedules have tightened. To be sure, recent years have seen sound crews hired early on major films to develop unique sounds—sound designer Erik Aadahl, for example, recalls spending time before production on *Superman Returns* (Bryan Singer, 2006) trying out different sounds for the effect of the earth splitting in half, and notes that on *Transformers* he started developing the signature sounds of the Transformers themselves before shooting even began.[27] But a very few well-publicized exceptions like the *Matrix* sequels aside, audio postproduction schedules on major features have been compressed in recent years. As sound designer Ben Burtt (George Lucas's *Star Wars* [1977], Andrew Stanton's *Wall-E* [2008]) explained early in the DAW era, "Tradition now is to do things faster than we were doing ten years ago—to deliver the film in a much shorter time. Therefore the people doing sound design really suffer more because they get hardly enough time to do anything other than throw stuff in the film and get out of there."[28] Postproduction schedules have continued to tighten since Burtt's observation, even as sound design has grown more complex, with seven-time Oscar winner Gary Rydstrom observing that "schedules and budgets are under downward pressure, while expectations are as high or higher."[29]

Film sound professionals have in some ways become victims of their own technologically aided efficiencies. Benjamin Wright, after interviewing numerous industry professionals, concluded that "there are distinct workflow advantages to using digital audio workstations, but these have proved to have an inverse effect on scheduling and budgeting."[30] As Wright points out, the fact that DAWs allow individual tasks to be done more quickly has led to disproportionate cuts in the time, money, and crew budgeted for audio post:

> The perceived speed and efficiency of computer editing has encouraged some facilities to trim their staff on individual film projects. . . . Instead of hiring six or seven editors to cut simultaneously, many high-budget features rely on a teams of two or three. . . . If a sound editor was given six weeks in the analog era to compile and cut sounds for a mix, the same job may be allotted three weeks. Although cutting and transfer times have been reduced with computer workstations, *digital tools have not accelerated the creative tasks of recording fresh effects, cutting effects, and designing new sound elements.*[31]

Wright's point that the creative process takes time is a crucial one. Combine that with the DAW-driven trend toward more complex soundtracks—requiring more sounds to be recorded, edited together, and mixed—and it is unclear how much digital technologies have sped up the overall post process.

The common assumption that "digital means 'faster'"[32] is not the only factor behind cuts in postproduction budgets and schedules. Producers, for instance, not infrequently try to make up for financial overruns during preproduction and production by cutting postproduction budgets. Schedule overruns are handled much the same way, particularly for major releases that have release dates locked in years ahead of time, and marketing campaigns beginning long before the movie is completed: if production runs long, or editing takes more time than expected, audio post must simply be done more quickly to meet the release date.

Regardless of cause, the compression of postproduction timeframes complicates audio post in several ways. For one, it means that audio post must often begin while picture editing is still happening—and digital picture editing systems, like their audio counterparts, make it so easy to quickly change things that changes to the picture edit often continue until close to the release date. Sound editor Mark Mangini (J. J. Abrams's *Star Trek* [2009], Josh Gordon and Will Speck's *Blades of Glory* [2007]) even suggests that ongoing picture changes are the greatest challenge to sound effects editors today, observing "what seems to be happening is that more and more versions of a cut are being generated, which means that they're working later and later and making more last-minute changes, and it's driving everybody crazy."[33]

A shortened postproduction schedule also makes it more difficult to get the necessary time with a film's director during the crucial final mix. As six-time Oscar-nominated rerecording mixer Paul Massey (James Mangold's *Walk the Line* [2005], Marc Webb's *The Amazing Spider-Man* [2012], *Star Trek*) notes, "Demands on directors at the end of their production periods, which is the time that we lay in, are great—they could be on the scoring stage because the music is still being written, they could be catching up on ADR sessions that are coming in late, and they could certainly be doing color timing for the picture and that is very time consuming and in the same period of time that we're in."[34]

The result is that despite already-tight mixing schedules, time is lost both working on ideas that a director ultimately doesn't like and rehashing prior work. Explaining the latter, Massey comments, "Often we will mix a reel of film without a director present and they'll come in [and] we will have explored an avenue that clearly didn't work or we thought didn't work and the director will want to undo everything and go back down that avenue again with you. And you can't say [to a director] 'Um, we've already tried that, it doesn't work.' [So] you try it again, and then typically they will go, 'Oh, that is not quite working, is it?'"[35]

Even when a director can focus solely on the mixing process, similar issues arise when tight schedules mean mixing must be spread across multiple dubbing stages working simultaneously, with the whole soundtrack only coming together to a single room late in the process.[36] In short, though DAWs have made some aspects of sound editing and mixing easier, their benefits have been tempered (and then some) by the tightening of schedules and budgets.

The realm of film music, the third and final broad category of film sound work, has been affected by some of the same technological and industrial changes as sound editing and mixing—and has similarly found many of them mixed blessings. For composition and music creation, as with sound editing and mixing, probably the most important technological shift since 2000 has been the use of DAWs. To be sure, technologically savvy composers had long been using computer-based systems as part of their writing process. Until fairly recently, however, getting an acceptable-sounding mock-up of a score out of a computer-based system required a massively complex setup and extensive additional work. Robert Ellis-Geiger, writing about the state of DAW-aided scoring in the late 1990s and early 2000s, explains: "Composers often had to use multiple sample libraries, multiple audio hardware samplers and multiple MIDI tracks assigned to multiple contrasting programs to construct a convincing single instrument part. . . . Composers had to employ the assistance of multiple audio and synthesiser technicians to realise their music. . . . If a composer was not able to afford the investment then there was little chance of success unless an individual was able to join an established production house operation."[37]

But as technology improved and the price of systems came down, this situation began to change. Ellis-Geiger notes as a watershed moment the creation of software samplers that could stream instrument sounds from anywhere on a hard drive, rather than only what could fit in a computer's active memory. This allowed the use of more and longer instrument samples, enabling DAWs to output realistic sound without the use of multiple hardware samplers: "Each sampled instrument . . . potentially sounded sufficiently realistic that a composer only had to create one MIDI track per instrument. This was a major breakthrough."[38] Today, composing on a computer is the norm. As Ellis-Geiger explains, "Most contemporary Hollywood film composers who create orchestral music are using a Digital Audio Workstation (DAW) sequencer and accompanying mock up orchestra as part of the composition process. . . . There are only a few composers such as James Horner, Christopher Young and John Williams who work in a traditional way where they watch the [movie] whilst composing at the piano and scribe music ideas onto manuscript using a pencil."[39]

As the quality of virtual instrument libraries improved and DAWs grew more powerful, eventually computer-based music found use not only in temporary or preview mixes but on actual releases. Films without the budget to hire and record a full orchestra could now get an orchestral-*sounding* score at a much lower cost. Although "the scene of a large orchestra playing under the baton of a composer as the film plays behind it may be the quintessential image" of film scoring, as James Buhler, David Neumeyer, and Rob Deemer write, this is an increasingly inaccurate view of the process: "Orchestral music has continued to serve as the foundation for scoring blockbusters, but the decreasing costs and increasing quality of synthesizers meant that, for most other films, composers drew more and more on the resources of the synthesizer, both as an independent instrument and as a substitute for orchestral instruments."[40] Composer and music professor Martin Sweidel puts it more concisely: "The [traditional orchestral-based] Hollywood process is dying for all but the giant mega films, and even many of those simply choose to take a different approach."[41] Today, an orchestral score is often the result of a primarily synthesized score being combined with live recordings of a few instruments.[42]

The current variety of approaches to film scoring is itself partly due to DAWs giving more people the tools to create scores and making new scoring workflows possible. Articulating the former change is composer Christophe Beck, who comments, "In recent years the price of entry for film composing has gone way down and for a few thousand dollars there is nothing stopping you from sounding totally pro, except your own skills, experience and/or talent."[43] Sweidel likewise highlights how technology has made entry into the composing field more democratic and enhanced the creative process: "Technology such as DAWs, coupled with affordable production software and sample libraries, put the basic tools in the hands of more composers with small project studios than was ever the case before 2000. Music notation skills and traditional orchestration, while extraordinarily useful, are no longer required. . . . The composer with the requisite tools and skills can spend considerably more time working creatively to develop the material and explore the use of that material in the actual context of the film."[44]

As to new scoring workflows, technological advances have allowed individual composers to try a number of previously impractical scoring approaches. A comprehensive listing of all such experiments would be impossible—the point here is the variety of new avenues possible—but a few examples demonstrate the importance of DAWs to these endeavors. Hans Zimmer tried working next to the picture editors, providing draft music cues as they went (Ridley Scott's *Gladiator* [2000]), as well as by giving the editors raw music tracks not tied to specific moments, to use as they saw fit (Ridley Scott's *Black Hawk Down* [2001]);[45] in both cases, it was crucial that Zimmer could quickly create and output audio files the editors could bring into their own systems and play with. For David Fincher's *Fight Club* (1999), the Dust Brothers created music and raw sounds based on the feel and tone of the movie but not synched to specific moments or scenes, and then left it to Fincher and the sound editors to mix, edit, and place them—here one key technological factor was the ability of the band to create large amounts of electronic music quickly on their own.[46] A similar collaborative design marked Christophe Beck's experimental approach to the scoring of parts of *Elektra* (Rob Bowman, 2005): recording orchestral material raw elements, then turning these materials over to the sound designers to create an underlying bed for the sound design.[47] Buhler, Neumeyer, and Deemer neatly summarize the recent trend toward new workflows, tying it in to the proliferation of low-budget films that cannot afford traditional orchestral recording: "The convergence of advanced digital technology with the enormous increase of independent filmmaking over the past thirty years has both allowed and forced composers to create a score in innovative ways, including performing and improvising the score themselves, creating a score entirely with electronic synthesizers or samplers, and using personal computers and home recording technology to record a score in the privacy of the composer's own home."[48]

The workflows used in *Fight Club* and *Elektra* highlight another shift in scoring: greater collaboration between composers and other members of the audio postproduction team. Historically, such interactions are uncommon: as Wright puts it, "The world of sound editing and mixing is professionally distinct from the world of film music composition and editing."[49] This still remains generally true, but it is no longer a hard-and-fast rule. In part this is because both composers and sound editors are working on DAWs, allowing them to easily exchange ideas and files. Indeed, Sweidel notes, the lines between their areas of responsibility are increasingly blurred: "The boundary between sound effects and music has often broken down to the point where it is all 'composed' in a unified way as to create [a] seamless universe of sound. . . . Composers are typically brought into the process earlier. Sound effects and music communicate and collaborate more."[50]

Despite all these advantages, not all of the effects of new technologies have been positive. Like sound editors and mixers, those in film music production have faced shrinking budgets and timeframes thanks to the perception that digital tools are more efficient. It is hardly surprising that once producers and executives heard high-quality scores created partially or solely through synthesis and sampling, they began questioning the need for full orchestras, and the music recording budgets on all but the biggest movies began to shrink. As in the rest of audio post, however, new technologies do not inherently mean everything can be done more cheaply or faster. Even setting aside the fundamental fact that the creative process takes time, demands on composers and their crews have grown while work timeframes have shrunk. For one thing, directors now expect to hear previews of the score more frequently and for each version to sound like a real orchestra. Notes Ellis-Geiger: "It is no longer acceptable for a composer to present their music at a piano or by humming a tune as directors expect to listen to music sketches and all completed cues through a DAW sequencer and accompanying mock-up orchestra."[51] These temp scores have to sound as good as possible, lest a poor rendition cause the director to call for rewrites or even to fire the composer. This means composers must spend time orchestrating full mock-ups of even rough ideas—time they could have otherwise used composing: "Because the stakes of the mock-up session are so high, composers often have to spend as much time preparing the mock-up musical files as they do writing the score itself," observe Buhler, Neumeyer, and Deemer.[52]

At the same time, picture lock is coming later and later in the filmmaking process. This decreases the time between final picture lock and the finished score being needed, and means composers' teams spend significant time adjusting to new cuts throughout the process; according to Ellis-Geiger, "More than one music editor is required to keep up with an evolving film editing process that changes on a daily basis."[53] This in turn puts a large burden on orchestrators and music editors even as downward budgetary pressures (driven by the belief that digital workflows have made all tasks cost less) shrink music production crews and schedules. Overall, new technologies have probably been a net creative positive for composers, but they have brought with them new challenges as well.

Exhibition Systems

From digital projection to a multitude of new surround formats to 3-D, theatrical exhibition technology may have undergone more, and more fundamental, changes in the last twenty years than it had over all the rest of cinema history. These changes have affected film sound in significant ways, if not as directly as developments like DAWs.

The most prominent change in the realm of exhibition since 2000 is, of course, the growth of digital projection. At the turn of the century this technology was very much in its infancy—when George Lucas (one of digital projection's chief early proponents) released his first *Star Wars* prequel in 1999, it showed digitally in only four theaters, and even by the 2002 release of the next prequel, Lucas found fewer than a hundred theaters worldwide, and only fifty-four in the U.S./Canada market, equipped for digital projection.[54] But as digital projectors improved and costs came down, adoption rates began to rise slowly, then skyrocketed after a 2008 deal in which studios agreed to help exhibitors with the high costs of converting theaters.[55] By 2012, over two-thirds of theater screens worldwide used digital projectors, including nearly 85 percent of those in the United States—an impressive number considering only 14 percent of U.S. screens were digital just four years earlier.[56] And when in 2014 Paramount became the first major studio to announce it would cease 35mm distribution entirely, it was clear the end was near for 35mm distribution industry-wide.[57]

For film sound, the principal impact of digital projection was that its use encouraged the development of new soundtrack formats by alleviating compatibility problems. A variety of factors affect the adoption of any new exhibition sound format: Does it have advantages over what it is replacing? Is it robust? Is it economical to use? But working with existing technology has generally been a necessary, if not sufficient, condition for any new format to see widespread adoption. Several multichannel sound formats, for instance, saw use in a few high-end theaters in the 1950s; none of them, though, became a broadly adopted exhibition standard, and in part this was because they required special prints incompatible with standard theatrical equipment.[58] In contrast, one major factor behind the quick success of Dolby Stereo after its introduction in the 1970s was its compatibility with existing technology—Dolby Stereo soundtracks would play back (without any multichannel effects) over monophonic systems, and monophonic soundtracks would play back correctly in Dolby Stereo–equipped theaters.[59] Similarly, digital surround sound (DSS) replaced Dolby Stereo as the exhibition standard only after the introduction of DSS formats that left analog soundtracks in place for backward compatibility. In fact, part of the reason that three different DSS formats (DTS, Dolby Digital, and SDDS) were able to survive and thrive for years was that all three—plus the Dolby Stereo track—could exist on the same print. Studios could make a single film print that would play in any theater, regardless of what sound system it had installed.[60]

By the late 1990s, current technology literally left little room for new innovations in sound exhibition; with major releases featuring four soundtracks, 35mm prints simply had no more free space for yet another soundtrack. Even if audiences or filmmakers had clamored for something beyond the current 5.1/6.1 channel configuration, it would have been difficult to find physical room for it on prints.[61] As Dolby consultant Thom Ehle explained in 2004, "To put more channels in the [Dolby Digital] system is rewriting the whole thing. . . . It's safe to say that we're fully utilizing the data we have on the film at this point."[62]

Digital projection, however, offered a fresh playing field, with hard drives offering plenty of room for multiple mixes and/or more channels of audio. Digital Cinema Packages, or DCPs, could include whatever mixes/channels the studio had created for a movie, and then each exhibitor could simply select the appropriate mix for its own theatrical configuration. Even for those multiplexes where different theaters in the same complex might have different sound systems—the largest auditoriums might be equipped with Dolby's Atmos or Surround 7.1 sound systems, for example, while smaller screens retained older 5.1 Dolby Digital setups—moving a film from one theater to another would involve merely selecting a different soundtrack file, not shipping a different print. Indeed, as studios move away from physical media entirely and use satellite or Internet transmission to send DCPs to theaters, it may become possible for exhibitors to download only the mixes they need.

Once they saw it was financially and practically feasible to create and distribute more sound mixes than could have fit on a 35mm film print, studios and audio companies were quick to introduce new formats—and digital projection also changed the way in which these formats differentiated themselves. In the 1990s, all digital surround-sound formats were built on the same (5.1) audio channel configuration, differing only in their compression algorithms—the ways they reduced 5.1 channels of high-quality audio enough to fit the data on a film print or CD.[63] With digital projection virtually eliminating the need for soundtrack data compression, new DSS formats introduced in the 2000s competed on channel configuration instead.

The first ten years of the new century thus saw films distributed in (and theaters equipped with) a wider variety of audio channel configurations than ever before—indeed, over the entire first 100 years of cinema, only about as many different theatrical audio channel configurations were ever tried as are in use simultaneously today. For an industry that had gone through only two standard exhibition formats (mono and Dolby Stereo) in the first sixty years of sync sound, this was quite a shift. Adding to the complexity of exhibition technology was that even systems with the same number of channels did not always configure them the same way—a 7.1-channel system, for example, could include five front channels and two surrounds (as in SDDS), allowing more precise placement of sounds across the screen, or three front channels and four surrounds (as in Dolby Surround 7.1), allowing for separation of sounds between those coming from the sides of the theater and those originating in the back.

Indeed, the early 2000s saw such a proliferation of formats and promotional names that sometimes it was difficult to even tell exactly what type of soundtrack a particular film or theater used. AMC's proprietary ETX system, for instance, promised twelve-channel, "breathtaking sound" without specifying whether ETX films were specially mixed in twelve channels or if ETX just electronically reprocessed 5.1 mixes.[64] Existing audio companies further confused audiences through a variety of monikers. The theatrical version of DTS was rebranded as

FIGURE 13: The early 2000s saw a large number of sound systems simultaneously in use. By 2014, a moviegoer might encounter any of a dozen logos denoting which sound system a particular theater had installed. Home systems often sported logos for nearly as many consumer formats.

Datasat, for example, while the home version of DTS continued to be marketed under the original brand name and logo. Dolby, meanwhile, simultaneously marketed four similarly named theatrical DSS formats (Dolby Digital, Dolby Digital Surround EX, Dolby Surround 7.1, and Dolby Atmos), leaving audiences at the many theaters where exhibitors simply displayed the Dolby logo unsure of which system was actually in use. Even excluding the many chain-proprietary, beta-testing, and large-screen sound formats, by 2014 at least eight different theatrical formats were still in common use (see figure 13).[65]

This explosion of formats was a positive development for marketers, as it allowed theaters a way to differentiate themselves based on their sound equipment. Among filmmakers themselves, views were more mixed. On the one hand, many appreciated the flexibility offered by some of the new formats. Sixteen-time Oscar-nominated rerecording mixer Greg Russell (Sam Mendes's *Skyfall* [2012], *Transformers*, Sam Raimi's *Spider-Man* [2002]) notes that while mixing Michael Bay's *Transformers: Dark of the Moon* (2011) in 7.1, both he and Bay found the new format's possibilities superior to those of 5.1: "I showed a couple of sequences to Michael early on, and he just commented, 'God, the surrounds just feel really cool. What's going on?' and I said, 'Well, that's the 7.1. . . . ' I can't think of a film ever with him that he's been this excited about the sound of his film. He continually talks about, 'There is just *so much* here for people to enjoy. This is a cinematic experience unlike anything we've ever done.'"[66]

Director Alfonso Cuarón had a similar reaction to the Dolby Atmos system when mixing *Gravity* (2013): "Every time throughout all my years, when I start mixing my films, I was always asking for possibilities in the mixing room that were not achievable. And now finally, with this system—that is, Dolby Atmos—you know, it's this dream come true, in which you really can explode the possibilities of depth and separation as never before."[67] Glowing reviews such as these are common to the introduction of any new sound format, certainly—in just the past two decades, filmmakers and sound enthusiasts reacted with similar delight to the launches of 5.1 and then 6.1.[68] But such praise does indicate that filmmakers could and did appreciate the expanded creative possibilities opened up by these new systems.

Yet while newer soundtrack formats allow for more precise placement of sounds and the creation of more immersive, realistic environments, that potential is only realized when filmmakers have the time and money to exploit it. The introduction of new sound formats, though, exacerbated the already troublesome issue of compressed postproduction schedules. Fully utilizing formats with more channels requires more sounds, as sound editors often cut different sounds for each channel in a surround environment.[69] But adding more channels without expanding postproduction schedules makes this difficult, raising the likelihood that the additional channels will remain empty or just duplicate sounds from other channels. Having more channels and more sound formats is an even bigger issue on the rerecording stage, where final panning and mixing decisions must be made. In an industry where mixing schedules can be so tight that already sometimes "there's not enough time to do the stuff in the surrounds" with 5.1 systems, as mixer Marti Humphrey comments, it is unclear how much practical benefit more complex surround systems offer.

That major studio releases may need to be mixed in several different formats to play in as many of the highest-end theaters as possible becomes another major time consideration. *Pacific Rim* (Guillermo del Toro, 2013), for instance, was mixed in six different sound formats, each with different channel configurations and panning possibilities.[70] To be sure, creating six versions of a soundtrack does not take six times the amount of time or effort as creating one—the sound crew creates one mix as a base and then tweaks it to create the others. Yet each version does take time to create, meaning that the more mixes a film requires, the less time is available to tweak each to exploit that particular format's advantages. As the number of mixes needed for major releases multiplies, the result is generally that the unique capabilities of each format are exploited a little less. On one superhero movie mixed for several different formats, including IMAX, for example, one of the film's sound editors recalls that by the time they got to the IMAX mix—the final one to be tackled—they literally had only enough time to change the placement of a single sound effect. Everything else remained identical to the 5.1 mix, not because the IMAX configuration was otherwise exactly like 5.1 but because they simply did not have time left after finishing the various other versions the studio required to do anything else.[71]

Ultimately, the increasing number and complexity of exhibition sound formats that have sprung up in the past two decades have been a mixed blessing. The increased flexibility and power of new systems offer expanded creative options, but the greater amount of time and work required to fully exploit these options and the demands to mix the same movie in ever-increasing numbers of formats have meant that films rarely take full advantage of these systems' potential. Even for those that do, moreover, only a fraction of theatergoers will hear the movie in its ideal sound format.

Dolby Atmos, the newest of the current generation of sound formats (introduced in 2012), encapsulates these competing advantages and challenges in a single design, making a deeper look at this particular system instructive about the state of exhibition sound. In my 2010 book on digital surround sound, *Beyond Dolby (Stereo)*, I postulated that 5.1 surround would remain the industry standard until digital projection had largely replaced 35mm exhibition.[72] What I did not predict was that shortly after this transition, a new sound system design would alter the underlying principles of how multichannel sound systems worked. Prior to the 2000s, all multichannel soundtracks were created using the same fundamental process: during mixing each sound was sent to one or more channels, everything going to a particular channel was recorded together to yield one finished audio track for each channel, and then each of these unique audio tracks would be specifically routed to one or more speakers during exhibition.

Dolby Atmos altered this process of channel-based mixing to incorporate the idea of "sound objects."[73] These are sounds that are not permanently mixed into a particular audio channel or speaker path, but instead are coded with metadata about where in the theater the sound should be placed. During playback, a theater's Atmos processor reads this information, determines which speaker(s) in that particular theater would best match the desired location, and then sends that sound to that speaker path.[74] For instance, if a sound was coded as playing from directly in the back of the theater, it would be sent to both the left and right surround channels in a 5.1-channel theater, but would be sent to the back surround channel, and neither of the other two surround channels, in a 6.1 installation. A full Dolby Atmos installation can route any sound object to any or all of sixty-two different locations within the theater.

To be clear, Dolby Atmos does not entirely abandon traditional channel-based mixing. Coding all the thousands of sounds in a feature film soundtrack with metadata would be a technological and practical nightmare, especially with sixty-two potential locations for each sound, so Atmos actually functions as a hybrid channel-based/object-based system. During the Atmos mixing process, the mixers follow conventional channel-based mixing practices to create a 9.1 mix (called a bed) that includes most of the film's sound elements (the 9.1 bed uses the Dolby Surround 7.1 channel configuration plus two height channels above the screen). Then they encode the remaining "sound objects" with metadata about desired location within the theater space. A finished Dolby Atmos soundtrack thus includes 9.1 channels of mixed audio and a number of "sound objects," each comprising placement data and one or more sound effects to be played together. During exhibition, the "sound objects" are added on the fly to the 9.1-channel sound bed to recreate the complete intended soundscape.[75]

A key design concept behind Dolby Atmos was that it should alleviate the problem of having to create many separate mixes for the same film. An Atmos mix, theoretically, can be played back over a 5.1, 6.1, or 7.1 system as long as the theater has an Atmos processor that can properly route each sound object and each channel in the 9.1 bed to the correct speakers for that particular installation. Indeed, Dolby's marketing of Atmos to studios and distributors makes this explicit, beginning its description with the headline "Package once, distribute everywhere with Dolby Atmos" and continuing with the claim, "Dolby Atmos builds intelligence into audio files, thereby *eliminating the need for multiple versions*. With Dolby Atmos, a single delivery file will play faithfully in any theatre."[76] Their marketing targeted at filmmakers similarly points out, "Dolby Atmos can automatically create 5.1 and 7.1 deliverables,"[77] which no doubt sounds appealing to sound professionals accustomed to manually remixing the same film for multiple output formats.

In theory, then, Atmos could eliminate a major problem with current practices; in the real world, predictably, the situation is more complicated. Although its ability to automatically create downmixes in particular channel configurations can greatly reduce the time needed to create multiple versions of a soundtrack, Atmos leaves mixers little recourse to manually tweak those downmixes. As Benjamin Wright, who interviewed rerecording mixers about the new system, explains, "These downmixes are done automatically based on room specs and approximate sound placement based on the mixer's 9.1 blueprint. It's actually *more difficult* for a mixer to make changes to the 7.1 downmix since it might fuss with the algorithm and mess up the whole deal. . . . Dolby is basically equating technical control with creative control."[78]

Downmixing would be a moot point were Dolby to realize its explicit long-term goal of Atmos being used in "every movie, every theatre,"[79] but even then a problem would remain: mixing for Atmos is more complicated than channel-based mixing and thus takes more time. Not only must filmmakers create a 9.1-channel bed mix (the addition of height channels meaning additional work beyond that of a 5.1 or 7.1 mix) and map position data for each sound object, they must also decide which sounds will be encoded as sound objects and which will be part of the bed—not necessarily easy decisions to make, and ones for which traditional channel-based mixing experience provides little guidance. Gianluca Sergi, in one of the first scholarly examinations of Dolby Atmos, considers whether filmmakers will find Atmos worth the trouble: "If 5.1 systems already presented filmmakers with a remarkable array of creative choices, a sound platform with a capacity for a 62.2 configuration could potentially take complexity to an almost unmanageable level. . . . In an increasingly compressed time-schedule is Atmos actually going to put more pressure on filmmakers? Will filmmakers feel confident that their Atmos' *über*-mixes play as coherently from a narrative standpoint, in simpler 5.1/6.1/7.1 configurations, in spite of Dolby's reassurances?"[80]

Atmos seemingly has the potential to alleviate the problem of creating multiple mixes, particularly if it becomes the standard for theatrical exhibition as Dolby hopes, but much depends on whether filmmakers find its advantages outweigh the creative and practical challenges it presents. At present, it appears filmmakers and studios may find mixing in Atmos too complicated, time-consuming, and/or expensive to use on all but a few flagship films each year.

Sound Design Trends

Ultimately, directors and most film sound professionals are not terribly concerned about the technical details of sound systems—what they really want to know about any format is simply whether it is well suited to their own creative plans. This raises a fundamental question about soundtracks today: How do contemporary filmmakers actually use sound design? Broadly speaking, recent decades have seen a move toward louder, busier, and more aggressive soundtracks.[81] Jeff Smith, for instance, sees modern sound design as an aural counterpart to the visual strategies described by David Bordwell as "intensified continuity": "The visceral effects and technological affordances of Dolby stereo and digital surround systems sit at the heart of the 'impact aesthetics' that came to be associated with intensified continuity techniques."[82] He argues that "the use of surround channels and directional sound effects creates an immersive aural environment for the viewer, which enhances the effect of contemporary cinema's impact aesthetic."[83] At the same time, he acknowledges that these elements (like the visual components of intensified continuity) do not represent a wholesale break with classic style, pointing out that "the paucity of specific deployments of directional sound effects suggests that this strategy merely enhances sound recording and mixing practices already well established within the Hollywood studio system."[84]

In *Beyond Dolby*, I acknowledge that much of contemporary cinema can rightly be described as "intensified continuity," but point out that digital surround systems have also led to a "digital surround style" that breaks the rules of traditional and intensified continuity both visually and aurally.[85] Key to this style, which uses heavily spatialized sound environments to take over the traditionally image-based function of providing continuity, is immersion within the diegetic space. This style has rarely been fully adopted for entire movies, but it has become more common as filmmakers have grown accustomed to working with digital surround and as new sound formats have grown more flexible. In short, while opinions differ on exactly how dramatic this shift has been and to what degree it represents a break from earlier practices, academics agree that modern soundtracks more actively impact and immerse audiences than their predecessors.

Filmmakers themselves offer mixed opinions on how much sound design has changed in the past couple of decades, particularly with regard to the use of surround sound. Certainly many appreciate the greater creative flexibility of new formats—recall Alfonso Cuarón's praise for Atmos—but not all seem interested in significantly changing their approaches to sound design. One factor is that some filmmakers are inherently skeptical of sound coming from anywhere other than the screen; as one director put it, "I'm hearing all the sound out here, but the movie's on the screen. I want to focus on the screen."[86] Mark Andrews, who with Brenda Chapman directed *Brave* (2012), had similar feelings when first approached about mixing the film in Atmos: "When they were pitching me the idea of kind of encapsulating sound, this dimensional sound, I was like, but wait a minute, the screen is there, why would I have sounds behind me or above me or underneath me, it's going to be weird."[87]

Another group, while not inherently opposed to multichannel sound, worries that any focus there hurts the more important elements of a film. As Gianluca

Sergi writes regarding Dolby Atmos, "It is likely to be seen by some scholars and filmmakers as yet another entry in a long list of technological innovations aimed at providing greater sensual engagement at the expense of film narrative."[88] Still, other filmmakers have found the ability to expand the sonic world of a film beyond the borders of the screen useful for a variety of reasons, such as helping audience members keep track of onscreen space in frenetically cut sequences (the Wachowski Brothers' *The Matrix* [1999], Michael Bay's *Transformers: Revenge of the Fallen* [2009]), differentiating real-world scenes from fantasy sequences (Lars von Trier's *Dancer in the Dark* [2000], Adam Shankman's *Hairspray* [2007]), placing the viewer psychologically in a character's head (Spike Jonze's *Being John Malkovich* [1999], James Cameron's *Terminator 2: Judgment Day* [1991]), and (most commonly) simply creating more realistic and immersive environments (Peter Weir's *Master and Commander: The Far Side of the World* [2003], John Dahl's *Joy Ride* [2001]).

Ultimately sound design in general is one creative tool in the filmmaking toolkit; just as different movies are shot and edited differently, different movies will use sound differently depending on their particular stories, directors, aesthetic approaches, and planned release format. There seems to be general agreement, for example, that 3-D movies should take a more aggressive approach to surround mixing.[89] One ongoing challenge for filmmakers is that sound formats have been changing so quickly that it is difficult to experiment with and learn how best to use each. For instance, by the time filmmakers began figuring out how to integrate 5.1 surround with other creative choices through late 1990s films such as *Saving Private Ryan* and *The Matrix*, the industry was already introducing 6.1 formats.

Factors beyond just technical capabilities or the creative needs of a particular movie affect trends in sound design, as broader issues of cultural experience shape expectations and tastes for both audiences and filmmakers. In the past twenty years, larger societal shifts have paradoxically both encouraged and discouraged aggressive exploitation of digital surround systems' unique capabilities, particularly their capacity for greater dynamic range, full-frequency surround channels, and precise placement of sounds around the theater.

Trends favoring use of these capabilities include the success of the DVD format in the early 2000s, the related growth of home theater, the adoption of Dolby Digital as the standard for high-definition television broadcasts, the increasingly complex use of surround sound in video games, and the critical fact that digital surround sound has now been the norm for theatrical exhibition for two decades. Audiences today are, in short, ever more accustomed to hearing audiovisual media in digital surround of one format or another. Experimental research in music has shown that the more experience listeners have with a particular type of sound playback system, the better they think it sounds. As I have written elsewhere, "Music listeners show preference bias toward the sound presentation mode to which they are most accustomed, even when that mode is compared to technically superior alternatives. Additionally, the more time listeners spend with a particular system, the more they prefer that system."[90] Thus as digital surround sound has become more common, and audiences have heard 5.1 (or 6.1, etc.) soundtracks more frequently, this data would suggest that tastes should have shifted to make surround sound, wide dynamic ranges, and all the other components of DSS formats more attractive, not only to audiences but also to filmmakers and studio executives, whose tastes are shaped by the same cultural shifts.

Additionally, the increasing availability of DSS formats on home video (e.g., DVD, Blu-ray) and the concurrent home theater boom partially assuaged concerns about soundtracks with aggressively spatialized mixes or dramatic variations in loudness not playing back well on home systems—an important consideration given that home viewing accounts for an ever-increasing portion of a major film's revenue.[91] One factor behind the fairly tame use of 5.1 in the early 1990s was that filmmakers knew multichannel effects would not be reproduced properly in the important home market. This made filmmakers understandably hesitant to take full advantage of the capabilities of DSS; as more and more homes were equipped to properly play back digital multichannel soundtracks, this became less of a worry.[92]

Yet neither the hope of increased audience familiarity with digital surround sound nor the promise of convergence between home and theater were realized as well as a simple technological history might imply, and these failures discouraged exploitation of DSS's capabilities in critical ways. Exposure to DSS soundtracks was certainly higher by the second decade of the 2000s than in years past—but still not at the level of exposure to traditional stereo. Despite the massive growth of home theater in the past two decades relative to its virtual nonexistence before the 1990s, even by 2012 only 39 percent of U.S. households had any sort of home theater system installed.[93] This growth in true multispeaker home systems also seems to be somewhat leveling off, as soundbars (single speakers designed to simulate surround sound) had "virtually supplanted separate speakers or home theater-in-a-box" by 2013.[94]

Meanwhile, even many of the true multichannel systems installed in homes are not set up correctly due to aesthetic concerns, less-than-ideal room configurations, wiring issues, technical competence, and lifestyle factors (e.g., parents moving speakers out of young children's reach). Indeed, the dismal reality is that even in movie theaters, it is difficult to find a sound system set up properly. "If you're not on the actual mix stage, the odds that you'll hear exactly what they want you to hear are very slim,"[95] comments sound editor Christopher Reeves. Given that reality, it is unlikely that more than a small percentage of even those homes with a home theater system can correctly reproduce a DSS soundtrack. Moreover, no home system can truly reproduce a soundtrack as it sounded in the theater for the same reasons that mixes done in editing suites rarely sound right:

differences in room size, organization, and acoustics mean that mixes designed in and for a theater space will not sound right in a living room–sized space, and vice-versa. And while theatrical box office might be a diminishing component of a film's overall revenue, filmmakers still mix for theatrical release. As three-time Oscar winner Richard King explains, "You just have to go for what's going to sound good in the best theaters in the biggest cities. . . . It's what's best for the film and what plays best in the best theaters. If it truly doesn't sound as good, then what we try to do is do a different mix for home release."[96]

As yet no standards exist as to how, when, and if home theater–specific mixes are done. In some cases these are done by the original sound team on the same rerecording stage as the theatrical mix, while in others they are done by a separate team on a smaller stage, while in yet others they are done in mock living rooms designed to mimic a home setup. In all of these situations, mixers face the challenge of creating a mix that will sound acceptable both in homes with multichannel home theater systems and in those without, knowing full well the problems with downmixing 5.1 mixes to stereo or mono. The dream of technological convergence has given way to the reality of adding yet another mix to the already lengthy list required for major releases.

In the long run, changes in consumption practices—how media is purchased, viewed (and heard), and stored—may end up having the most significant cultural impact on film sound. The proliferation of movie channels and pay-per-view options on cable and satellite, combined with new technologies (high-speed Internet connections, Netflix, Hulu, etc.) allowing movies to be cheaply streamed on demand, have given people more options for watching movies outside theaters than ever before. This greater accessibility of movies at home has made studios and exhibitors eager for any way to differentiate the theatrical experience, which has in turn encouraged the development and use of new sound systems. Indeed, the recent glut of new sound formats, the return of 3-D, and Hollywood's embrace of IMAX illustrate how eager the film industry has been to re-spectacularize the moviegoing experience. Thus far these strategies have helped hold theater attendance levels in the United States fairly steady over the past decade.[97]

Yet if the growth of secondary distribution channels has sparked innovations in film exhibition, it has also resulted in an audience less attuned to sound quality. Often movies screened through streaming or other secondary distribution channels do not include the original soundtrack; even those that do are rarely screened on sound systems that can correctly reproduce the intended mix. Media is increasingly played back through television or computer speakers, over headphones, or even through tiny smart phone or tablet speakers—all systems lacking the multichannel, frequency response, and dynamics capabilities of the theatrical systems for which movies are mixed. Since listeners come to prefer the systems they're accustomed to hearing, even in the face of superior playback options, as audiences (and filmmakers themselves) increasingly hear soundtracks played back on inferior systems, they may come to feel that those systems sound better than—or at least no different from—higher-quality systems. This has already happened in the music realm, with younger listeners who have grown up listening to compressed audio on mp3 players often unable to hear the difference between mp3s and higher-quality formats such as CDs. One game sound designer even mentioned that his company has recently had trouble finding younger people to hire for its sound teams, as so many of them have spent so much time listening to compressed audio that they cannot distinguish between good and bad recordings well enough to work in the industry.[98]

It is impossible to know whether current trends that would seem to encourage a gradual diminishment of appreciation for high-quality sound will continue, or how much of an effect they will have. But it does suggest that in the future the film industry may be challenged—particularly if it continues using sound to differentiate itself from the home market—to find both film artists who appreciate and want to exploit the full potential of advanced sound systems, and audiences who believe these systems are worth hearing.

The Future of Movie Sound

The first few years of the 2000s have seen changes in film sound production technology, practices, and workflows; changes in film exhibition ranging from digital projection to 3-D to new sound formats; and changes in aesthetic practices and tastes spurred by new technologies and shifts in media consumption habits. Although some of these were very public while others went unnoticed by anyone outside the industry, all have influenced the ways film soundtracks are created and how they sound. For an industry that has long relied on tradition, and where change often comes slowly, this has been a tumultuous period—and the future remains unclear in many of the areas where significant changes are already under way. Behind the scenes, sound editing and sound mixing might be reestablished as distinct crafts, for instance, or the lines between the two might disintegrate completely. In theaters, Dolby Atmos or a new format not yet conceived might emerge as the standard for exhibition, or the industry may continue to simultaneously support a range of systems competing with each other. Culturally, small-screen movie viewing on tablets, computers, and smart phones might prove to be a passing fad, with consumers eventually deciding they prefer big screens and big sound, or perhaps the reverse will happen and filmmakers will have to design their soundtracks to play best over earbuds or on tinny laptop speakers. The next few years will begin to resolve some of these questions, but for now film sound production, exhibition, and consumption all remain in flux, and no one within or outside the industry can say for sure where they will go next.

ACADEMY AWARDS FOR SOUND   Compiled by Joseph Sherry

The following list accounts for the Academy Awards, also known as Oscars, in the various categories of sound. At numerous times throughout the years, the Academy of Motion Picture Arts and Sciences (AMPAS) has changed its categories and methods for nominating and awarding Oscars in sound. The list below is based on information from AMPAS's own Academy Awards database, Oscars .org, and reflects the changing categories used by the Academy over the years. Note that AMPAS's database lists no winners in some sound categories for some years, reflecting the fact that Oscars were not always awarded in each category in each year. Numerous scientific and technical Oscars have been awarded for sound during the Academy's history. Only those designated as Special Achievement Awards are included here.

1929/30   SOUND RECORDING, Metro-Goldwyn-Mayer Studio Sound Department,
            ·   Douglas Shearer, Sound Director: *The Big House*

1930/31   SOUND RECORDING, Paramount Publix Studio Sound Department (not associated with a specific film)

1931/32 SOUND RECORDING, Paramount Publix Studio Sound Department (not associated with a specific film)

1932/33 SOUND RECORDING, Paramount Studio Sound Department, Franklin B. Hansen, Sound Director:
A Farewell to Arms

1934 SOUND RECORDING, Columbia Studio Sound Department, John Livadary, Sound Director:
One Night of Love

1935 SOUND RECORDING, Metro-Goldwyn-Mayer Studio Sound Department,
Douglas Shearer, Sound Director: *Naughty Marietta*

1936 SOUND RECORDING, Metro-Goldwyn-Mayer Studio Sound Department,
Douglas Shearer, Sound Director: *San Francisco*

1937 SOUND RECORDING, United Artists Studio Sound Department, Thomas T. Moulton, Sound Director:
The Hurricane

1938 SOUND RECORDING, United Artists Studio Sound Department, Thomas T. Moulton, Sound Director:
The Cowboy and the Lady

1939 SOUND RECORDING, Universal Studio Sound Department, Bernard B. Brown, Sound Director:
When Tomorrow Comes

1940 SOUND RECORDING, Metro-Goldwyn-Mayer Studio Sound Department,
Douglas Shearer, Sound Director: *Strike Up the Band*

1941 SOUND RECORDING, General Service Sound Department, Jack Whitney, Sound Director:
That Hamilton Woman

1942 SOUND RECORDING, Warner Bros. Studio Sound Department, Nathan Levinson, Sound Director:
Yankee Doodle Dandy

1943 SOUND RECORDING, RKO Radio Studio Sound Department, Stephen Dunn, Sound Director:
This Land Is Mine

1944 SOUND RECORDING, Twentieth Century–Fox Studio Sound Department, E. H. Hansen, Sound Director:
Wilson

1945 SOUND RECORDING, RKO Radio Studio Sound Department, Stephen Dunn, Sound Director:
The Bell's of St. Mary's

1946 SOUND RECORDING, Columbia Studio Sound Department, John Livadary, Sound Director:
The Jolson Story

1947   SOUND RECORDING, Samuel Goldwyn Studio Sound Department, Gordon Sawyer, Sound Director:
              The Bishop's Wife

1948   SOUND RECORDING, Twentieth Century–Fox Studio Sound Department,
              Thomas T. Moulton, Sound Director: *The Snake Pit*

1949   SOUND RECORDING, Twentieth Century–Fox Studio Sound Department,
              Thomas T. Moulton, Sound Director: *Twelve O'Clock High*

1950   SOUND RECORDING, Twentieth Century–Fox Studio Sound Department,
              Thomas T. Moulton, Sound Director: *All About Eve*

1951   SOUND RECORDING, Metro-Goldwyn-Mayer Studio Sound Department,
              Douglas Shearer, Sound Director: *The Great Caruso*

1952   SOUND RECORDING, London Film Sound Department: *Breaking the Sound Barrier*

1953   SOUND RECORDING, Columbia Studio Sound Department, John P. Livadary, Sound Director:
              From Here to Eternity

1954   SOUND RECORDING, Universal-International Studio Sound Department,
              Leslie I. Carey, Sound Director: *The Glenn Miller Story*

1955   SOUND RECORDING, Todd-AO Sound Department, Fred Hynes, Sound Director: *Oklahoma!*

1956   SOUND RECORDING, Twentieth Century–Fox Studio Sound Department,
              Carl Faulkner, Sound Director: *The King and I*

1957   SOUND RECORDING, Warner Bros. Studio Sound Department, George Groves, Sound Director:
              Sayonara

1958   SOUND,   Todd-AO Sound Department, Fred Hynes, Sound Director: *South Pacific*

1959   SOUND,   Metro-Goldwyn-Mayer Studio Sound Department,
              Franklin E. Milton, Sound Director: *Ben-Hur*

1960   SOUND,   Samuel Goldwyn Studio Sound Department, Gordon E. Sawyer, Sound Director;
              and Todd-AO Sound Department, Fred Hynes, Sound Director: *The Alamo*

1961   SOUND,   Todd-AO Sound Department, Fred Hynes, Sound Director: *West Side Story*

1962   SOUND,   Shepperton Studio Sound Department, John Cox, Sound Director: *Lawrence of Arabia*

1963   SOUND,   Metro-Goldwyn-Mayer Studio Sound Department, Franklin E. Milton, Sound Director:
              How the West Was Won

| | SOUND EFFECTS, | Walter G. Elliott: *It's a Mad, Mad, Mad, Mad World* |

| 1964 | SOUND, | Warner Bros. Studio Sound Department, George R. Groves, Sound Director: *My Fair Lady* |
| | SOUND EFFECTS, | Norman Wanstall: *Goldfinger* |

| 1965 | SOUND, | Twentieth Century-Fox Studio Sound Department, James P. Corcoran, Sound Director, and Todd A-O Sound Department, Fred Hynes, Sound Director: *The Sound of Music* |
| | SOUND EFFECTS, | Tregoweth Brown: *The Great Race* |

| 1966 | SOUND, | Metro-Goldwyn-Mayer Studio Sound Department, Franklin E. Milton, Sound Director: *Grand Prix* |
| | SOUND EFFECTS, | Gordon Daniel: *Grand Prix* |

| 1967 | SOUND, | Samuel Goldwyn Studio Sound Department: *In the Heat of the Night* |
| | SOUND EFFECTS, | John Poyner: *The Dirty Dozen* |

| 1968 | SOUND, | Shepperton Studio Sound Department: *Oliver!* |

| 1969 | SOUND, | Jack Solomon, Murray Spivack: *Hello, Dolly!* |

| 1970 | SOUND, | Douglas Williams, Don Bassman: *Patton* |

| 1971 | SOUND, | Gordon K. McCallum, David Hildyard: *Fiddler on the Roof* |

| 1972 | SOUND, | Robert Knudson, David Hildyard: *Cabaret* |

| 1973 | SOUND, | Robert Knudson, Chris Newman: *The Exorcist* |

| 1974 | SOUND, | Ronald Pierce, Melvin Metcalfe Sr.: *Earthquake* |

| 1975 | SOUND, | Robert L. Hoyt, Roger Heman, Earl Madery, John Carter: *Jaws* |
| | SPECIAL ACHIEVEMENT AWARD (SOUND EFFECTS), | Peter Berkos: *The Hindenburg* |

| 1976 | SOUND, | Arthur Piantadosi, Les Fresholtz, Dick Alexander, Jim Webb: *All the President's Men* |

1977	SOUND,	Don MacDougall, Ray West, Bob Minkler, Derek Ball: *Star Wars*
	SPECIAL ACHIEVEMENT AWARD (SOUND EFFECTS EDITING)	Frank Warner: *Close Encounters of the Third Kind*
	SPECIAL ACHIEVEMENT AWARD	Benjamin Burtt Jr., for the creation of the alien, creature, and robot voices featured in *Star Wars*

| 1978 | SOUND, | Richard Portman, William McCaughey, Aaron Rochin, Darin Knight: *The Deer Hunter* |

1979 SOUND,   Walter Murch, Mark Berger, Richard Beggs, Nat Boxer: *Apocalypse Now*
          SPECIAL ACHIEVEMENT AWARD (SOUND EDITING),   Alan Splet: *The Black Stallion*

1980 SOUND,   Bill Varney, Steve Maslow, Gregg Landaker, Peter Sutton:
                                The Empire Strikes Back

1981 SOUND,   Bill Varney, Steve Maslow, Gregg Landaker, Roy Charman:
                                Raiders of the Lost Ark
          SPECIAL ACHIEVEMENT AWARD (SOUND EFFECTS EDITING),
                                Ben Burtt, Richard L. Anderson: *Raiders of the Lost Ark*

1982 SOUND,   Robert Knudson, Robert Glass, Don Digirolamo, Gene Cantamessa:
                                E.T. The Extra-Terrestrial
          SOUND EFFECTS EDITING,   Charles L. Campbell, Ben Burtt: *E.T. The Extra-Terrestrial*

1983 SOUND,   Mark Berger, Tom Scott, Randy Thom, David MacMillan: *The Right Stuff*
          SOUND EFFECTS EDITING,   Jay Boekelheide: *The Right Stuff*

1984 SOUND,   Mark Berger, Tom Scott, Todd Boekelheide, Chris Newman: *Amadeus*
          SPECIAL ACHIEVEMENT AWARD (SOUND EFFECTS EDITING),   Kay Rose: *The River*

1985 SOUND   Chris Jenkins, Gary Alexander, Larry Stensvold, Peter Handford: *Out of Africa*
          SOUND EFFECTS EDITING   Charles L. Campbell, Robert Rutledge: *Back to the Future*

1986 SOUND   John K. Wilkinson, Richard Rogers, Charles "Bud" Grenzbach, Simon Kaye:
                                Platoon
          SOUND EFFECTS EDITING,   Don Sharpe: *Aliens*

1987 SOUND.   Bill Rowe, Ivan Sharrock: *The Last Emperor*
          SPECIAL ACHIEVEMENT AWARD (SOUND EFFECTS EDITING),   Stephen Flick, John Pospisil: *RoboCop*

1988 SOUND,   Les Fresholtz, Dick Alexander, Vern Poore, Willie D. Burton: *Bird*
          SOUND EFFECTS EDITING,   Charles L. Campbell, Louis L. Edemann: *Who Framed Roger Rabbit?*

1989 SOUND,   Donald O. Mitchell, Gregg C. Rudloff, Elliot Tyson, Russell Williams II: *Glory*
          SOUND EFFECTS EDITING,   Ben Burtt, Richard Hymns: *Indiana Jones and the Last Crusade*

1990 SOUND,   Jeffrey Perkins, Bill W. Benton, Greg Watkins, Russell Williams II:
                                Dances with Wolves
          SOUND EFFECTS EDITING,   Cecelia Hall, George Watters II: *The Hunt for Red October*

1991 SOUND   Tom Johnson, Gary Rydstrom, Gary Summers, Lee Orloff:
                                Terminator 2: Judgment Day
          SOUND EFFECTS EDITING,   Gary Rydstrom, Gloria S. Borders: *Terminator 2: Judgment Day*

1992   SOUND,   Chris Jenkins, Doug Hemphill, Mark Smith, Simon Kaye, *The Last of the Mohicans*
        SOUND EFFECTS EDITING,   Tom C. McCarthy, David E. Stone: *Bram Stoker's Dracula*

1993   SOUND,   Gary Summers, Gary Rydstrom, Shawn Murphy, Ron Judkins: *Jurassic Park*
        SOUND EFFECTS EDITING,   Gary Rydstrom, Richard Hymns: *Jurassic Park*

1994   SOUND,   Gregg Landaker, Steve Maslow, Bob Beemer, David R. B. MacMillan: *Speed*
        SOUND EFFECTS EDITING,   Stephen Hunter Flick: *Speed*

1995   SOUND,   Rick Dior, Steve Pederson, Scott Millan, David MacMillan: *Apollo 13*
        SOUND EFFECTS EDITING,   Lon Bender, Per Hallberg: *Braveheart*

1996   SOUND,   Walter Murch, Mark Berger, David Parker, Chris Newman: *The English Patient*
        SOUND EFFECTS EDITING,   Bruce Stambler: *The Ghost and the Darkness*

1997   SOUND,   Gary Rydstrom, Tom Johnson, Gary Summers, Mark Ulano: *Titanic*
        SOUND EFFECTS EDITING,   Tom Bellfort, Christopher Boyes: *Titanic*

1998   SOUND,   Gary Rydstrom, Gary Summers, Andy Nelson, Ronald Judkins:
                             Saving Private Ryan
        SOUND EFFECTS EDITING,   Gary Rydstrom, Richard Hymns: *Saving Private Ryan*

1999   SOUND,   John Reitz, Gregg Rudloff, David Campbell, David Lee: *The Matrix*
        SOUND EFFECTS EDITING,   Dane A. Davis: *The Matrix*

2000   SOUND,   Scott Millan, Bob Beemer, Ken Weston: *Gladiator*
        SOUND EDITING,   Jon Johnson: *U-571*

2001   SOUND,   Michel Minkler, Myron Nettinga, Chris Munro: *Black Hawk Down*
        SOUND EDITING,   George Watters II, Christopher Boyes: *Pearl Harbor*

2002   SOUND,   Michael Minkler, Dominick Tavella, David Lee: *Chicago*
        SOUND EDITING,   Ethan Van der Ryn, Michael Hopkins:
                             The Lord of the Rings: The Two Towers

2003   SOUND MIXING,   Christopher Boyes, Michael Semanick, Michael Hedges, Hammond Peek:
                             The Lord of the Rings: The Return of the King
        SOUND EDITING,   Richard King: *Master and Commander: The Far Side of the World*

2004   SOUND MIXING,   Scott Millan, Greg Orloff, Bob Beemer, Steve Cantamessa: *Ray*
        SOUND EDITING,   Michael Silvers, Randy Thom: *The Incredibles*

2005   SOUND MIXING,   Christopher Boyes, Michael Semanick, Michael Hedges, Hammond Peek: *King Kong*
        SOUND EDITING,   Mike Hopkins, Ethan Van der Ryn: *King Kong*

2006 SOUND MIXING,   Michael Minkler, Bob Beemer, Willie Burton: *Dreamgirls*
     SOUND EDITING,   Alan Robert Murray, Bub Asman: *Letters from Iwo Jima*

2007 SOUND MIXING,   Scott Millan, David Parker, Kirk Francis: *The Bourne Ultimatum*
     SOUND EDITING,   Karen Baker Landers, Per Hallberg: *The Bourne Ultimatum*

2008 SOUND MIXING,   Ian Tapp, Richard Pryke, Resul Pookutty: *Slumdog Millionaire*
     SOUND EDITING,   Richard King: *The Dark Knight*

2009 SOUND MIXING,   Paul N.J. Ottosson, Ray Becket: *The Hurt Locker*
     SOUND EDITING,   Paul N.J. Ottosson: *The Hurt Locker*

2010 SOUND MIXING,   Lora Hirschberg, Gary A. Rizzo, Ed Novick: *Inception*
     SOUND EDITING,   Richard King: *Inception*

2011 SOUND MIXING,   Tom Fleishman, John Midgley: *Hugo*
     SOUND EDITING,   Phillip Stockton, Eugene Gearty: *Hugo*

2012 SOUND MIXING,   Andy Nelson, Mark Paterson, Simon Hayes: *Les Misérables*
     SOUND EDITING (tie), Per Hallberg, Karen Baker Landers: *Skyfall*
                        Paul N.J. Ottosson: *Zero Dark Thirty*

2013 SOUND MIXING,   Skip Lievsay, Niv Adiri, Christopher Benstead, Chris Munro: *Gravity*
     SOUND EDITING,   Glenn Freemantle: *Gravity*

ACADEMY AWARDS FOR MUSIC Compiled by Joseph Sherry

The following list accounts for the Academy Awards, also known as Oscars, in several categories for music, including Original Score and Original Song. Note that throughout the years the Academy of Motion Picture Arts and Sciences (AMPAS) has changed the categories and methods for nominating and awarding its Oscars for music numerous times and as recently as 1999. The list below is based on information from AMPAS's own Academy Awards database, Oscars.org, and both denotes the specific categories of recognition for each individual film and reflects the changing language used by the Academy over the years (for instance, the change from "lyrics" to "lyric" in 1979 in the Original Song category).

1934	SCORING,	Columbia Studio Music Department, Louis Silvers (score by Victor Schertzinger and Gus Kahn): *One Night of Love*
	SONG,	"The Continental" from *The Gay Divorcee* Music by Con Conrad, Lyrics by Herb Magidson
1935	SCORING,	RKO Radio Studio Music Department, Max Steiner (score also by Steiner): *The Informer*

SONG, "Lullaby of Broadway" from *Gold Diggers of 1935*
Music by Harry Warren, Lyrics by Al Dubin

1936 SCORING, Warner Bros. Studio Music Department, Leo Forbstein
(score by Erich Wolfgang Korngold): *Anthony Adverse*
SONG, "The Way You Look Tonight" from *Swing Time*
Music by Jerome Kern, Lyrics by Dorothy Fields

1937 SCORING, Universal Studio Music Department, Charles Previn (no composer credit):
One Hundred Men and a Girl
SONG, "Sweet Leilani" from *Waikiki Wedding*
Music and Lyrics by Harry Owens

1938 ORIGINAL SCORE, Erich Wolfgang Korngold: *The Adventures of Robin Hood*
SCORING, Alfred Newman: *Alexander's Ragtime Band*
SONG, "Thanks for the Memory" from *The Big Broadcast of 1938*
Music by Ralph Rainger, Lyrics by Leo Robin

1939 ORIGINAL SCORE, Herbert Stothart: *The Wizard of Oz*
SCORING, Richard Hageman, Frank Harling, John Leipold, Leo Shuken: *Stagecoach*
SONG, "Over the Rainbow" from *The Wizard of Oz*
Music by Harold Arlen, Lyrics by E. Y. Harburg

1940 ORIGINAL SCORE, Leigh Harline, Paul J. Smith, Ned Washington: *Pinocchio*
SCORING, Alfred Newman: *Tin Pan Alley*
SONG, "When You Wish upon a Star" from *Pinocchio*
Music by Leigh Harline, Lyrics by Ned Washington

1941 MUSIC SCORE OF A DRAMATIC PICTURE, Bernard Herrmann: *All That Money Can Buy*
SCORING OF A MUSICAL PICTURE, Frank Churchill, Oliver Wallace: *Dumbo*
SONG, "The Last Time I Saw Paris" from *Lady Be Good*
Music by Jerome Kern, Lyrics by Oscar Hammerstein II

1942 MUSIC SCORE OF A DRAMATIC OR COMEDY PICTURE, Max Steiner: *Now, Voyager*
SCORING OF A MUSICAL PICTURE, Ray Heindorf, Heinz Roemeld: *Yankee Doodle Dandy*
SONG, "White Christmas" from *Holiday Inn*, Music and Lyrics by Irvin Berlin

1943 MUSIC SCORE OF A DRAMATIC OR COMEDY PICTURE, Alfred Newman: *The Song of Bernadette*
SCORING OF A MUSICAL PICTURE, Ray Heindorf: *This Is the Army*
SONG, "You'll Never Know" from *Hello, Frisco, Hello*
Music by Harry Warren, Lyrics by Mack Gordon

1944 MUSIC SCORE OF A DRAMATIC OR COMEDY PICTURE, Max Steiner: *Since You Went Away*
SCORING OF A MUSICAL PICTURE, Morris Stoloff, Carmen Dragon: *Cover Girl*
SONG, "Swinging on a Star" from *Going My Way*
Music by James Van Heusen, Lyrics by Johnny Burke

1945   MUSIC SCORE OF A DRAMATIC OR COMEDY PICTURE,   Miklós Rózsa: *Spellbound*
    SCORING OF A MUSICAL PICTURE,   Georgie Stoll: *Anchors Aweigh*
    SONG,   "It Might as Well Be Spring" from *State Fair*
               Music by Richard Rodgers, Lyrics by Oscar Hammerstein II

1946   MUSIC SCORE OF A DRAMATIC OR COMEDY PICTURE,   Hugo Friedhofer: *The Best Years of Our Lives*
    SCORING OF A MUSICAL PICTURE,   Morris Stoloff: *The Jolson Story*
    SONG,   "On the Atchison, Topeka and the Santa Fe" from *The Harvey Girls*
               Music by Harry Warren, Lyrics by Johnny Mercer

1947   MUSIC SCORE OF A DRAMATIC OR COMEDY PICTURE,   Dr. Miklós Rózsa: *A Double Life*
    SCORING OF A MUSICAL PICTURE,   Alfred Newman: *Mother Wore Tights*
    SONG,   "Zip-a-Dee-Doo-Dah" from *Song of the South*
               Music by Allie Wrubel, Lyrics by Ray Gilbert

1948   MUSIC SCORE OF A DRAMATIC OR COMEDY PICTURE,   Brian Easdale: *The Red Shoes*
    SCORING OF A MUSICAL PICTURE,   Johnny Green, Roger Edens: *Easter Parade*
    SONG,   "Buttons and Bows" from *The Paleface*
               Music and Lyrics by Jay Livingston and Ray Evans

1949   MUSIC SCORE OF A DRAMATIC OR COMEDY PICTURE,   Aaron Copland: *The Heiress*
    SCORING OF A MUSICAL PICTURE,   Roger Edens, Lennie Hayton: *On the Town*
    SONG,   "Baby, It's Cold Outside" from *Neptune's Daughter*
               Music and Lyrics by Frank Loesser

1950   MUSIC SCORE OF A DRAMATIC OR COMEDY PICTURE,   Franz Waxman: *Sunset Blvd.*
    SCORING OF A MUSICAL PICTURE,   Adolph Deutsch, Roger Edens: *Annie Get Your Gun*
    SONG,   "Mona Lisa" from *Captain Carey, U.S.A.*
               Music and Lyrics by Ray Evans and Jay Livingston

1951   MUSIC SCORE OF A DRAMATIC OR COMEDY PICTURE,   Franz Waxman: *A Place in the Sun*
    SCORING OF A MUSICAL PICTURE,   Johnny Green, Saul Chaplin: *An American in Paris*
    SONG,   "In the Cool, Cool, Cool of the Evening" from *Here Comes the Groom*
               Music by Hoagy Carmichael, Lyrics by Johnny Mercer

1952   MUSIC SCORE OF A DRAMATIC OR COMEDY PICTURE,   Dimitri Tiomkin: *High Noon*
    SCORING OF A MUSICAL PICTURE,   Alfred Newman: *With a Song in My Heart*
    SONG,   "High Noon (Do Not Forsake Me, Oh My Darlin')" from *High Noon*
               Music by Dimitri Tiomkin, Lyrics by Ned Washington

1953   MUSIC SCORE OF A DRAMATIC OR COMEDY PICTURE,   Bronislau Kaper: *Lili*
    SCORING OF A MUSICAL PICTURE,   Alfred Newman: *Call Me Madam*
    SONG,   "Secret Love" from *Calamity Jane*
               Music by Sammy Fain, Lyrics by Paul Francis Webster

1954   MUSIC SCORE OF A DRAMATIC OR COMEDY PICTURE,   Dimitri Tiomkin: *The High and the Mighty*
      SCORING OF A MUSICAL PICTURE,   Adolph Deutsch, Saul Chaplin: *Seven Brides for Seven Brothers*
      SONG,   "Three Coins in the Fountain" from *Three Coins in the Fountain*
      Music by Jule Styne, Lyrics by Sammy Cahn

1955   MUSIC SCORE OF A DRAMATIC OR COMEDY PICTURE,   Alfred Newman: *Love Is a Many-Splendored Thing*
      SCORING OF A MUSICAL PICTURE,   Robert Russell Bennett, Jay Blackton, Adolph Deutsch: *Oklahoma!*
      SONG,   "Love Is a Many-Splendored Thing" from *Love Is a Many-Splendored Thing*
      Music by Sammy Fain, Lyrics by Paul Francis Webster

1956   MUSIC SCORE OF A DRAMATIC OR COMEDY PICTURE,   Victor Young: *Around the World in 80 Days*
      SCORING OF A MUSICAL PICTURE,   Alfred Newman, Ken Darby: *The King and I*
      SONG,   "Whatever Will Be, Will Be (Que Sera, Sera)" from *The Man Who Knew Too Much*
      Music and Lyrics by Jay Livingston and Ray Evans

1957   SCORING,   Malcolm Arnold: *The Bridge on the River Kwai*
      SONG,   "All The Way" from *The Joker Is Wild*
      Music by James Van Heusen, Lyrics by Sammy Cahn

1958   MUSIC SCORE OF A DRAMATIC OR COMEDY PICTURE,   Dimitri Tiomkin: *The Old Man and the Sea*
      SCORING OF A MUSICAL PICTURE,   André Previn: *Gigi*
      SONG,   "Gigi" from *Gigi*
      Music by Frederick Loewe, Lyrics by Alan Jay Lerner

1959   MUSIC SCORE OF A DRAMATIC OR COMEDY PICTURE,   Miklós Rózsa: *Ben-Hur*
      SCORING OF A MUSICAL PICTURE,   André Previn, Ken Darby: *Porgy and Bess*
      SONG,   "High Hopes" from *A Hole in the Head*
      Music by James Van Heusen, Lyrics by Sammy Cahn

1960   MUSIC SCORE OF A DRAMATIC OR COMEDY PICTURE,   Ernest Gold: *Exodus*
      SCORING OF A MUSICAL PICTURE,   Morris Stoloff, Harry Sukman: *Song without End*
      (The Story of Franz Liszt)
      SONG,   "Never On Sunday" from *Never on Sunday:* Music and Lyrics by Manos Hadjidakis

1961   MUSIC SCORE OF A DRAMATIC OR COMEDY PICTURE,   Henry Mancini: *Breakfast at Tiffany's*
      SCORING OF A MUSICAL PICTURE,   Saul Chaplin, Johnny Green, Sid Ramin, Irwin Kostal:
      West Side Story
      SONG,   "Moon River" from *Breakfast at Tiffany's*
      Music by Henry Mancini, Lyrics by Johnny Mercer

1962   MUSIC SCORE–SUBSTANTIALLY ORIGINAL,   Maurice Jarre: *Lawrence of Arabia*
      SCORING OF MUSIC–ADAPTATION OR TREATMENT,   Ray Heindorf: *The Music Man*
      SONG,   "Days of Wine and Roses" from *Days of Wine and Roses*
      Music by Henry Mancini, Lyrics by Johnny Mercer

1963   MUSIC SCORE–SUBSTANTIALLY ORIGINAL,   John Addison: *Tom Jones*
   SCORING OF MUSIC–ADAPTATION OR TREATMENT,   André Previn: *Irma La Douce*
   SONG,   "Call Me Irresponsible" from *Papa's Delicate Condition*
         Music by James Van Heusen, Lyrics by Sammy Cahn

1964   MUSIC SCORE–SUBSTANTIALLY ORIGINAL,   Richard M. Sherman, Robert B. Sherman: *Mary Poppins*
   SCORING OF MUSIC–ADAPTATION OR TREATMENT,   André Previn: *My Fair Lady*
   SONG,   "Chim Chim Cher-ee" from *Mary Poppins*
         Music and Lyrics by Richard M. Sherman and Robert B. Sherman

1965   MUSIC SCORE–SUBSTANTIALLY ORIGINAL,   Maurice Jarre: *Doctor Zhivago*
   SCORING OF MUSIC–ADAPTATION OR TREATMENT,   Irwin Kostal: *The Sound of Music*
   SONG,   "The Shadow of Your Smile" from *The Sandpiper*
         Music by Johnny Mandel, Lyrics by Paul Francis Webster

1966   ORIGINAL MUSIC SCORE,   John Barry: *Born Free*
   SCORING OF MUSIC–ADAPTATION OR TREATMENT,   Ken Thorne: *A Funny Thing Happened on the Way*
         to the Forum
   SONG,   "Born Free" from *Born Free*
         Music by John Barry, Lyrics by Don Black

1967   ORIGINAL MUSIC SCORE,   Elmer Bernstein: *Thoroughly Modern Millie*
   SCORING OF MUSIC–ADAPTATION OR TREATMENT,   Alfred Newman, Ken Darby: *Camelot*
   SONG,   "Talk to the Animals" from *Doctor Dolittle*
         Music and Lyrics by Leslie Bricusse

1968   ORIGINAL SCORE–FOR A MOTION PICTURE, NOT A MUSICAL,   John Barry: *The Lion in Winter*
   SCORE OF A MUSICAL PICTURE–ORIGINAL OR ADAPTATION,   John Green: *Oliver!* (adaptation)
   SONG–ORIGINAL FOR THE PICTURE,   "The Windmills of Your Mind" from *The Thomas Crown Affair*
         Music by Michel Legrand, Lyrics by Alan Bergman and Marilyn Bergman

1969   ORIGINAL SCORE–FOR A MOTION PICTURE, NOT A MUSICAL,   Burt Bacharach: *Butch Cassidy and the*
         Sundance Kid
   SCORE OF A MUSICAL PICTURE–ORIGINAL OR ADAPTATION,   Lennie Hayton, Lionel Newman: *Hello, Dolly!*
         (adaptation)
   SONG–ORIGINAL FOR THE PICTURE,   "Raindrops Keep Fallin' on My Head" from
         Butch Cassidy and the Sundance Kid: Music by Burt Bacharach, Lyrics by Hal David

1970   ORIGINAL SCORE   Francis Lai: *Love Story*
   ORIGINAL SONG SCORE,   The Beatles: *Let It Be*
   SONG–ORIGINAL FOR THE PICTURE,   "For All We Know" from *Lovers and Other Strangers*
   Music by Fred Karlin, Lyrics by Robb Royer (aka Robb Wilson) and James Griffin (aka Arthur James)

1971   ORIGINAL DRAMATIC SCORE,   Michel Legrand: *Summer of '42*
   SCORING: ADAPTATION AND ORIGINAL SONG SCORE,   John Williams: *Fiddler on the Roof* (adaptation)

SONG–ORIGINAL FOR THE PICTURE,   "Theme from Shaft" from *Shaft*
    Music and Lyrics by Isaac Hayes

1972 ORIGINAL DRAMATIC SCORE,   Charles Chaplin, Raymond Rasch, Larry Russell: *Limelight*
    SCORING: ADAPTATION AND ORIGINAL SONG SCORE,   Ralph Burns: *Cabaret* (adaptation)
    SONG–ORIGINAL FOR THE PICTURE,   "The Morning After" from *The Poseidon Adventure*
        Music and Lyrics by Al Kasha and Joel Hirschhorn

1973 ORIGINAL DRAMATIC SCORE,   Marvin Hamlisch: *The Way We Were*
    SCORING: ORIGINAL SONG SCORE AND ADAPTATION,   Marvin Hamlisch: *The Sting* (adaptation)
    SONG,   "The Way We Were" from *The Way We Were*
        Music by Marvin Hamlisch, Lyrics by Alan Bergman and Marilyn Bergman

1974 ORIGINAL DRAMATIC SCORE,   Nino Rota, Carmine Coppola: *The Godfather Part II*
    SCORING: ORIGINAL SONG SCORE AND ADAPTATION,   Nelson Riddle: *The Great Gatsby* (adaptation)
    SONG,   "We May Never Love Like This Again" from *The Towering Inferno*
        Music and Lyrics by Al Kasha and Joel Hirschhorn

1975 ORIGINAL SCORE,   John Williams: *Jaws*
    SCORING: ORIGINAL SONG SCORE AND ADAPTATION,   Leonard Rosenman: *Barry Lyndon* (adaptation)
    ORIGINAL SONG   "I'm Easy" from *Nashville*
        Music and Lyrics by Keith Carradine

1976 ORIGINAL SCORE.   Jerry Goldsmith: *The Omen*
    ORIGINAL SONG SCORE AND ITS ADAPTATION,   Leonard Rosenman: *Bound for Glory* (adaptation)
    ORIGINAL SONG,   "Evergreen (Love Theme from *A Star Is Born*)" from *A Star Is Born*
        Music by Barbra Streisand, Lyrics by Paul Williams

1977 ORIGINAL SCORE,   John Williams: *Star Wars*
    ORIGINAL SONG SCORE AND ITS ADAPTATION,   Jonathan Tunick: *A Little Night Music* (adaptation)
    ORIGINAL SONG,   "You Light Up My Life" from *You Light Up My Life*
        Music and Lyrics by Joseph Brooks

1978 ORIGINAL SCORE,   Giorgio Moroder: *Midnight Express*
    ADAPTATION SCORE, Joe Renzetti: *The Buddy Holly Story*
    ORIGINAL SONG,   "Last Dance" from *Thank God It's Friday*
        Music and Lyrics by Paul Jabara

1979 MUSIC (ORIGINAL SCORE),   Georges Delerue: *A Little Romance*
    MUSIC (ORIGINAL SONG SCORE AND ITS ADAPTATION),   Ralph Burns: *All That Jazz* (adaptation)
    ORIGINAL SONG,   "It Goes Like It Goes" from *Norma Rae*
        Music by David Shire, Lyrics by Norman Gimbel

1980 ORIGINAL SCORE,   Michael Gore: *Fame*
    ORIGINAL SONG,   "Fame" from *Fame*: Music by Michael Gore, Lyrics by Dean Pitchford

1981   ORIGINAL SCORE,   Vangelis: *Chariots of Fire*
      ORIGINAL SONG,   "Arthur's Theme (Best That You Can Do)" from *Arthur*: Music and Lyrics
           by Burt Bacharach, Carole Bayer Sager, Christopher Cross, and Peter Allen

1982   ORIGINAL SCORE,   John Williams: *E.T. The Extra-Terrestrial*
      ORIGINAL SONG SCORE AND ITS ADAPTATION,   Henry Mancini (adaptation score); Henry Mancini and
           Leslie Bricusse (song score): *Victor/Victoria*
      ORIGINAL SONG,   "Up Where We Belong" from *An Officer and a Gentleman*
           Music by Jack Nitzsche and Buffy Sainte-Marie, Lyrics by Will Jennings

1983   ORIGINAL SCORE,   Bill Conti: *The Right Stuff*
      MUSIC (ORIGINAL SONG SCORE OR ADAPTATION SCORE),   Michel Legrand, Alan Bergman, Marilyn Bergman:
           Yentl (song score)
      ORIGINAL SONG,   "Flashdance . . . What a Feeling" from *Flashdance*
           Music by Giorgio Moroder, Lyrics by Keith Forsey and Irene Cara

1984   ORIGINAL SCORE,   Maurice Jarre: *A Passage to India*
      ORIGINAL SONG SCORE,   Prince: *Purple Rain*
      ORIGINAL SONG,   "I Just Called to Say I Love You" from *The Woman in Red*
           Music and Lyrics by Stevie Wonder

1985   ORIGINAL SCORE,   John Barry: *Out of Africa*
      ORIGINAL SONG,   "Say You, Say Me" from *White Night*
           Music and Lyrics by Lionel Richie

1986   ORIGINAL SCORE,   Herbie Hancock: *'Round Midnight*
      ORIGINAL SONG,   "Take My Breath Away" from *Top Gun*
           Music by Giorgio Moroder, Lyrics by Tom Whitlock

1987   ORIGINAL SCORE,   Ryuichi Sakamoto, David Byrne, Cong Su: *The Last Emperor*
      ORIGINAL SONG,   "(I've Had) The Time of My Life" from *Dirty Dancing*: Music by Franke Previte,
           John DeNicola, and Donald Markowitz, Lyrics by Franke Previte

1988   ORIGINAL SCORE,   Dave Grusin: *The Milagro Beanfield War*
      ORIGINAL SONG,   "Let The River Run" from *Working Girl:* Music and Lyrics by Carly Simon

1989   ORIGINAL SCORE,   Alan Menken: *The Little Mermaid*
      ORIGINAL SONG,   "Under the Sea" from *The Little Mermaid*
           Music by Alan Menken, Lyrics by Howard Ashman

1990   ORIGINAL SCORE,   John Barry: *Dances with Wolves*
      ORIGINAL SONG,   "Sooner or Later (I Always Get My Man)" from *Dick Tracy*
           Music and Lyrics by Stephen Sondheim

1991   ORIGINAL SCORE,   Alan Menken: *Beauty and the Beast*
      ORIGINAL SONG,   "Beauty and the Beast" from *Beauty and the Beast*
      Music by Alan Menken, Lyrics by Howard Ashman

1992   ORIGINAL SCORE,   Alan Menken: *Aladdin*
      ORIGINAL SONG,   "A Whole New World" from *Aladdin*: Music by Alan Menken, Lyrics by Tim Rice

1993   ORIGINAL SCORE,   John Williams: *Schindler's List*
      ORIGINAL SONG,   "Streets of Philadelphia" from *Philadelphia*
      Music and Lyrics by Bruce Springsteen

1994   ORIGINAL SCORE,   Hans Zimmer: *The Lion King*
      ORIGINAL SONG,   "Can You Feel the Love Tonight" from *The Lion King*
      Music by Elton John, Lyrics by Tim Rice

1995   ORIGINAL DRAMATIC SCORE,   Luis Enrique Bacalov: *The Postman (Il Postino)*
      ORIGINAL MUSICAL OR COMEDY SCORE,   Alan Menken, Stephen Schwartz: *Pocahontas*
      ORIGINAL SONG,   "Colors of the Wind" from *Pocahontas*
      Music by Alan Menken, Lyrics by Stephen Schwartz

1996   ORIGINAL DRAMATIC SCORE,   Gabriel Yared: *The English Patient*
      ORIGINAL MUSICAL OR COMEDY SCORE,   Rachel Portman: *Emma*
      ORIGINAL SONG,   "You Must Love Me" from *Evita*
      Music by Andrew Lloyd Webber, Lyrics by Tim Rice

1997   ORIGINAL DRAMATIC SCORE,   James Horner: *Titanic*
      ORIGINAL MUSICAL OR COMEDY SCORE,   Anne Dudley: *The Full Monty*
      ORIGINAL SONG,   "My Heart Will Go On" from *Titanic*
      Music by James Horner, Lyrics by Will Jennings

1998   ORIGINAL DRAMATIC SCORE,   Nicola Piovani: *Life Is Beautiful*
      ORIGINAL MUSICAL OR COMEDY SCORE,   Stephen Warbeck: *Shakespeare in Love*
      ORIGINAL SONG,   "When You Believe" from *The Prince of Egypt*
      Music and Lyrics by Stephen Schwartz

1999   ORIGINAL SCORE,   John Corigliano: *The Red Violin*
      ORIGINAL SONG,   "You'll Be in My Heart" from *Tarzan*: Music and Lyrics by Phil Collins

2000   ORIGINAL SCORE,   Tan Dun: *Crouching Tiger, Hidden Dragon*
      ORIGINAL SONG,   "Things Have Changed" from *Wonder Boys*
      Music and Lyrics by Bob Dylan

2001   ORIGINAL SCORE,   Howard Shore: *The Lord of the Rings: The Fellowship of the Ring*
      ORIGINAL SONG,   "If I Didn't Have You" from *Monsters, Inc.*: Music and Lyrics by Randy Newman

2002 ORIGINAL SCORE,   Elliot Goldenthal: *Frida*
      ORIGINAL SONG,   "Lose Yourself" from *8 Mile*
                        Music by Eminem, Jeff Bass, and Luis Resto, Lyrics by Eminem

2003 ORIGINAL SCORE,   Howard Shore: *The Lord of the Rings: The Return of the King*
      ORIGINAL SONG,   "Into the West" from *The Lord of the Rings: The Return of the King*
                        Music and Lyrics by Fran Walsh and Howard Shore

2004 ORIGINAL SCORE,   Jan A. P. Kaczmarek: *Finding Neverland*
      ORIGINAL SONG,   "Al Otro Lado Del Rio" from *The Motorcycle Diaries*
                        Music and Lyrics by Jorge Drexler

2005 ORIGINAL SCORE,   Gustavo Santaolalla: *Brokeback Mountain*
      ORIGINAL SONG,   "It's Hard Out Here for a Pimp" from *Hustle & Flow*
                        Music and Lyrics by Jordon Houston, Cedric Coleman, and Paul Beauregard

2006 ORIGINAL SCORE,   Gustavo Santaolalla: *Babel*
      ORIGINAL SONG,   "I Need to Wake Up" from *An Inconvenient Truth*
                        Music and Lyrics by Melissa Etheridge

2007 ORIGINAL SCORE,   Dario Marianelli: *Atonement*
      ORIGINAL SONG,   "Falling Slowly" from *Once*: Music and Lyrics by Glen Hansard and Marketa Irglova

2008 ORIGINAL SCORE,   A. R. Rahman: *Slumdog Millionaire*
      ORIGINAL SONG,   "Jai Ho" from *Slumdog Millionaire*: Music by A. R. Rahman, Lyrics by Gulzar

2009 ORIGINAL SCORE,   Michael Giacchino: *Up*
      ORIGINAL SONG,   "The Weary Kind (Theme from Crazy Heart)" from *Crazy Heart*
                        Music and Lyrics by Ryan Bingham and T Bone Burnett

2010 ORIGINAL SCORE,   Trent Reznor, Atticus Ross: *The Social Network*
      ORIGINAL SONG,   "We Belong Together" from *Toy Story 3:* Music and Lyrics by Randy Newman

2011 ORIGINAL SCORE,   Ludovic Bource: *The Artist*
      ORIGINAL SONG,   "Man or Muppet" from *The Muppets*: Music and Lyrics by Bret McKenzie

2012 ORIGINAL SCORE,   Mychael Danna: *Life of Pi*
      ORIGINAL SONG,   "Skyfall" from *Skyfall*: Music and Lyrics by Adele Adkins and Paul Epworth

2013 ORIGINAL SCORE,   Steven Price: *Gravity*
      ORIGINAL SONG,   "Let It Go" from *Frozen*: Music and Lyrics by Kristen Anderson-Lopez and
                        Robert Lopez

NOTES

Introduction

1 "I Have Seen Two More Great Completed Cinemascope Features" (advertisement), *Variety*, December 2, 1953.

2 Quoted in Gianluca Sergi, "Knocking at the Door of Cinematic Artifice: Dolby *Atmos*, Challenges, and Opportunities," *New Soundtrack* 3, no. 2 (September 2013): 116.

3 "Musical Union Strong in but 150 U.S. Towns Where Minimum Enforceable—50,000 Out of Work," *Variety*, August 22, 1928, 24.

4 Page Cook, "The Sound Track," *Films in Review*, March 1968, 162.

1 The Silent Screen, 1894–1927

1 So-called reasons for the existence of film music are quoted in, for example, Charles Merrell Berg, *An Investigation of the Motives and Realization of Music to Accompany the American Silent Film, 1896–1927* (New York: Arno Press, 1976), 24, and Roy M. Prendergast, *Film Music: A Neglected Art* (New York: W. W. Norton, 1977), 4–5.

2 Tom Gunning, "The Cinema of Attraction: Early Film, Its Spectator, and the Avant-Garde," *Wide Angle* 8, nos. 3–4 (1986): 63–70. Although in the title the word "attraction" is singular, throughout the article Gunning uses it in the plural, and a later article (in *Velvet*

Light Trap 32 [Fall 1993]: 3–12) is titled "'Now You See It, Now You Don't': The Temporality of the Cinema of Attractions." For recent commentary, see the twenty-four essays in *The Cinema of Attractions Reloaded,* ed. Wanda Strauven (Amsterdam: Amsterdam University Press, 2006).

3 See, for example, Roy Prendergast, *Film Music: A Neglected Art;* Russell Lack, *Twenty-four Frames Under: A Buried History of Film Music* (London: Quartet Books, 1997); Roger Hickman, *Reel Music: Exploring 100 Years of Film Music* (New York: W. W. Norton, 2005); Peter Larsen, *Film Music,* trans. John Irons (London: Reaktion, 2007); Mervyn Cooke, *A History of Film Music* (Cambridge: Cambridge University Press, 2008); and James Wierzbicki, *Film Music: A History* (New York: Routledge, 2009).

4 For descriptions, and photographs, of Kinetoscope parlors, see Rick Altman, *Silent Film Sound* (New York: Columbia University Press, 2004), 78–83.

5 Probably the best-known type of Asian shadow-puppet theater is the *wayang kulit* native to the Indonesian island of Java. But Asian shadow-puppet theater ranges from the *karagöz* in Turkey and the *jalamandapika* in India to the *yuanshen zhiying* in China and the *nang yai* in Thailand. See Fan Pen Chen, "Shadow Theaters of the World," *Asian Folklore Studies* 62, no. 1 (2003): 25–64; and Inge C. Orr, "Puppet Theatre in Asia," *Asian Folklore Studies* 33, no. 1 (1974): 69–84.

   Traditional Asian shadow-puppet theater involves both a translucent screen that separates the audience from the manipulators of the puppets and a light source that emanates from *behind* the puppets; invariably, traditional Asian shadow-puppet theater is sonically accompanied by a combination of sound effects, music both vocal and instrumental, and—importantly—spoken or sung narrative.

6 "The Allegory of the Cave" is part of Book VII of Plato's *The Republic* (ca. 380 B.C.). In the allegory, a population of prisoners has been chained underground in such a way so that for their entire lives all they have been able to see are the shadows of figures moving behind them. When one of the prisoners is released, he does not recognize the various objects whose mere shadows had hitherto constituted his "real" world.

   The link between cinematic illusion and the shadowy images in "The Cave" has long fascinated film theorists, perhaps best known among them the French writer Jean-Louis Baudry. Baudry's ideas first appeared in an article titled "Le Dispositif" in *Communications* 23 (1975): 56–72; translated by Bertrand Augst, the article was published as "The Apparatus" in the journal *Camera Obscura* 1 (Fall 1976): 104–126; since then the article has been much anthologized, sometimes under the title "The Apparatus: Metapsychological Approaches to the Impression of Reality in Cinema."

7 The venue was the Salon Indie located below the Grand Café at 14 Boulevard des Capucines in Paris.

8 The Maraval poster dates not from the initial screenings but from 1896 or even later, and it is "highly unlikely that the Lumière brothers' first showings can have been accompanied by some sort of musical performance in the hall." Gianni Rondolino, *Cinema e musica: Breve storia della musica cinematografica* (Torino: Unione Tipografico-Editrice Torinese, 1991), 14. Quoted, in translation, in Larsen, *Film Music,* 14.

9 Information on these can be found in, for example, Roger Manvell and John Huntley, *The Technique of Film Music* (London: Focal Press, 1957), 17; Emmanuelle Toulet, *Birth of the Motion Picture,* trans. Susan Emanuel (New York: Harry N. Abrams, 1995), 20–21; Charles Musser, *Before the Nickelodeon: Edwin S. Porter and the Edison Manufacturing Company* (Berkeley: University of California Press, 1992), 60–62; and—in impressive detail—Altman, *Silent Film Sound,* 83–115.

10 *Philadelphia Record,* August 11, 1896. Quoted in Charles Musser, *The Emergence of Cinema: The American Screen to 1907* (New York: Scribner's, 1990), 178.

11 *Providence Evening Times,* September 7, 1896, and September 9, 1896. Quoted in Altman, *Silent Film Sound,* 86.

12 *New York Times,* October 21, 1896. Quoted in Kemp R. Niver, *Biograph Bulletins, 1896–1908* (Los Angeles: Locare Research Group, 1971), 14.

13 Kemp R. Niver, *Klaw and Erlanger: Famous Plays in Pictures* (London: Renovare, 1985), 11.

14 *New York World,* February 27, 1898. Quoted in Altman, *Silent Film Sound,* 87.

15 Altman, *Silent Film Sound,* 136–137.

16 Ibid., 137, emphasis added.

17 Richard Crangle, "'Next Slide Please': The Lantern Lecture in Britain, 1890–1910," in *The Sounds of Early Cinema,* ed. Richard Abel and Rick Altman (Bloomington: Indiana University Press, 2001), 39. As its title suggests, Crangle's chapter focuses on so-called magic lantern lectures in the UK, but its gist applies easily to activities in the United States. For more on illustrated lectures in the UK, see, for example, Joe Kember, "'Go Thou and Do Likewise': Advice to Lantern and Film Lecturers in the Trade Press, 1897–1909," *Early Popular Visual Culture* 8, no. 4 (2010): 419–430; and Joe Kember, "Professional Lecturing in Early British Film Shows," in *The Sounds of the Silents in Britain,* ed. Julie Brown and Annette Davison (Oxford: Oxford University Press, 2013), 17–37.

18 Gunning, "The Cinema of Attraction," 64 (Gunning bases the comment on information gleaned from Robert C. Allen, *Vaudeville and Film, 1895–1915: A Study in Media Interaction* [New York: Arno Press, 1980], 159, 212–213); James Lastra, *Sound Technology and the American Cinema: Perception, Representation, Modernity* (New York: Columbia University Press, 2000), 97; John Belton, *American Cinema/American Culture* (New York: McGraw-Hill, 1994), 10.

19 The term comes from the name of a small movie theater that opened in Pittsburgh in 1905; the name of The Nickelodeon was based on the price of admission.

20 In alphabetical order, the members of the Motion Picture Patents Company were Biograph, Edison, Essanay, Lubin, Kalen, Méliès, Pathé, Selig, and Vitagraph. The Méliès and Pathé companies were French, but by 1908 they were not just distributing but manufacturing films in the United States.

21 Early movie palaces in New York included the 2,460-seat Regent Theater (1913), the 3,500-seat Strand (1914), the 1,900-seat Rialto (1916), the 2,100-seat Rivoli (1917), and the 5,300-seat Capitol (1919). For information on movie palaces throughout the United States, see, for example, Ben M. Hall, *The Best Remaining Seats: The Story of the Golden Age of the Movie Palace* (New York: Bramhall House, 1961); David Naylor, *American Picture Palaces: The Architecture of Fantasy* (New York: Van Nostrand Reinhold, 1981); Janna Jones, *The Southern Movie Palace: Rise, Fall, and Resurrection* (Gainesville: University Press of Florida, 2003); and Ross Melnick, *Cinema Treasures: A New Look at Classic Movie Theaters* (St. Paul: MBI, 2004).

22 The term "song illustrator" is sometimes used to describe such a performer, but more often the term "illustrated song" is used to describe the performance. See, for example, Richard Abel, "That Most American of Attractions, the Illustrated Song," in *The Sounds of Early Cinema,* ed. Abel and Altman, 143–155; Altman, *Silent Film Sound,* 106–115 and 183–192; and Paul S. Moore, "The Grand Opening of the Movie Theatre in the Second Birth of Cinema," *Early Popular Visual Culture* 11, no. 2 (2013): 113–125. In any case, "illustrated songs," which typically involved audience members singing, date back to the pre-cinema vaudeville theater.

23 To date the best source of information is the fourth section ("Nickelodeon Sound") of Altman, *Silent Film Sound,* 119–230.

24 An online search for "Sam Fox Moving Picture Music" will lead to numerous downloadable .pdf files.

25 For a survey of music in nineteenth-century British melodrama, see Michael Pisani, "Music for the Theatre: Style and Function in Incidental Music," in *The Cambridge Companion to Victorian and Edwardian Theatre,* ed. Kerry Powell (Cambridge: Cambridge University Press, 2005), 70–92.

26 I have demonstrated this often in the tutorials for the "Survey of Film Music" class that I teach at the University of Sydney. For these I request the services of a volunteer pianist equipped only with moderate keyboard skills and sight-reading ability. While the volunteer quickly looks over the material in one or another of the *Sam Fox* volumes, I remind the other students of the volumes' Tables of Contents, and then I solicit nominations for three selections. With the chosen selections on the music rack, the pianist starts to play and I enact a spontaneously invented scenario that involves, for example, a cowboy who is first beset by a storm and then visited by a fairy; on my cue, the pianist switches from one piece to another, and almost always the result is effective enough to prove the point.

27 For detailed information on collections of generic film music, arranged not just for solo piano but also for various combinations of instruments, see Gillian B. Anderson, *Music for Silent Films, 1894–1929: A Guide* (Washington, DC: Library of Congress, 1988).

28 Max Winkler, *A Penny from Heaven* (New York: Appleton-Century-Crofts, 1951), 171; emphases in original.

29 Frank A. Edson, "The Movies," *Metronome*, April 1915, 38.

30 The "Incidental Music for Edison Pictures" suggestions were published in the *Edison Kine-togram*, September 15, 1909, 12–13; they are reproduced in Berg, *An Investigation of the Motives and Realization of Music to Accompany the American Silent Film, 1896–1927*, 103, and in *Celluloid Symphonies: Texts and Contexts in Film Music History*, ed. Julie Hubbert (Berkeley: University of California Press, 2011), 39–41.

31 Joseph Medill Patterson, "The Nickelodeons: The Poor Man's Elementary Course in the Drama," *Saturday Evening Post*, November 23, 1907, 10.

32 For vivid details on the "crisis of the late aughts" that beset nickelodeon operators as both the number of venues and the number of film products reached a peak, see Altman, *Silent Film Sound*, 119–132.

33 Sinn, who wrote for *Moving Picture World*, had been music director for both the Orpheum Theater and the Criterion Theatre in Chicago; Harrison, who wrote for *Moving Picture World* from 1908 until 1920, had worked as a journalist and a scriptwriter, and in 1916 he authored a book titled *Screencraft*; Martin, who wrote for *Film Index*, was the pianist at Dodge's Theatre in Keokuk, Iowa; Luz, who wrote for *Moving Picture News*, was an orchestra conductor who in 1912 became musical director for the nationwide chain of Loew's Theaters; Barnhardt, who wrote for *Film Index*, was the orchestra conductor at the Palace Theatre in Charleroi, Pennsylvania. For more on these writers, see Altman, *Silent Film Sound*, 231–246.

34 Probably the best-known column on what accompanists should not do, and certainly the most entertainingly vitriolic, is Louis Reeves Harrison's "Jackass Music," *Moving Picture World* 8, no. 3, January 21, 1911, 124–125. The column is reproduced in both Hubbert, *Celluloid Symphonies: Texts and Contexts in Film Music History*, 42–44, and *The Routledge Film Music Sourcebook*, ed. James Wierzbicki, Nathan Platte, and Colin Roust (New York: Routledge, 2012), 11–16. For commentary on Harrison's column, see Tim Anderson, "Reforming 'Jackass Music': The Problematic Aesthetics of Early Film Music Accompaniment," *Cinema Journal* 37, no. 1 (Autumn 1997): 3–22.

35 Clyde Martin, "Playing the Pictures," *Film Index*, December 10, 1910, 5.

36 *New York Dramatic Mirror*, October 9, 1909.

37 Winkler, *A Penny from Heaven*, 168–169.

38 H. L. Barnhart, "Orchestral Music in Pictures," *Film Index*, May 20, 1911, 15.

39 Samuel L. Rothapfel, "Management of the Theater," *Moving Picture World*, April 9, 1910, 548.

40 Eugene A. Ahren, *What and How to Play for Pictures* (Twin Falls, ID: Newsprint, 1913), 12.

41 Clarence E. Sinn, "Music for the Picture," *Moving Picture World*, November 26, 1910, 1227.

42   Ibid.

43   Clyde Martin offers a long list of sound-effects devices that accompanists would do well to have on hand; these include a "baby cry, rooster crow, hen cackle, mocking bird whistle, steamboat whistle, sleigh bells, tugboat whistle, locomotive whistle, horse hoof imitation, train imitation, midway musette, dog bark, chimes, cow bawl, revolver, wind machine, auto horn [and] thunder sheet." He adds, though, that "it is seldom that you will find use for some of these effects." Clyde Martin, "Playing the Pictures," 5. The article is reproduced in Wierzbicki et al., *The Routledge Film Music Sourcebook*, 8–11.

44   Altman, *Silent Film Sound*, 241

45   Following its very successful New York premiere, Griffith's *The Birth of a Nation* was, in fact, exhibited in smaller theaters, and copies of the film were released in tandem with a variety of versions of Joseph Breil's score; along with the full orchestral arrangement, these include arrangements for eight-, nine-, and ten-piece ensembles and two separate keyboard arrangements that are marked "piano" but which were probably played, in venues rich enough to be equipped with the instrument, on the so-called theater organ. For details on the different versions of the score, and for facsimile reproductions of pages from the keyboard arrangements, see Martin M. Marks, *Music and the Silent Film: Contexts and Case Studies, 1895–1924* (New York: Oxford University Press, 1997), 112–131.

46   The score composed and compiled by Elinor, performed by a forty-piece orchestra and a twelve-voice chorus, was heard at showings at the 2,700-seat Clune's Auditorium in Los Angeles. The score composed and compiled by Breil was first heard at New York's 1,055-seat Liberty Theatre.

47   A month after the first New York showings of *The Birth of a Nation*, Altschuler led the Russian Symphony Orchestra in the American premiere of Alexander Scriabin's colossal *Prometheus: The Poem of Fire*.

48   For a thorough analysis of Breil's score for *The Birth of a Nation*, see Marks, *Music and the Silent Film*, 109–166.

49   Marks, *Music and the Silent Film*, 189–194.

50   For more on the road show film, see Wierzbicki, *Film Music: A History*, 61–63.

51   Clifford McCarty's encyclopedic *Film Composers in America: A Filmography, 1911–1970* (New York: Oxford University Press, 2000) lists just thirty or so composers who produced film scores for local consumption.

52   The popular literature contains many well-illustrated books on the history of the theater organ, the first example of which was demonstrated in 1910 by the Rudolf Wurlitzer Company. For scholarly treatments, see, for example, John W. Landon, "Long Live the Mighty Wurlitzer," *Journal of Popular Film* 2, no. 1 (1973): 3–13; and Thomas J. Mathiesen, "Silent Film Music and the Theatre Organ," *Indiana Theory Review* 11 (1990): 81–117.

Because the theater organ was a keyboard instrument, its players in the large movie palaces could easily do—but much more loudly, and with a great variety of tone colors—whatever pianists had done in the small nickelodeon theaters. But the player of the theater organ, especially the player of the theater organ developed for the Wurlitzer company by the British engineer Robert Hope-Jones, could also provide sound effects, of the sort enumerated above in note 43, but loud enough to fill the space of a capacious movie palace. The Hope-Jones theater organ is, in fact, the musical instrument that gave rise to the modern-day cliché that describes a sophisticated technological device as being equipped with "all the bells and whistles"; as Rick Altman puts it (in *Silent Film Sound*, 333), the Hope-Jones theater organ made available to organists "an entire toy counter of percussion sounds, and in particular dozens of traditional moving picture sound effects."

53   Winkler, *A Penny from Heaven*, 236.

54   Hugo Riesenfeld, "Music and the Motion Picture," *Annals of the American Academy of Political and Social Science*, November 1, 1926, 60. Riesenfeld was one of the many composers

who wrote license-free music for Carl Fischer and other publishers. He also composed original scores for the occasional road show film. Importantly, he was the musical director for several large movie palaces in New York.

55 The composer for *Don Juan* was William Axt, who had previously written scores for such road show films as MGM's 1925 *The Big Parade* and *Ben-Hur* and who since 1921 had been on the music staff of New York's Capitol Theatre. The principal composer for *The Better 'Ole* was Maurice Baron, assisted by Fred Heff and Edward Kilenyi; previously, Baron had done the orchestrations for *Don Juan* and the two just-mentioned MGM films. Although they were for the most part originally composed, the scores for both *Don Juan* and *The Better 'Ole* did include public domain popular tunes and pieces of library material.

56 Edison typically gets credit for inventing the motion picture, but many historians agree that the work was done not by Edison but by his employee William Kennedy Laurie Dickson. Some historians argue that the motion picture was in fact invented, in England, by William Friese-Greene in 1889 or by Louis Le Prince in 1888. See Christopher Rawlence, *The Missing Reel: The Untold Story of the Lost Inventor of Moving Pictures* (New York: Fontana, 1990).

57 In a published memoir Dickson claimed to have invented the kineto-phonograph as early as 1889, but Douglas Gomery has convincingly argued that this is no more than "a myth [that has been] repeated in the popular culture." See W.K.L. Dickson and Antonia Dickson, *The History of the Kinetograph, Kinetoscope, and Kineto-phonograph* (New York: Albert Brunn, 1895), 8, and Douglas Gomery, *The Coming of Sound: A History* (New York: Routledge, 2005), 159.

58 See, for example, Douglas Gomery, "The Coming of Sound: Technological Change in the American Film Industry," in *The American Film Industry*, ed. Tino Balio (Madison: University of Wisconsin Press, 1985), 231; Scott Eyman, *The Speed of Sound: Hollywood and the Talkie Revolution, 1926–30* (New York: Simon and Schuster, 1997), 32–37; and Gomery, *The Coming of Sound: A History*, 28–29.

59 "Reserved His Decisions," *New York Times*, June 20, 1895, 6. For details on the patent hearings, see Wierzbicki, *Film Music: A History*, 72–74.

Loie Fuller, it should be noted, performed onstage her "Serpentine Dance" not to arguably "serpentine" music but to Wagner's forceful "The Ride of the Valkyries." For commentary on Fuller's performances and their relationship to Wagner, see Elizabeth Coffman, "Women in Motion: Loie Fuller and the 'Interpenetration' of Art and Science," *Camera Obscura* 17, no. 1 (2002): 73–104; and Matthew William Smith, "American Valkyries: Richard Wagner, D. W. Griffith, and the Birth of Classical Cinema," *Modernism/modernity* 15, no. 2 (April 2008): 221–242.

60 Whereas Edison sold more than a thousand of his Kinetoscope machines to operators of Kinetoscope parlors nationwide, he was able to sell only forty-five of his Kinetophones. See Eyman, *The Speed of Sound*, 26.

61 For details on these and other colorfully named devices, see Altman, *Silent Film Sound*, 158–175.

62 A film projector is based on the idea of intermittent motion, similar to the start-stop-start-stop action of a sewing machine: the aperture opens and an image is shown, the aperture closes, the film is advanced, the aperture opens and closes again, the film advances again, and so on. A phonograph, whose stylus rests in a groove and is sensitive to hills and valleys analogous to sound waves, is based on the idea of continuous motion.

63 The sound-on-film system was called Tri-Ergon because it resulted from the work of three engineers: Josef Engle, Josef Massolle, and Hans Vogt. It should be noted that the American engineer Lee de Forest—who in 1906–07 had invented the prototype of the vacuum tube that eventually led to Western Electric's postwar development of the PA system—in 1919 patented a comparable sound-on-film process whose resultant product he called the DeForest Phonofilm, and that even as the patent for the Tri-Ergon process was under consideration he was attempting to market so-called Phonofilms internationally. For more on

this, and on other efforts to record sound on film, see Wierzbicki, *Film Music: A History*, 86–87.

64 The orchestral score for *The Jazz Singer* is by Louis Silvers. In addition to Silvers's "Mother of Mine, I Still Have You" (written especially for the film), the songs that Jolson's character sings are "Dirty Hands, Dirty Face," "Toot, Toot, Tootsie," "Blue Skies," and "My Mammy." Early in the film, the character of the jazz singer as a child sings "My Gal Sal" and "Waiting for the Robert E. Lee"; late in the film various characters, including Jolson's, sing the traditional "Kol Nidre" and "Kaddish."

65 The score for *Mother Knows Best* features both music composed by Erno Rapee and music compiled by theater entrepreneur S. I. "Roxy" Rothafel. The words and music for the theme song, "Sally of My Dreams," are by William Kernell.

2 Classical Hollywood, 1928–1946

1   William De Mille, "The Screen Speaks," *Scribner's Magazine* 85, no. 4 (April 1929): 367.

2   Attendance data pre-1930 can be variable and unreliable, but most sources cite attendance figures of 57–60 million in 1927 and 80–90 million in 1930. See, for instance, William and Nancy Young, *The Great Depression in America: A Cultural Encyclopedia* (Westport, CT: Greenwood Publishing, 2007), 319–322 (http://books.google.com/books?id=VBljswT-LaIEC, accessed January 29, 2009); Richard Koszarski, *An Evening's Entertainment: The Age of the Silent Picture 1915–1928* (Berkeley: University of California Press, 1994), 25; Joel W. Finler, *The Hollywood Story* (London: Wallflower Press, 2003), 288; and David Cook, *A History of Narrative Film*, 4th ed. (New York: Norton, 2004), 214. According to *Southern California Business*, theater weekly attendance rose from 98 million in 1927–28 to 113 million by 1929. See Campbell MacCulloch, "Not Entirely Dumb," *Southern California Business*, January 1930, 14. But by anyone's figures, the rise in attendance was precipitous.

3   Fitzhugh Green, *The Film Finds Its Tongue* (New York: G. P. Putnam, 1929), 272.

4   Kenneth MacGowan, quoted in James Wierzbicki, *Film Music: A History* (New York: Routledge, 2009), 103.

5   Fox Movietone publicity brochure, "*The Silent Screen Takes Voice,*" 1928.

6   Samuel Goldwyn, quoted in Garry Allighan, *The Romance of the Talkies* (London: C. Stacey, 1929), i.

7   B. P. Schulberg, quoted in "Progress Report," supplement to *Academy Bulletin* 24 (August 6, 1929): 1. See also "Niblo Advises Cautious Steps in Sound Field," *Los Angeles Examiner*, July 29, 1928, n.p. and "'Talkies Won't Oust Silent Films' Zukor," *Los Angeles Examiner*, November 27, 1928, n.p. All references to Los Angeles and San Francisco newspapers are from the "Sound" clippings files at the Margaret Herrick Library, Academy of Motion Picture Arts and Sciences.

8   Harry Carr, "The Lancer in Hollywood," *Los Angeles Times*, November 25, 1929, 1.

9   De Mille, "The Screen Speaks," 368.

10 Alexander Walker, *The Shattered Silents* (New York: William Morrow, 1979), vii.

11 Douglas Gomery, *The Coming of Sound: A History* (New York: Routledge, 2004), 1.

12 Green, *The Film Finds Its Tongue*, 272.

13 De Mille, "The Screen Speaks," 368.

14 Jesse Lasky, quoted in John Hobart, "Stars Are Born by Special Delivery," *San Francisco Chronicle*, January 22, 1929, n.p.

15 Allighan, *The Romance of the Talkies*, 78.

16 Green, *The Film Finds Its Tongue, 268.*

17 Theories abound as to Gilbert's demise. Scott Eyman's, for instance, is that Gilbert had nothing worse than a light baritone but that that particular vocal register clashed with Gilbert's passionate onscreen persona. Thomas Schatz surmises that it was "his inability to adjust an exaggerated pantomime style to the subtler techniques of talking pictures." See Eyman, *The Speed of Sound: Hollywood and the Talkie Revolution* (New York: Simon and Schuster, 1997), 300–301, and Schatz, *The Genius of the System: Hollywood Filmmaking in the Studio Era* (New York: Pantheon, 1988), 103.

18 "Bill Hart Seen a Talker Bet," *Sound Waves* 2, no. 11 (June 15, 1929): 7.

19 De Mille, "The Screen Speaks," 369.

20 Green, *The Film Finds Its Tongue,* 288.

21 Egli, quoted in "Inexperienced Record Well," *Sound Waves* 1, no. 1 (August 15, 1929): 1.

22 "Picking Future Talkie-Movie Stars from Telephone 'Central,'" *American Weekly* 1929, n.p.

23 "Sound Script Experiences Talked by Screen Writers," Academy of Motion Picture Arts and Sciences, "Progress Report": Supplement to the *Academy Bulletin,* August 6, 1929, 3.

24 Jesse Lasky, quoted in "Early End of Silent Film Seen," *Los Angeles Times,* June 2, 1928, 1.

25 Condon, quoted in "Condon Discusses Talker Technique," *Los Angeles Record,* August 6, 1929, n.p.

26 Albert Lewin, quoted in "Talking Pictures Will Remove Films from 'Apologetic Class,'" *Los Angeles Record,* October 27, 1929, n.p. Lewin, assistant to Irving Thalberg, was in charge of play acquisition at MGM.

27 Advertisement, *Variety,* June 19, 1929, 33.

28 "An Oral History with Daniel Taradash," interviewed by Barbara Hall (Beverly Hills: Academy of Motion Picture Arts and Sciences, Oral History Program, 2001), 20.

29 William A. Johnston, "The World War of Talking Pictures," *Saturday Evening Post,* July 19, 1930, 31.

30 Johnston, "The World War of Talking Pictures," 124.

31 "Panel Pictures Help U.S. Pictures in Near East," *Variety,* November 21, 1933, 19.

32 "N.Y. Musicians and Organists Get Body Blow of All Time from 'Sound,'" *Variety,* November 21, 1929, 57.

33 H. P. Moore, "Opposed to Mechanical Substitution" (letter to the editor), *Sound Waves* 1, no. 1 (August 15, 1928): 1.

34 "N.Y. Musicians and Organists Get Body Blow," 57.

35 "Musical Union Strong in but 150 U.S. Towns Where Minimum Enforceable—50,000 Out of Work," *Variety,* August 22, 1928, 24.

36 "L.A. Union Swamped by Migration," *Variety,* February 5, 1930, 59.

37 Katherine Spring, *Saying It with Songs* (New York: Oxford University Press, 2013), 3.

38 Luella Parsons, quoted in "Big Change Predicted in Screen Work," *Los Angeles Examiner,* June 11, 1928, n.p.

39 "Lasky Tells of Triple Opportunities in Store," *Los Angeles Record,* February 8, 1929, n.p.

40 "Hollywood Has Tin Pan Alley," *Sound Waves* 2, no. 4 (March 1, 1929): 11.

41 "Need for Better Music Is Voiced," *Sound Waves* 1, no. 4 (October 1, 1928): 2.

42 Ibid.

43 Wierzbicki, *Film Music: A History,* 113.

44 "300 Musicians in L.A. Enough for Studios," *Variety,* February 26, 1930, 69.

45 Edwin Schallert, "Sound Gains More Impetus," *Los Angeles Times,* July 15, 1929, n.p.

46 "Musicians $600–$700," *Variety*, September 5, 1928, 4.

47 Max Steiner, "Scoring the Film," in *We Make the Movies*, ed. Nancy Naumberg (New York: Norton, 1937), 218.

48 Myrtle Gebhart, "Tin Pan Alley Says Goodbye," *Los Angeles Times*, May 10, 1931, K9, quoted in Wierzbicki, *Film Music: A History*, 121.

49 "N.Y. and Transfer Musicians on Verge of Battle over Job Scarcity," *Variety*, December 3, 1930, 65.

50 See Todd Decker, *Music Makes Me: Fred Astaire and Jazz* (Berkeley: University of California Press, 2012), 329n3.

51 "An Oral History with Hans J. Salter," interviewed by Warren Sherk (Beverly Hills: Academy of Motion Picture Arts and Sciences, Oral History Program, 1994), 34.

52 Margaret Driscoll, "New Language Originated by 'Talking' Films," *Los Angeles Examiner*, December 2, 1928, n.p.

53 Norman Foster, "Sh!—They're Filming 'Talkies'!," *Popular Science Monthly*, April 1929, 176.

54 "Blanket Tents Used for Filming Sound," *Sound Waves* 1, no. 9 (December 20, 1928): 6.

55 See Douglas Shearer, "Sound," in *Behind the Screen*, ed. Stephen Watts (New York: Dodge, 1938), 133, 135.

56 Ibid., 136.

57 "Quiet Air Zones Asked as Planes Disturb Talkies," *Los Angeles Times*, December 17, 1928, 1.

58 William C. De Mille, "Preface," in *Recording Sound for Motion Pictures*, ed. Lester Cowan (New York: McGraw-Hill, 1931), v.

59 Lea Jacobs, "The Innovation of Re-recording in the Hollywood Studios," *Film History* 24, no. 1 (2012): 6.

60 See Helen Hanson, "Sound Affects: Post-production Sound, Soundscapes, and Sound Design in Hollywood's Studio Era," *Music Sound and the Moving Image* 1, no. 1 (Spring 2007): 27–49.

61 "An Oral History with Murray Spivack," interviewed by Charles Degelman (Beverly Hills: Academy of Motion Picture Arts and Sciences, Oral History Program, 1995), 56.

62 Ibid.

63 "Sound's Interesting," *Cinema Progress* (May-June 1938): n.p.

64 See, for instance, Jacobs, "The Innovation of Re-recording in the Hollywood Studios," 5–34, and Helen Hanson and Steve Neale, "Commanding the Sounds of the Universe: Classical Hollywood Sound in the 1930s and Early 1940s," in *The Classical Hollywood Reader*, ed. Steve Neale (London: Routledge, 2012), 249–261.

65 "'Noise Morgue' Is Latest in Pictures," *Sound Waves* 1, no. 9 (December 20, 1928): 5.

66 Ibid.

67 Ray Hoadley and Roman Freulich, "Sound," in *How They Make a Motion Picture* (New York: Thomas Y. Cromwell, 1939), 68.

68 De Mille, "Preface," v.

69 Hanson and Neale, "Commanding the Sounds," 251.

70 "Talkers Seeking Perfected Voice," *Sound Waves* 1, no. 5 (October 15, 1928): 7.

71 "Silent Cameramen Trained for Sound," *Sound Waves* 2, no. 2 (February 1, 1929): 9.

72 Frederick James Smith, "The Silent Drama Speaks," *Liberty*, 1928, 35.

73 Pierre Norman Sands, *A Historical Study of the Academy of Motion Picture Arts and Sciences, 1927–1947* (New York: Arno, 1973), 135.

74 See David Bordwell, Janet Staiger, and Kristin Thompson, *The Classical Hollywood Cinema: Film Style and Mode of Production to 1960* (New York: Routledge, 1985).

75 William A. Johnston, "Writer's Gold," *New York Herald Tribune*, March 29, 1931, magazine section, 6.

76 "Claim Ace Scenarists," *Variety*, October 8, 1934, 4.

77 Johnston, "Writer's Gold," 6.

78 Writers Guild of America West, *Guide to the Guild*, http://www.wga.org/searchresults.aspx-?q=frances%20marion, accessed August 20, 2014.

79 Frances Marion, "Scenario Writing," in Watts, *Behind the Screen*, 38.

80 Reginald Owen, "Substantial," in *Hollywood's Who's Who* 1 (1941): n.p.

81 Bette Davis, "The Actress Plays Her Part," in *We Make the Movies*, ed. Nancy Naumberg (New York: Norton, 1937), 123.

82 Martin Shingler, "Breathtaking: Bette Davis's Performance at the End of *Now, Voyager*," *Journal of Film and Video* 58, no. 1–2 (Spring/Summer 2006): 52.

83 Josef Berne, "In the Realm of Sound—Reviews and Previews," *Sound Waves* 2, no. 7 (April 15, 1929): 10.

84 Ibid.

85 Hammell, quoted in Fred Karlin, *Listening to Movies: The Film Lover's Guide to Film Music* (New York: Schirmer, 1994), 58.

86 See Nathan Platte, "Before *Kong* Was King: Competing Methods in Hollywood Under-score," *Journal of the Society for American Music* 8, no. 3 (2014): 311–337, and Michael Slowik, "Diegetic Withdrawal and Other Worlds: Film Music Strategies before *King Kong*, 1927–1933," *Cinema Journal* 53, no. 1 (Fall 2013): 1–25.

87 To the best of my knowledge, this term was first used by Roy M. Prendergast in *Film Music: A Neglected Art* (New York: Norton, 1992), 29.

88 The film's two uncredited composers, Gerard Carbonara and Stephan Pasternacki, went unacknowledged at Oscar time; another composer, Louis Gruenberg, who had screen credit, was not awarded an Oscar because the nominating letter from producer Walter Wanger did not include Gruenberg's name in the list of composers, likely an oversight on Wanger's part.

89 "An Oral History with Hans J. Salter," 62.

90 Dimitri Tiomkin, quoted in Dave Epstein, Studio Publicity, "Biography," 5.

91 Stravinsky would, however, famously contribute his *The Rite of Spring* to Disney's *Fantasia*. But that piece was not originally created for the film, having been composed over twenty years earlier, and it constituted only a portion of the film's score.

92 Max Steiner, "The Music Director," in *The Real Tinsel*, ed. Bernard Rosenberg and Harry Silverstein (London: Macmillan, 1970), 392.

93 Salter, "An Oral History," 57.

94 Max Steiner, quoted in "Film Music," *Hollywood Bowl Monthly Magazine*, February 1948, 16.

95 R.V.S., "Magnitude of Music Department of Pictures," *Pacific Coast Musician*, March 6, 1937, 12.

96 Paramount Music Department Notes, "ca. 1946," 1.

97 R.V.S., "Magnitude of Music Department," 12.

98 Notable exceptions includes Erich Wolfgang Korngold, who insisted on retaining copyright, which gave him the right to recycle his film music in his concert work. Dimitri Tiomkin also negotiated for copyright for many of the songs he produced in his film scores, but this was later, in the 1950s. In the 1960s Henry Mancini, who was in a position to do so, demanded the copyright for his music.

99   "Sound Film Fete Planned," *Los Angeles Examiner*, April 17, 1946, I7.

100 Warner Bros. publicity release, April 19, 1946.

3 Postwar Hollywood, 1947 –1967

1   Page Cook, "The Sound Track," *Films in Review*, March 1968, 162.

2   Ibid.

3   Ibid.

4   *The Graduate* includes limited underscore by Dave Grusin, preexisting songs from Simon and Garfunkel's album *Sounds of Silence* (1966), and an original Simon and Garfunkel song, "Mrs. Robinson."

5   From 1939 to 1962, films featuring exceptional sound effects could be nominated in the "Special Effects" category, where they competed alongside visual effects.

6   Barry Langford, *Post-Classical Hollywood: Film Industry, Style, and Ideology Since 1945* (Edinburgh: Edinburgh University Press, 2010), 41.

7   Frederick Sternfeld, "Music and the Feature Films," *Musical Quarterly* 33, no. 4 (October 1947): 522.

8   Louis Applebaum, "The Best Years of Our Lives," *Film Music Notes* 6, no. 5 (April-May 1947): 12.

9   Sternfeld, "Music and the Feature Films," 520.

10 Ibid., 529; Applebaum, "Best Years," 13.

11 Applebaum, "Best Years," 15.

12 Ibid.

13 By 1955, the same journal that published Applebaum's article (*Film Music Notes*) would publish lists of film soundtrack albums, including a 1954 Decca record, "Love Themes from the Motion Pictures," featuring a portion of Friedhofer's *Best Years* score. See Alan Morrison, "Film Music on Record," *Film Music* 14, no. 4 (March-April 1955): 19.

14 Applebaum, "Best Years," 12; Sternfeld, "Music and the Feature Films," 520.

15 Gordon Sawyer, whose Hollywood career spanned from the late 1920s to the late 1970s, worked for Samuel Goldwyn for over forty years. During this time, "the Goldwyn sound department gained an industry-wide reputation for excellence, with other studios frequently employing Goldwyn facilities and Sawyer's expertise" ("Gordon E. Sawyer, 75, Sound Pioneer, Dies in Hollywood," *Variety*, May 21, 1980, 33). In 1981 the Academy named a special award after him; it is given to individuals "whose technological contributions have brought credit to the industry" ("Gordon E. Sawyer Award," Academy of Motion Picture Arts and Sciences, accessed November 25, 2013, http://www.oscars.org/awards/academy-awards/about/awards/sawyer.html).

16 Sternfeld, "Music and the Feature Films," 530.

17 At the end of the film, the sounds of a bomber and Friedhofer's music merge almost seamlessly as Fred explores an abandoned plane in a junkyard. According to an interview with Friedhofer, this later passage includes musical imitations of an engine—heard in the low brass—along with actual engine noise. See Linda Danly, *Hugo Friedhofer: The Best Years of His Life* (Lanham, MD: Scarecrow Press, 1999), 87; Sarah Kozloff, *The Best Years of Our Lives* (London: BFI, 2011), 75–76.

18 Joel W. Finler, *The Hollywood Story* (London: Wallflower Press, 2003), 376–377. For a more nuanced breakdown of attendance numbers and sources, see Peter Lev, *Transforming the Screen, 1950-1959* (New York: Scribner's, 2003), 7–9.

19 Lev, *Transforming the Screen*, 9.

20 Ibid.

21 John Belton, "Glorious Technicolor, Breathtaking CinemaScope, and Stereophonic Sound," in *Hollywood in the Age of Television*, ed. Tino Balio (Boston: Unwin Hyman, 1990), 187.

22 Barbara Berch Jamison, "And Now Super-Colossal Headaches," *New York Times Sunday Magazine*, January 10, 1954, 20.

23 Miklós Rózsa, *Double Life* (New York: Wynwood Press, 1982, 1989), 185–186.

24 Ibid., 196.

25 Paul Monaco, *The Sixties* (New York: Scribner's, 2001), 107.

26 Matthew Malsky, "Stretched from Manhattan's Back Alley to MOMA: A Social History of Magnetic Tape and Recording," in *Music and Technoculture*, ed. René Lysloff and Leslie Gay Jr. (Middletown, CT: Wesleyan University Press, 2003), 234.

27 David L. Morton Jr., *Sound Recording: The Life Story of a Technology* (Baltimore: Johns Hopkins University Press, 2006), 50–54.

28 Malsky, "Stretched," 245.

29 Stephen Handzo, "A Narrative Glossary of Film Sound Technology," in *Film Sound: Theory and Practice*, ed. Elisabeth Weis and John Belton (New York: Columbia University Press, 1985), 391.

30 Monaco, *The Sixties*, 105.

31 Vincent LoBrutto, *Sound-on-Film* (Westport, CT: Praeger, 1994), 13.

32 Ibid., 14.

33 Morton, *Sound Recording*, 124.

34 Handzo, "A Narrative Glossary of Film Sound Technology," 391; LoBrutto, *Sound-on-Film*, 16.

35 Rick Altman, "The Evolution of Sound Technology," in Weis and Belton, *Film Sound: Theory and Practice*, 48.

36 *Film Music* 14, no. 1 (September-October 1954): 21.

37 Mark Katz, *Capturing Sound: How Technology Has Changed Music* (Berkeley: University of California Press, 2004), 45–46.

38 For a detailed history and analysis of this unusual score, see James Wierzbicki, *Louis and Bebe Barron's "Forbidden Planet": A Film Score Guide* (Lanham, MD: Scarecrow Press, 2005).

39 Morton, *Sound Recording*, 144.

40 Katz, *Capturing Sound*, 41.

41 Albin Zak III, *I Don't Sound Like Nobody: Remaking Music in 1950s America* (Ann Arbor: University of Michigan Press, 2010), 47.

42 LoBrutto, *Sound-on-Film*, 17.

43 Bosley Crowther, "The Screen in Review," *New York Times*, April 11, 1953.

44 "New Magnetic Recorder Developed at Warners," *Variety*, August 25, 1948, 23.

45 "I Have Seen Two More Great Completed Cinemascope Features" (advertisement), *Variety*, December 2, 1953.

46 "Act II—A Demonstration of Stereophonic Sound," *This Is Cinerama* (1952; Los Angeles: Flicker Alley, 2012), DVD.

47 Although the screen credits list only Lou Forbes as music director, Max Steiner, Roy Webb, Paul Sawtell, Leo Shuken, and Sidney Cutner composed music for *This Is Cinerama* (see James V. D'Arc and John N. Gillespie, eds., *The Max Steiner Collection* [Provo, UT: Brigham Young University Press, 1996], 88).

48 Bosley Crowther, "CinemaScope Seen at Roxy Preview," *New York Times*, April 25, 1953.

49 For more on these short films, see Nathan Platte, "Performing Prestige: The American Cinema Orchestra, 1910–1958," in *The Oxford Handbook of Film Music Studies*, ed. David Neumeyer (New York: Oxford University Press, 2014), 628–636.

50 Lev, *Transforming the Screen*, 112.

51 Ibid., 119.

52 "Dialog and Sound Effects: Comments of Showmen on Current Trends," *Variety*, May 19, 1954, 20.

53 Jay Beck, "The Evolution of Sound in Cinema," in *The Routledge Companion to Film History*, ed. William Guynn (New York: Routledge, 2011), 72. It is also important to note that although early stereophonic features were recorded in stereo on the set, filmmakers planning to release magnetic stereophonic prints also returned to recording in mono on the set; stereo effects could be rendered later in postproduction, just as they were done with the Perspecta system. See John Belton, *Widescreen Cinema* (Cambridge, MA: Harvard University Press, 1992), 203–204.

54 As *Variety* reported after the system's demonstration: "Observers were unanimous on one point—Perspecta sound, in terms of performance, is equal in every respect to the magnetic multi-track sound adopted by Twentieth Century–Fox for its CinemaScope pictures." Fred Hift, "Perspecta Test Impressive But Film Men Separate into 'Boon' vs. 'Nuisance' Groupings," *Variety*, April 21, 1954, 4 and 16.

55 Belton, *Widescreen Cinema*, 135–136.

56 "MGM's Policy on CinemaScope Pictures and Stereophonic Sound," *Variety*, May 5, 1954, 17.

57 Ibid.

58 Louis Reeves Harrison, "Jackass Music," *Moving Picture World*, January 21, 1911, 125.

59 Beck, "The Evolution of Sound," 71; Belton, *Widescreen Cinema*, 205–206.

60 Bosley Crowther, "Sound and (or) Fury," *New York Times*, January 31, 1954.

61 Ibid.

62 LoBrutto, *Sound-on-Film*, 24.

63 Jeff Smith, *The Sounds of Commerce: Marketing Popular Film Music* (New York: Columbia University Press, 1998), 32–44.

64 Jeff Smith tells of how "United Artists released the Beatles' *A Hard Day's Night* in the summer of 1964 with modest expectation for the film, but very high hopes for the soundtrack album. . . . The album sold some 1.5 million copies within its first two weeks" (ibid., 54–55).

65 Joel Friedman, "What Price Pic Scores?," *Billboard*, May 13, 1957, 31.

66 Altman, "The Evolution of Sound Technology," 48.

67 Henry Mancini was particularly proactive in making sure his albums satisfied listeners as records, not just music from films. See Smith, "That Money-Making 'Moon River' Sound: Thematic Organization and Orchestration in the Film Music of Henry Mancini," in *Music and Cinema*, ed. James Buhler, Caryl Flinn, and David Neumeyer (Hanover, NH: Wesleyan University Press, 2000), 251–252.

68 "Coming Up Strong" and "This Week's Best Buys," *Billboard*, March 24, 1956, 40.

69 Friedman, "What Price Pic Scores?," *Billboard*, May 13, 1957, 31.

70 *Bernstein: Backgrounds for Brando*, Dot DLP 3107, 1958, 33 1/3 RPM, LP.

71 "Elmer Bernstein Warns of Hazards in Trying to Write Pic Tunes as Pop Hits," *Variety*, February 10, 1965, 55.

72 "Pressure of Getting Pop Hit Plagues Film Scorer, Says Elmer Bernstein," *Variety*, February 13, 1967, 43.

73 Ibid.

74 Elmer Bernstein took the rejection of Herrmann's *Torn Curtain* score seriously. He helped restore Herrmann's music by releasing an LP in 1977 of himself conducting excerpts of the score with the Royal Philharmonic Orchestra. For the remake of *Cape Fear* (1991), Bernstein incorporated passages from Herrmann's *Torn Curtain* as homage to the late composer, who had also scored the original *Cape Fear* (1962).

75 Zak, *I Don't Sound Like Nobody*, 10–11.

76 Ibid., 47.

77 For recent discussions of this postwar divergence, see James Wierzbicki, *Film Music: A History* (New York: Routledge, 2009), 165ff.; Mervyn Cooke, *A History of Film Music* (Cambridge: Cambridge University Press, 2009), 183ff.

78 Variations on this point have been made elsewhere, although directed at more specific eras and trends. In particular, Ethan Mordden has argued that composers became increasingly focused on developing unique sounds for individual films in the 1960s. Jeff Smith has argued that this preoccupation characterized pop scores of the late 1950s and 1960s. See Mordden, *Medium Cool: The Movies of the 1960s* (New York: Alfred A. Knopf, 1990); Smith, *The Sounds of Commerce*, 9–10.

79 Charles Drazin, *In Search of The Third Man* (New York: Proscenium Publishers, 2000), 95.

80 Charles Emge, "Coast in Big Dither over Popularity of the Zither," *Down Beat*, March 24, 1950, 9.

81 Lawrence Morton, "Film Music of the Quarter," *Hollywood Quarterly* 5, no. 1 (Autumn 1950), 49.

82 Emge, "Coast in Big Dither," 9.

83 Hy Hollinger, "Pictures: Film Music Not So Over-Written Now, Says Green," *Variety*, March 9, 1955, 4, 16.

84 "Wider Horizons Loom for Picture Scorers, Andre Previn Contends," *Variety*, March 21, 1962, 51.

85 Charles Emge, "Movies' 'Musician DPs' Shifting to TV Studios," *Down Beat*, November 18, 1953, 5.

86 "RKO First Major Studio to Drop Staff Orchestra," *Down Beat*, April 21, 1954, 1.

87 Wierzbicki, *Film Music: A History*, 158.

88 Mark Harris, *Pictures at a Revolution: Five Movies and the Birth of the New Hollywood* (New York: Penguin Press, 2008), 1.

89 Mike Matessino, liner notes to *The Sand Pebbles: Complete Original Motion Picture Soundtrack*, Intrada MAF 7116, 2011, 2 CDs. One hundred and thirteen musicians are listed as contributing to the recording.

90 "*The Sand Pebbles* Roadshow Souvenir Program," reproduced in *The Sand Pebbles* (1966; Beverly Hills, CA: Twentieth Century–Fox Home Entertainment, 2007), 2 DVDs.

91 Monaco, *The Sixties*, 114.

92 Leonard Feather, "'Cold Blood' Music Hot Property," *Los Angeles Times*, March 24, 1968.

93 Chuck Crisafulli, "Q'd Up: Jones on His Most Memorable Musical Moments," *Billboard*, March 22, 2008, 34.

94 Cook, "The Sound Track," 163.

95 Quincy Jones, quoted by Norman Jewison in the original LP liner notes for *In the Heat of the Night*, reproduced in *Quincy Jones, In the Heat of the Night/They Call Me Mr. Tibbs: Original MGM Motion Picture Soundtrack*, Ryko RCD 10712, 1997, CD.

96 As Julie Hubbert has noted, compilation scores also drew from classical repertoires, as in the case of Stanley Kubrick's *2001: A Space Odyssey* (1968) and *A Clockwork Orange* (1971).

See Julie Hubbert, "The Compilation Soundtrack from the 1960s to the Present," in *The Oxford Handbook of Film Music Studies*, ed. David Neumeyer (New York: Oxford University Press, 2014), 295.

97 Leonard Feather, "Jazz Scene: Quincy in Hollywood," *Melody Maker*, March 30, 1968, 8.

98 Jeff Smith, "'The Tunes They Are A-changing': Moments of Historical Rupture and Reconfiguration in the Production and Commerce of Music in Film," in *The Oxford Handbook of Film Music Studies*, ed. David Neumeyer (New York: Oxford University Press, 2014), 280.

99 Hubbert, "The Compilation Soundtrack," 295–297.

4 The Auteur Renaissance, 1968–1980

1 See Peter Biskind, *Easy Riders and Raging Bulls: How the Sex-Drugs-and Rock 'n' Roll Generation Saved Hollywood* (New York: Simon and Schuster, 1998), 18–19.

2 Mark Harris, *Pictures at a Revolution: Five Movies and the Birth of the New Hollywood* (New York: Penguin Press, 2008).

3 Jay Beck, "A Quiet Revolution: Changes in American Film Sound Practices, 1967–1979" (Ph.D. diss., University of Iowa, 2003), 338–340.

4 Harris, *Pictures at a Revolution*, 289–290.

5 F. J. Kolb Jr., "Sound Committee," *Journal of the SMPTE* 78, no. 7 (July 1969): 566–567.

6 See John Belton, "1950s Magnetic Sound: The Frozen Revolution," in *Sound Theory/Sound Practice*, ed. Rick Altman (New York: Routledge, 1992), 154–167.

7 Loren L. Ryder, "Magnetic Sound Recording in the Motion Picture and Television Industries," *SMPTE Journal* 85, no. 7 (July 1976): 530.

8 Vincent LoBrutto, *Sound-on-Film: Interviews with Creators of Film Sound* (Westport, CT: Praeger, 1994), 126–127.

9 Ryder, "Magnetic Sound Recording," 530.

10 "About New Tools & Old Jobholders," *Variety*, May 10, 1967, 11. For a more complete account of the implications of these changes on existing labor structures, see Jay Beck's "A Quiet Revolution," 229–285.

11 The *Journal of the SMPTE* changed its name to *SMPTE Journal* at the end of 1975.

12 Ryder, "Magnetic Sound Recording," 530.

13 "Synchro, Edit-Rite, Producers Sound Merge, Year End," *Variety*, November 25, 1970, 3, 23.

14 Don Carle Gillette, "Atom Bombs on Celluloid," *Variety*, January 7, 1948, 54.

15 See Charles Schreger, "Sounding Off for the Movies," *Los Angeles Times*, April 29, 1980, G1.

16 LoBrutto, *Sound-on-Film*, 85. For a more complete analysis of Murch's sound design for *THX 1138*, see William Whittington, *Sound Design and Science Fiction* (Austin: University of Texas Press, 2007), 68–90.

17 John G. Frayne, Arthur C. Blaney, George R. Groves, and Harry F. Olson, "A Short History of Motion-Picture Sound Recording in the United States," *SMPTE Journal* 85, no. 7 (July 1976): 523–524.

18 Robert Orban and John Delantoni, "An Improved System for Theatrical Reproduction of 35mm Optical Sound," *Journal of the SMPTE* 81, no. 12 (December 1972): 927.

19 Beck, "Quiet Revolution," 31.

20 Ibid., 32.

21 Ioan Allen, "The Production of Wide-Range, Low-Noise Optical Soundtracks Utilizing the Dolby Noise Reduction System," *Journal of the SMPTE* 84, no. 9 (September 1975): 720.

22 Beck, "Quiet Revolution," 33–36.

23 Allen, "Wide-Range, Low-Noise Optical Soundtracks," 721.

24 Beck, "Quiet Revolution," 38.

25 Allen, "Wide-Range, Low-Noise Optical Soundtracks," 721.

26 Ibid.

27 Ibid., 728; Beck, "Quiet Revolution," 39.

28 William D. Hedden, "Progress Committee Report for 1975," *Journal of the SMPTE* 85, no. 5 (May 1976): 275.

29 Charles Schreger, "The Second Coming of Sound," *Film Comment* 14, no. 5 (September/ October 1978): 35–36.

30 For more on the cocktail party effect, see Jessica Hamzelou, "'Cocktail Party Effect' Identified in the Brain," *New Scientist,* April 18, 2012, http://www.newscientist.com/article/ mg21428613.800-cocktail-party-effect-identified-in-the-brain.html#.UgAoc5WyT0s.

31 See Mark Minett, "Expanding the Standard Story: Rethinking 'Early Altman' and the Elaboration of Classical Hollywood Storytelling" (Ph.D. diss., University of Wisconsin-Madison, 2014), 238–312.

32 LoBrutto, *Sound-on-Film,* 70.

33 Ibid., 44–45.

34 For more on *Planet of the Apes,* see Randall D. Larson, *Musique Fantastique: A Survey of Film Music in the Fantastic Cinema* (Metuchen, NJ: Scarecrow Press, 1985), 253–255; and Jeff Bond, liner notes for *Planet of the Apes Original Soundtrack,* Varese Sarabande Compact Disc, VSD-5848.

35 See Royal S. Brown, *Overtones and Undertones: Reading Film Music* (Berkeley: University of California Press, 1994), 178–180.

36 Julie Hubbert, "'Whatever Happened to Great Movie Music?': Cinéma Vérité and Hollywood Film Music of the Early 1970s," *American Music* 21, no. 2 (2003): 180–213.

37 Christopher Sieving, "Super Sonics: Song Scores as Counter-Narration in *Super Fly*," *Journal of Popular Music Studies* 13, no. 1 (March 2001): 77–91.

38 Susan Peterson, "Selling a Hit Soundtrack," *Billboard,* October 6, 1979, ST-2.

39 For a more detailed overview of John Williams's career, see Emilio Audissino, *John Williams' Film Music:* Jaws, Star Wars, Raiders of the Lost Ark*, and the Return of the Classical Hollywood Score* (Madison: University of Wisconsin Press, 2014).

40 For more on *Star Wars'* temp track, see Michael Matessino, liner notes for John Williams, *Star Wars: A New Hope, Original Motion Picture Soundtrack,* BMG Compact Disc 09026–68772-2.

41 James Buhler, "Star Wars, Music, and Myth," in *Music and Cinema,* ed. James Buhler, Caryl Flinn, and David Neumeyer (Hanover, NH: Wesleyan University Press, 2000), 33–57.

42 Grover Hensley, quoted in Fred Karlin's *Listening to Movies: The Film Lover's Guide to Film Music* (New York: Schirmer Books, 1994), 244.

43 Beck, "Quiet Revolution," 303.

44 Michael Ondaatje, *The Conversations: Walter Murch and the Art of Editing Film* (New York: Borzoi Books, 2002), 53.

45 For a thorough overview of these sound designers' unique styles, see Beck, "Quiet Revolution," 291–308.

46 Ibid., 303.

47 LoBrutto, *Sound-on-Film,* 85. For a more complete discussion of Murch's pioneering sound effects work, see William Whittington, *Sound Design and Science Fiction* (Austin: University of Texas Press, 2007), 55–90.

48 See LoBrutto, *Sound-on-Film*, 87–88; Ondaatje, *The Conversations*, 119.

49 For a comparison of Murch's and Burtt's sound styles, see Stephen Keane, "Walter Murch and Ben Burtt: The Sound Designer as Composer," in *Sound and Music in Film and Visual Media*, ed. Graeme Harper, Ruth Doughty, and Jochen Eisentraut (New York: Continuum, 2009), 452–462.

50 For more on *Star Wars'* sound effects, see Keely Parrack, "Let's Go Listen to a Movie," *Christian Science Monitor*, May 17, 2005, 18; Lynde McCormick, "Do You Know What Wookies Sound Like?," *Christian Science Monitor*, June 17, 1980; B6–B7; Aljean Harmetz, "Space Sounds for 'Empire' Had Terrestrial Genius," *New York Times*, June 9, 1980, C12; and Bill DeLapp, "Star Tech," *Syracuse New Times*, March 8, 2000, 7.

51 Judith Shulevitz, "When Sound Is a Character," *New York Times*, August 18, 1991, H11.

52 Steve Harvey, "*Star Wars* Sounds: Deep Roots, Lasting Impact," *Pro Sound News* 29, no. 8 (August 2007): 39.

53 Ric Gentry, "Alan Splet and Sound Effects for *Dune*," *American Cinematographer* 65, no. 12 (December 1984): 62.

54 "Ann Kroeber Special: Exclusive Interview," *Designing Sound*, October 25, 2011, http://designingsound.org/2011/10/ann-kroeber-special-exclusive-interview/.

55 Gentry, "Alan Splet," 72.

56 "Ann Kroeber Special."

57 Ibid.

58 For more on Lynch's debt to the art world, see Martha Nochimson, *The Passion of David Lynch: Wild at Heart in Hollywood* (Austin: University of Texas Press, 1997), 21–32.

59 It is worth remembering that the original *Star Wars* was produced for the tidy sum of $11 million. Compare that to the $24 million budget of *King Kong* (1976) or the $35 million budget of *Star Trek: The Motion Picture* (1979).

5 The New Hollywood, 1981–1999

1 Walter Murch, "Clear Density—Dense Clarity," presented at the "Walter Murch and the Art of Sound Design" conference, Iowa City, IA, April 1, 1999.

2 Jordan Fox, "Walter Murch: Making Beaches Out of Grains of Sand," *Cinefex* no. 3 (1980): 52.

3 Mark Cousins, "Walter Murch: Designing Sound for *Apocalypse Now*," in *Projections* 6, ed. John Boorman and Walter Donohue (New York: Faber and Faber, 1996), 159–160.

4 Michael Rivlin, "Motion Picture Sound Re-recording and Mixing: Dawn of a Digital Decade," *Millimeter* 8, no. 5 (May 1980): 115.

5 Walter Murch, "Foreword," in Michel Chion, *Audio-Vision: Sound on-Screen* (New York: Columbia University Press, 1994), xxii.

6 Frank Serafine, "The New Motion Picture Sound," *American Cinematographer* 61, no. 8 (August 1980): 767.

7 "Serafine Designs for *Tron*," *Back Stage* 23, no. 18 (April 30, 1982): 23.

8 Frank Serafine, "Sound Effects Design and Synthesis for *TRON*," *American Cinematographer* 63, no. 8 (August 1982): 830.

9 Randy Thom, "Sounding Off in a Visual Medium," in *Sound For Picture: An Inside Look at Audio Production For Film and Television*, ed. Jeff Forlenza and Terri Stone (Emeryville, CA: Mix Books/Hal Leonard Publishing, 1993), 8.

10 Mark Mangini, "Making Sound Career Choices," *Variety* (April 22, 1998), A4.

11 Vincent LoBrutto, *Sound-on-Film: Interviews with Creators of Film Sound* (Westport, CT: Praeger, 1994), 141.

12 Steve Barnett, "Film Sound Editing Techniques [Part Two]," *Recording Engineer/Producer* 13, no. 1 (February 1982): 65–66.

13 Larry Blake, *Film Sound Today: An Anthology of Articles from Recording Engineer/Producer* (Hollywood: Reveille Press, 1984), 35.

14 Aljean Harmetz, "Space Sounds for *Empire Had Terrestrial Genesis*," *New York Times*, June 9, 1980, C12.

15 Barnett, "Film Sound Editing Techniques," 67.

16 LoBrutto, *Sound-on-Film*, 148.

17 Ibid., 63.

18 Steve Gowin, "Sound by Splet: *Mosquito Coast*'s Bugs, Birds, and Burps," *Theatre Crafts* 21, no. 2 (February 1987): 71.

19 LoBrutto, *Sound-on-Film*, 190.

20 Gowin, "Sound by Splet," 71.

21 Ric Gentry, "Alan Splet and Sound Effects for *Dune*," *American Cinematographer* 65, no. 12 (December 1984): 63.

22 Ann Kroeber, Skype interview with Vanessa Theme Ament, July 24, 2013.

23 Lisa Vincenzi, "The Sound of *Blue Velvet*," *Millimeter*, issue 14 (November 1986): 122.

24 Gentry, "Alan Splet and Sound Effects for *Dune*," 64, emphasis in original.

25 Ibid.

26 Ibid., 66.

27 Tom Kenny, *Sound for Picture: The Art of Sound Design in Film and Television*, 2nd ed. (Vallejo, CA: Mix Books, 2000), 138.

28 Frank Spotnitz, "Stick It in Your Ear," *American Film* 15, no. 1 (October 1989): 45.

29 Gentry, "Alan Splet and Sound Effects for *Dune*," 66.

30 Spotnitz, "Stick It in Your Ear," 45.

31 Gowin, "Sound by Splet," 71.

32 *Indiana Jones and the Temple of Doom* (Steven Spielberg, 1984), *Always* (Spielberg, 1989); *Forrest Gump* (Robert Zemeckis, 1994), *Contact* (Zemeckis, 1997), *Cast Away* (Zemeckis, 2000); *Sex, Lies, and Videotape* (Steven Soderbergh, 1989), *Out of Sight* (Soderbergh, 1998), *Erin Brockovich* (Soderbergh, 2000).

33 Larry Blake, "A Sound Designer by Any Other Name . . . ," *Mix* 25, no. 10 (October 2001): 226.

34 Thom, "Sounding Off," 10.

35 Terry Atkinson, "Scoring with Synthesizers," in *Celluloid Symphonies: Texts and Contexts in Film Music History*, ed. Julie Hubbert (Berkeley: University of California Press, 2011), 424.

36 Ibid., 425.

37 Ibid., 427.

38 Colin Larkin, ed., *The Virgin Encyclopedia of Eighties Music* (London: Virgin/Muze UK, 1997), 492.

39 Tim Greiving, "How Does Hans Zimmer Keep His Film Scores Fresh? He Invents New Instruments," *LA Weekly*, June 20, 2013, http://www.laweekly.com/2013–06–20/film-tv/hans-zimmer-lone-ranger/.

40 Randall D. Larson, "Danny Elfman: From Boingo to Batman," in Hubbert, *Celluloid Symphonies*, 445.

41 Ibid., 444.

42 Julie Hubbert, "The Postmodern Soundtrack: Film Music in the Video and Digital Age (1978-Present)," in Hubbert, *Celluloid Symphonies*, 396.

43 Stephen Holden, "How Rock Is Changing Hollywood's Tune," in Hubbert, *Celluloid Symphonies*, 437.

44 Peter Occiogrosso, "Reelin' and Rockin'," *American Film* 9, no. 6 (April 1, 1984): 47.

45 Jeff Rona, "Making Soundtracks, Part 1," in *The Routledge Film Music Sourcebook*, ed. James Wierzbicki, Nathan Platte, and Colin Roust (New York: Routledge, 2012), 260.

46 Paul Grein, "The Soundtrack Explosion: Big Hits from the Big Screen," *Billboard* 96, no. 51 (December 22, 1984): TA40.

47 Jeff Smith, *The Sounds of Commerce: Marketing Popular Music* (New York: Columbia University Press, 1998), 199.

48 Grein, "The Soundtrack Explosion," TA6.

49 Smith, *The Sounds of Commerce*, 201.

50 Marianne Meyer, "Rock Movideo," in Hubbert, *Celluloid Symphonies*, 431.

51 Grein, "The Soundtrack Explosion," TA6.

52 Ibid.

53 Occiogrosso, "Reelin' and Rockin'," 49.

54 *St. Elmo's Fire* (Joel Schumacher, 1985), *Back to the Future* (Robert Zemeckis, 1985), and *Mad Max Beyond Thunderdome* (George Miller and George Ogilvie, 1985), respectively.

55 Kip Kirby, "Hollywood Finally Flashes That Proud Soundtrack Smile," *Billboard* 97, no. 47 (November 23, 1985): VM6.

56 David T. Friendly, "Seeking the Groove in Movie Sound Tracks," *Los Angeles Times*, October 2, 1986, sec. 6, 1.

57 Mel Lambert, "Digital Audio for Film: The Cinema Digital Sound Process From Kodak/ORC," *Mix* 14, no. 9 (September 1990): 18.

58 Blake, *Film Sound Today*, 3–4.

59 Ibid., 7.

60 Ibid., 9.

61 David Stone, "Cinema Digital Sound: New Multi-Track Format to Debut," *Moviesound Newsletter* 1, no. 12 (May 1990): 1.

62 Blake, *Film Sound Today*, 45, emphasis in original.

63 Mel Lambert, "Digital Audio for Film," 23.

64 Gentry, "Alan Splet and Sound Effects for *Dune*," 68, 70.

65 See Ioan Allen, Joseph Hull, and Robert Peterson, "Stereo Sound in the Theater," prepared for TEA Convention, Scottsdale, AZ, May 1981, and Stephen St. Croix, "Mongrel Dogs at the Movies," *Mix* 14, no. 9 (September 1990): 14–16.

66 See Jay Beck, "Citing the Sound: *The Conversation, Blow Out*, and the Mythological Ontology of the Soundtrack in '70s Film," *Journal of Popular Film and Television* 29, no. 4 (Winter 2002): 156–163.

67 Larry Blake, "Mixing Techniques for Dolby Stereo Film and Video Releases," *Recording Engineer/Producer* 16, no. 3 (June 1985): 94.

68 See John Belton, "1950s Magnetic Sound: The Frozen Revolution," in *Sound Theory/Sound Practice*, ed. Rick Altman (New York: Routledge/AFI, 1993), 154–170.

69 *Dolby Surround Mixing Manual*, issue 2 (San Francisco: Dolby Laboratories, Inc., 2005), 5.5–5.6.

70 Ibid., 5.4.

71 Blake, *Film Sound Today*, 45, emphasis in original.

72 David Stone, "Indy Splits," *Moviesound Newsletter* 1, no. 5 (July 1989): 1.

73 "Walla" refers to the non-semantic background sounds of speech, usually provided by specialized "walla groups" in postproduction.

74 Stone, "Indy Splits," 1.

75 See David Stone, "*The Hunt for Red October*," *Moviesound Newsletter* 1, no. 12 (May 1990): 2–3, and Jay Beck, "The Sounds of 'Silence:' Dolby Stereo, Sound Design, and *The Silence of the Lambs*," in *Lowering the Boom*, ed. Jay Beck and Tony Grajeda (Urbana: University of Illinois Press, 2008), 68–83.

76 Steven B. Cohen, "A New Audio Age: Digital Offers Artistic Choices and Presentational Challenges," *Film Journal International* (October 1, 1996): 82.

77 Michel Chion, *Audio-Vision*, ed. and trans. Claudia Gorbman (New York: Columbia University Press, 1994), 150.

78 Mark Kerins, *Beyond Dolby (Stereo): Cinema in the Digital Sound Age* (Bloomington: Indiana University Press, 2011), 92.

79 Michael Rivlin, "Motion Picture Sound Re-recording and Mixing," 106.

80 Lou CasaBianca and Joe Van Witsen, "*Time Code*—A Brief Review," *Mix* 8, no. 4 (April 1984): 46.

81 Ken Pohlmann, "A Primer on Time Code and Synchronization," *Mix* 8, no. 4 (April 1984): 44, 46.

82 Peter Bergren, "Sound Effects: New Tools and Techniques—Part One," *Mix* 10, no. 4 (April 1986): 92–93.

83 Nicholas Pasquariello, "Trends in Film Sound—Part One," *Mix* 11, no. 11 (November 1987): 72.

84 David Gans, "David Byrne's *True Stories* at Russian Hill Recording," *Mix* 10, no. 9 (September 1986): 44.

85 Larry Blake, "Digital Sound for Motion Pictures: Including Production Recording and Random-Access Editing," *Recording Engineer/Producer* 16, no. 5 (October 1985): 128–129.

86 Kenny, *Sound for Picture*, 137.

87 Ibid., 140.

88 Randy Thom, "Designing a Movie for Sound," *iris* no. 27 (Spring 1999): 10.

89 Gans, "David Byrne's *True Stories*," 44, emphasis in original.

90 Jeff Smith, "The Sound of Intensified Continuity," in *The Oxford Handbook of New Audio-visual Aesthetics*, ed. John Richardson, Claudia Gorbman, and Carol Vernallis (New York: Oxford University Press, 2013), 343.

91 Vanessa Theme Ament, *The Foley Grail: The Art of Performing Sound for Film, Games, and Animation* (Burlington, MA: Focal Press, 2009), 10–14; Jerry Trent, interview with Vanessa Theme Ament, Burbank, CA, August 27, 2007; Ken Dufva and David Lee Fein, interview with Vanessa Theme Ament, Los Angeles, August 2, 2006.

92 The practice of a hierarchy between feature and television was quite prevalent in all facets of postproduction in the 1980s and 1990s. Most Foley artists specialized in one or the other. However, some crossed over with ease.

93 Tim Sadler, a music engineer who became the Foley mixer at TAJ Soundworks in the 1980s, is credited with introducing the twenty-four-track format to Foley recording, according to John Roesch.

94 The special role of the music librarian is often misunderstood. Rather than just being responsible for coordinating and categorizing, the more gifted of these professionals were

able to find the perfect recordings for sound editors and present special "finds" that contributed greatly to the soundtracks themselves.

95 Gordon Ecker Jr., telephone interview with Vanessa Theme Ament, October 11, 2013.

96 Ibid.

97 Tom Kenny, "Walter Murch: The Search for Order in Sound & Picture," *Mix* 22, no. 4 (April 1998): 22, 24.

6 The Modern Entertainment Marketplace, 2000–Present

1 For an excellent overview of changes to the business side of film sound, see Benjamin Wright, "Sound from Start to Finish: Professional Style and Practice in Modern Hollywood Sound Production" (Ph.D. diss., Carleton University, 2011), 65–118.

2 Ibid., 168–169.

3 Ibid., 136–137.

4 For a discussion on why Pro Tools succeeded, see ibid., 138–146.

5 Quoted in ibid., 339.

6 Glenn Morgan, personal interview by the author, July 31, 2006.

7 Anonymous rerecording mixer, personal interview by the author, summer 2006.

8 Morgan, personal interview.

9 The addition of sound designers somewhat complicated this dichotomy, but today they are generally placed within the category of sound editors.

10 Wright, "Sound from Start to Finish," 334.

11 Ibid., 331.

12 Morgan, personal interview.

13 Erik Aadahl, personal interview by the author, August 9, 2006.

14 Richard King, personal interview by the author, July 28, 2006.

15 Marti Humphrey, personal interview by the author, August 5, 2006.

16 Aadahl, personal interview, 2006.

17 Mike Knobloch, personal interview by the author, July 20, 2004.

18 Humphrey, personal interview.

19 Morgan, personal interview.

20 King, personal interview.

21 Midge Costin, personal interview by the author, July 1, 2006.

22 Quoted in Wright, "Sound from Start to Finish," 336.

23 King, personal interview.

24 Quoted in Wright, "Sound from Start to Finish," 339.

25 Humphrey, personal interview.

26 Wright, "Sound from Start to Finish," 149.

27 Erik Aadahl, personal interview by the author, July 20, 2004, and Aadahl, personal interview, 2006.

28 Quoted in Vincent LoBrutto, *Sound-on-Film: Interviews with Creators of Film Sound* (Westport, CT: Praeger, 1994), 148.

29 Quoted in Wright, "Sound from Start to Finish," 345.

30 Ibid., 125.

31 Ibid., 147–148, emphasis added.

32 Ibid., 121.

33 Quoted in Wright, "Sound from Start to Finish," 335.

34 Paul Massey, personal interview by the author, August 8, 2006.

35 Ibid.

36 Humphrey, personal interview, and King, personal interview.

37 Robert Jay Ellis-Geiger, "Trends in Contemporary Hollywood Film Scoring: A Synthesized Approach for Hong Kong Cinema" (Ph.D. diss., University of Leeds, 2007), 49.

38 Ibid., 45–47.

39 Ibid., 30.

40 James Buhler, David Neumeyer, and Rob Deemer, *Hearing the Movies: Music and Sound in Film History* (New York: Oxford University Press, 2010), 407, 401.

41 Martin Sweidel, "Re: changes in composition for film," e-mail message to the author, December 21, 2013.

42 Buhler, Neumeyer, and Deemer, *Hearing the Movies*, 407.

43 Quoted in Ellis-Geiger, "Trends in Contemporary Hollywood Film Scoring," 51.

44 Sweidel, "Re: changes in composition."

45 Ellis-Geiger, "Trends in Contemporary Hollywood Film Scoring," 37.

46 Knobloch, personal interview.

47 Ellis-Geiger, "Trends in Contemporary Hollywood Film Scoring." 40.

48 Buhler, Neumeyer, and Deemer, *Hearing the Movies*, 402.

49 Wright, "Sound from Start to Finish," 15.

50 Sweidel, "Re: changes in composition."

51 Ellis-Geiger, "Trends in Contemporary Hollywood Film Scoring," 30.

52 Buhler, Neumeyer, and Deemer, *Hearing the Movies*, 405.

53 Ellis-Geiger, "Trends in Contemporary Hollywood Film Scoring," 36.

54 Paul Eng, "The Digital Death of Film?," May 9, 2002, *ABC News*, accessed February 2, 2014, http://abcnews.go.com/Technology/story?id=98007, and Brandon Gray, "'Attack of the Clones' to Invade 3,161 Theaters," May 14, 2002, *Box Office Mojo*, accessed February 2, 2014, http://boxofficemojo.com/news/?id=1166.

55 Dawn C. Chmielewski, "Major Studios Agree to Back Switch to Digital Projection," *Los Angeles Times*, October 2, 2008, accessed February 2, 2014, http://articles.latimes.com/2008/oct/02/business/fi-studios2.

56 "Theatrical Market Statistics 2012," Motion Picture Association of America (MPAA), accessed October 14, 2013, http://www.mpaa.org/resources/3037b7a4–58a2–4109–8012–58fca3abdf1b.pdf, 6 and 22.

57 Richard Verrier, "Paramount Stops Releasing Major Movies on Film," *Los Angeles Times*, January 18, 2014, accessed January 30, 2014, http://www.latimes.com/entertainment/envelope/cotown/la-et-ct-paramount-end-to-film-20140118,0,806855.story#axzz2rwFaxwwv.

58 Mark Kerins, *Beyond Dolby (Stereo): Cinema in the Digital Sound Age* (Bloomington: Indiana University Press, 2010), 24–31.

59 See Jay Beck, "A Quiet Revolution: Changes in American Film Sound Practices, 1967–1979" (Ph.D. diss., University of Iowa, 2003), 91–108.

60 For more on the introduction and adoption of digital surround sound, see Kerins, *Beyond Dolby*, 35–44.

61 SDDS originally used a 7.1 system, but by 2007 all SDDS releases were being mixed in 5.1. DTS and Dolby Digital, meanwhile, found room in their codecs to expand to 6.1 but no further. See Kerins, *Beyond Dolby*, 50–51.

62 Thom Ehle, personal interview by the author, July 21, 2004.

63 For details, see Kerins, *Beyond Dolby*, 41–42.

64 "AMC Enhanced Theatre Experience ETX," March 4, 2010, accessed February 2, 2014, http://www.disneydreaming.com/2010/03/04/amc-enhanced-theatre-experience-etx/.

65 Dolby Digital, DTS/Datasat, SDDS, Dolby Digital Surround EX, DTS-ES/Datasat, Dolby Surround 7.1, Dolby Atmos, Auro 11.1

66 "The Sound of Transformers 3," accessed November 26, 2013, http://www.youtube.com/watch?v=UqIzKZHxSRo.

67 "In 'Gravity,' music—and Dolby Atmos—recreate the disorientation of space," Dolby Laboratories, accessed November 26, 2013, http://blog.dolby.com/2013/10/gravity-music-dolby-atmos-recreate-disorientation-space/.

68 See, for instance, Kerins, *Beyond Dolby*, 39, 67, and 163, for sound designers and other industry professionals explaining how various new sound systems allowed them to do things not possible with older systems.

69 Midge Costin, personal interview by the author, July 21, 2004.

70 The six formats were IMAX, Dolby Atmos, 7.1, 5.1, LtRt (Dolby Stereo), and a DVD mix. Lauren Hadaway, "Re: different mixes?," e-mail message to the author, October 16, 2013.

71 Anonymous sound editor, personal interview by the author, summer 2004.

72 Kerins, *Beyond Dolby*, 52.

73 Atmos is not the only sound system to include object-based mixing (video games have long relied on sound objects in creating multichannel soundtracks), but has been far and away the most successful and widely installed cinematic implementation of this idea.

74 Technical information on Atmos: "Dolby Atmos Next-Generation Audio for Cinema," Dolby Laboratories, accessed November 27, 2013, http://www.dolby.com/uploadedFiles/Assets/US/Doc/Professional/Dolby-Atmos-Next-Generation-Audio-for-Cinema.pdf. For a less technical explanation of Atmos, see Gianluca Sergi, "Knocking at the Door of Cinematic Artifice: Dolby *Atmos, Challenges and Opportunities*," *New Soundtrack* 3, no. 2 (September 2013): 107–121.

75 Sergi, "Knocking at the Door," 111.

76 "Dolby Atmos for Distributors," Dolby Laboratories, accessed November 26, 2013, http://www.dolby.com/us/en/professional/technology/cinema/dolby-atmos-distributors.html; emphasis added.

77 "Dolby Atmos for Content Creators," Dolby Laboratories, accessed November 27, 2013, http://www.dolby.com/us/en/professional/technology/cinema/dolby-atmos-creators.html.

78 Benjamin Wright, "Re: use of dissertation," personal e-mail message to the author, January 26, 2014; emphasis added.

79 Matt Cuson, Senior Marketing Director of Cinema for Dolby Laboratories, quoted in Sergi, "Knocking at the Door," 108.

80 Sergi, "Knocking at the Door," 115.

81 See, for instance, Jeff Smith, "The Sound of Intensified Continuity," in *The Oxford Handbook of New Audiovisual Aesthetics*, ed. John Richardson, Claudia Gorbman, and Carol Vernallis (New York: Oxford University Press, 2013), 338–347, and Kerins, *Beyond Dolby*, 53–83.

82 Smith, "Sound of Intensified Continuity," 338. See also David Bordwell, "Intensified Continuity: Visual Style in Contemporary American Film," *Film Quarterly* 55, no. 3 (2002): 16–28.

83   Smith, "Sound of Intensified Continuity," 343.

84   Ibid.

85   Kerins, *Beyond Dolby*, 121–122.

86   Anonymous sound editor, personal interview, summer 2006.

87   Quoted in Sergi, "Knocking at the Door," 116.

88   Ibid., 118.

89   Jeffrey Katzenberg, "3-D and Monsters vs. Aliens," lecture, Cinemark Theaters, Dallas, TX, December 10, 2008.

90   Mark Kerins, "Understanding the Impact of Surround Sound in Multimedia," in *The Psychology of Music in Multimedia*, ed. Siu-Lan Tan, Annabel J. Cohen, Scott D. Lipscomb, and Roger A. Kendall (Oxford: Oxford University Press, 2013), 375.

91   See, for instance, S. Mark Young, James C. Gong, and Wim A. Van der Stede, who argue that "more than four-fifths of a film's revenue typically comes from home video, pay TV, and other downstream sources." "The Business of Making Money with Movies," *Strategic Finance*, February 2010, 35.

92   David Bondelevitch, personal interview by the author, July 28, 2006.

93   "Digital America 2012," Consumer Electronics Association (CEA), accessed September 19, 2013, http://content.ce.org/PDF/DigitalAmerica2012_abridged.pdf, 69.

94   "Digital America 2013," Consumer Electronics Association (CEA), accessed September 19, 2013, http://content.ce.org/PDF/2013DigitalAmerica_abridged.pdf, 17.

95   Christopher Reeves, personal interview by the author, July 31, 2006. See also Kerins, *Beyond Dolby*, 161–163.

96   King, personal interview.

97   "Theatrical Market Statistics 2012," 10–11.

98   Anonymous game sound designer, personal interview, July 7, 2010.

GLOSSARY

5.1: pronounced "five-point-one" or "five-one," the standard base channel configuration for digital soundtrack format, featuring three front channels across the
width of the screen (left, center, right), two surround channels (left surround,
right surround), and a low-frequency effects (or LFE) channel devoted solely to
very low sounds.

cocktail party effect: a phenomenon that refers to the capacity to focus on a single
element in a sound stream by filtering out competing audio stimuli. It gets its
name from a partygoer's ability to pick out the frequency and timbre of a single
speaking voice from the chatter of other discussions occurring in a crowded
room. Director Robert Altman used overlapping dialogue to evoke the cocktail
party effect, sometimes using wireless radio microphones to record as many as
fourteen different actors at the same time.

compander: a key device in Dolby's Type-A noise reduction technology that simultaneously compresses and expands the audio signal by using bandpass filters to
isolate particular frequency ranges that can be boosted during recording. The
process is then reversed during playback with a comparable deemphasis given
to those same frequency ranges that previously were enhanced. The end result
is a cleaner recording that lacks the high-frequency tape hiss and background
noise commonly found in more traditional recording techniques.

compiled score/compilation score: in the silent era, a compiled score is a musical accompaniment for a film that is not originally composed but rather compiled from preexisting material; in the sound era, a compilation score uses prerecorded songs in place of or in conjunction with an orchestral score.

cue sheet: in the silent era, a printed sheet that indicated specific moments within the film that would cue, or signal, music of one sort or another to be played; in the sound era, a legal document that listed each and every bit of music—originally composed or borrowed from an existing repertoire—that figured into a film.

digital audio workstations (DAWs): a stand-alone computerized sound editing system, allowing for large numbers of sounds to be stored, edited, played back, processed and mixed, and designed to accommodate nondestructive editing and random access of digitized sounds. Past and current DAWs include Pro Tools, Logic Pro, Digital Performer, Nuendo, WaveFrame, and Fairlight.

digital projection: a theatrical exhibition system that plays movies back from digital files rather than by shining light through celluloid. Movie files used for digital projection include one or more digital soundtracks in addition to the image data.

digital sound systems: a variety of theatrical sound systems that either encoded multichannel audio as digital data directly on the 35mm film (Dolby Digital, SDDS) or on a separate CD-R played in sync with the film (DTS).

digital surround sound (DSS): the generic term for any digital sound format capable of playing back at least 5.1 discrete channels of sound.

Dolby Stereo (35mm SVA and 70mm magnetic): Dolby Laboratories' proprietary system for recording multichannel sound onto analog film media. Dolby SVA used a matrix to combine four channels of sound (Left, Right, Center, and Surround) into two channels (Left-total, Right-total) on the 35mm optical soundtrack. Dolby 70mm applied Dolby noise reduction to the six discrete magnetic channels on 70mm film and used proprietary encoding to enhance low frequency response and provide split-surround channels.

dubbing stage: in the studio era, a room where the final rerecording of a film's soundtrack took place. It was more like a theater than a soundstage with a screen at one end, seats in the middle, and a sound booth at the back.

effects list: in the studio era, a list of sound effects keyed to individual scenes compiled by a studio's sound department for use in a specific film.

Fantasound: an early form of stereophonic sound developed at the Disney studio, named after *Fantasia* (1940), the film that first utilized it. The system propelled stereophonic sound through speakers positioned throughout specially outfitted theaters to surround audiences in sound, not unlike Dolby systems of today, and utilized forerunners of noise reduction systems that were decades away. Less than stellar box office returns for *Fantasia* as well as the expense of outfitting theaters doomed the venture.

Foley artist: a sound professional responsible for the creation of performed sound effects synched to the image.

Foley effects: named after sound editor Jack Foley (1891–1967), Foley effects are specially—and sometimes elaborately—rendered sounds (such as footsteps, clothing sounds, and additional sound design effects) that are recorded and synched to the film during postproduction.

Kinetophone: a device invented by Thomas Edison ca. 1895 but never patented that combined the viewing of motion pictures via a Kinetoscope with the hearing of recorded sound played via a phonograph.

Kinetoscope: a device invented and patented by Thomas Edison ca. 1894 that allowed individual paying customers to view motion pictures through peep-holes.

looping: rerecording dialogue in postproduction.

magnetic recording: adopted by Hollywood studios beginning in the 1940s, magnetic recording offered many advantages over the then standard practice of recording soundtracks onto optical film. Magnetic recording provided greater audio detail and immediate playback, and facilitated a number of mixing and manipulative techniques not possible with optical film.

mickey mousing: pioneered by Walt Disney, the practice of precisely synchronizing music to screen action; so named after the cartoon character for whom Disney devised the practice.

Movietone: a process, invented in Germany in 1922 and licensed by Fox in 1926, that allowed sound to be recorded—by means of motion-picture photography that captured light triggered by sound waves—directly onto celluloid film.

multichannel recording: recording sound with multiple microphones; an early technological achievement in the sound era.

multichannel sound system: a sound system allowing different elements of a soundtrack to be placed in different locations around the listening space. Most multichannel soundtracks are completely premixed, with a separate audio waveform (analog or digital) recorded for each unique playback channel.

multitrack recorders: tape recorders that accommodated the simultaneous recording and playback of several audio tracks in sync with film or video.

music supervisor: the individual responsible for negotiating the reproduction rights and often the selections involved in a compilation score, including hiring composers to write new songs.

Nagra: a series of Swiss-made, quarter-inch magnetic tape recorders that were popularized during the Auteur Renaissance. Appearing in 1961, the Nagra III was the company's first lightweight, portable, battery-operated audio recorder engineered for film work, making it much easier to get high-quality production sound on location shoots.

original score: a musical accompaniment for a film that is composed specifically for the film.

Perspecta sound: a pseudo-stereophonic system that MGM developed for use in its CinemaScope productions. Sub-audible tones embedded in the soundtrack indicated variable volumes for the right, center, and left speakers, thereby rendering a stereo-like experience from one audio signal.

postsynchronization: synchronizing sound and image in postproduction. Postsynchronization was produced by filming the image track silent and adding sound effects in postproduction, thus freeing up the camera during production. It proved a crucial stage in the development of sound film since it demonstrated that the production of sound could be separate from the production of images.

Pro Tools: the dominant DAW in the film industry; formerly produced by DigiDesign, currently owned by Avid.

production sound: audio, generally dialogue with some occasional effects and background ambiences, recorded during the shooting of a film.

recording cue sheet: commonly used in the studio era, a list of all the sound effects, dialogue, and music cues keyed to the script for use in postproduction.

rerecording (also known as dubbing): the rerecording of a film's soundtrack in postproduction. Rerecording allows multiple tracks for dialogue, sound effects, and music that could potentially have been recorded at different places and at different times to be mixed in postproduction and rerecorded for the final theatrical soundtrack.

rerecording mixer: the individual responsible for mixing all the tracks prepared in postproduction by the sound editors into the final theatrical soundtrack.

sound designer: the individual responsible for the overall sound of a motion picture, akin to the production designer supervising the overall look of a film.

sound editing: the general term encompassing the processes of selecting, cutting, and placing sound recordings for a soundtrack. It can also include the electronic processing and/or creation of new sounds to be used in the soundtrack. On any given film, a single sound editor generally edits only a specific type of sound: dialogue, sound effects, music, Foley, etc.

sound editor: one of the many individuals in postproduction who select, edit, and synchronize sounds (dialogue, effects, music, ambience) with the final edited image track. Often the sound editor will also create sound effects when needed.

sound library: originally called a noise library, a studio's collection of recorded sounds for postproduction use. Having a variety of sound effects available at a moment's notice cut down on costs as the same sound effects could be (and were) recycled across dozens—even hundreds—of a studio's films.

sound mixing: a general term in filmmaking covering two categories of work. One is recording original sounds, either on set or in a studio (as with Foley or ADR mixing); the best-known job in this realm is that of production mixer, the head of the on-set sound crew. The other is combining various sonic elements into a finished soundtrack in postproduction. This can include panning sounds, adjusting volume levels, processing sounds, adding reverb, etc.; the job primarily responsible for this is that of the rerecording mixer.

sound-on-disc: the mode of presentation, early in the sound era, that involved attempts to coordinate motion pictures with sounds recorded on phonograph discs.

sound-on-film: the mode of presentation, early in the sound era, that involved the playback of both sound and images that had been recorded on a single roll of celluloid film.

spotting session: typically the first step in the creation of a film's score. After a provisional work print of the film was edited, it was generally the composer, the director, the producer, and the head of the music department who met to decide which "spots" needed music. The music editor would then create a list of the specific scenes and their timings, which generally served as the composer's road map in creating music cues for the film.

stereophonic sound: a variety of playback systems, developed in the 1950s, in which distinct yet complementary audio signals were sent simultaneously to two or more speakers, giving the composite sound a spatial, stereophonic dimension that monaural soundtracks (one signal sent to all speakers) lacked.

synthesis: in music, the creation of new sounds electronically, either from scratch or by electronically processing original sound samples.

temp track: a temporary music track used during postproduction that is eventually replaced by a music score specially composed for the film. Initially, the temp track was created to guide the work of the picture editor, but it now serves a wider variety of functions, including serving as a role model for the film composer.

Vitaphone: a process, patented and first demonstrated by Warner Bros. in 1926, that combined the projection of motion pictures with the amplified playback of sounds recorded on phonograph discs.

walla (also known as group ADR): the specialized sound effect of background conversations.

SELECTED BIBLIOGRAPHY

Abel, Richard, and Rick Altman, eds. *The Sounds of Early Cinema*. Bloomington: Indiana University Press, 2001.

Allen, Ioan. "The Production of Wide-Range, Low-Noise Optical Soundtracks Utilizing the Dolby Noise Reduction System." *Journal of the SMPTE* 84, no. 9 (September 1975): 720–729.

Altman, Rick. *Silent Film Sound*. New York: Columbia University Press, 2004.

Ament, Vanessa Theme. *The Foley Grail: The Art of Performing Sound for Film, Games, and Animation*. Burlington, MA: Focal Press, 2009.

Anderson, Gillian B. *Music for Silent Films, 1894–1929: A Guide*. Washington, D.C.: Library of Congress, 1988.

Audissino, Emilio. *John Williams' Film Music: Jaws, Star Wars, Raiders of the Lost Ark, and the Return of the Classical Hollywood Score*. Madison: University of Wisconsin Press, 2014.

Barnett, Steve. "Film Sound Editing Techniques [Part Two]." *Recording Engineer/Producer* 13, no. 1 (February 1982): 56, 58, 60, 62, 64–67.

Beck, Jay. "The Evolution of Sound in Cinema." In *The Routledge Companion to Film History*, edited by William Guynn, 64–76. New York: Routledge, 2011.

———. "A Quiet Revolution: Changes in American Film Sound Practices, 1967–1979." Ph.D. diss., University of Iowa, 2003.

Belton, John. *Widescreen Cinema.* Cambridge, MA: Harvard University Press, 1992.

Berg, Charles Merrell. *An Investigation of the Motives and Realization of Music to Accompany the American Silent Film, 1896–1927.* New York: Arno Press, 1976.

Biskind, Peter. *Easy Riders and Raging Bulls: How the Sex-Drugs-and Rock 'n' Roll Generation Saved Hollywood.* New York: Simon and Schuster, 1998.

Blake, Larry. *Film Sound Today: An Anthology of Articles from Recording Engineer/Producer.* Hollywood: Reveille Press, 1984.

Bordwell, David. "Intensified Continuity: Visual Style in Contemporary American Film." *Film Quarterly* 55, no. 3 (2002): 16–28.

Buhler, James, David Neumeyer, and Rob Deemer. *Hearing the Movies: Music and Sound in Film History.* New York: Oxford University Press, 2010.

Chion, Michel. *Audio-Vision.* Edited and translated by Claudia Gorbman. New York: Columbia University Press, 1994.

Cooke, Mervyn. *A History of Film Music.* Cambridge: Cambridge University Press, 2009.

Crafton, Donald. *The Talkies: America's Transition to Sound, 1926–1931.* New York: Scribner's, 1997.

Ellis-Geiger, Robert Jay. "Trends in Contemporary Hollywood Film Scoring: A Synthesized Approach for Hong Kong Cinema." Ph.D. diss., University of Leeds, 2007.

Eyman, Scott. *The Speed of Sound: Hollywood and the Talkie Revolution.* New York: Simon and Schuster, 1997.

Flinn, Caryl. *Strains of Utopia: Gender, Nostalgia, and Hollywood Film Music.* Princeton, NJ: Princeton University Press, 1992.

Forlenza, Jeff, and Terri Stone, eds. *Sound for Picture: An Inside Look at Audio Production for Film and Television.* Emeryville, CA: Mix Books/Hal Leonard Publishing, 1993.

Gentry, Ric. "Alan Splet and Sound Effects for Dune." *American Cinematographer* 65, no. 12 (December 1984): 62–64, 66, 68, 70, 72.

Gomery, Douglas. *The Coming of Sound: A History.* New York: Routledge, 2004.

Gorbman, Claudia. *Unheard Melodies: Narrative Film Music.* Bloomington: Indiana University Press, 1987.

Gowin, Steve. "Sound by Splet: *Mosquito Coast*'s Bugs, Birds and Burps." *Theatre Crafts* 21, no. 2 (February 1987): 71–72.

Gunning, Tom. "The Cinema of Attraction: Early Film, Its Spectator, and the Avant-Garde." *Wide Angle* 8, nos. 3–4 (1986): 63–70.

Handzo, Stephen. "A Narrative Glossary of Film Sound Technology." In *Film Sound: Theory and Practice*, edited by Elisabeth Weis and John Belton, 383–426. New York: Columbia University Press, 1985.

Hanson, Helen. "Sound Affects: Post-production Sound, Soundscapes, and Sound Design in Hollywood's Studio Era." *Music, Sound and the Moving Image* 1, no. 1 (Spring 2007): 27–49.

Hanson, Helen, and Steve Neale. "Commanding the Sounds of the Universe: Classical Hollywood Sound in the 1930s and Early 1940s." In *The Classical Hollywood Reader*, edited by Steve Neale, 249–261. London: Routledge, 2012.

Harris, Mark. *Pictures at a Revolution: Five Movies and the Birth of the New Hollywood*. New York: Penguin Press, 2008.

Hubbert, Julie, ed. *Celluloid Symphonies, Texts and Contexts in Film Music History*. Berkeley: University of California Press, 2011.

Jackson, Blair. "What's That Sound? It Takes Big Work to Make Even the Smallest Movie Sound Effects." *Mix* 14, no. 9 (September 1990): 116–117, 119–123.

Jacobs, Lea. "The Innovation of Re-recording in the Hollywood Studios." *Film History* 24, no. 1 (2012): 5–34.

Kalinak, Kathryn. *Settling the Score: Music and the Classical Hollywood Film*. Madison: University of Wisconsin Press, 1992.

Keane, Stephen. "Walter Murch and Ben Burtt: The Sound Designer as Composer." In *Sound and Music in Film and Visual Media*, edited by Graeme Harper, Ruth Doughty, and Jochen Eisentraut, 452–462. New York: Continuum, 2009.

Kenny, Tom, ed. *Sound for Picture: The Art of Sound Design in Film and Television*. 2nd ed. Vallejo, CA: Mix Books, 2000.

Kerins, Mark. *Beyond Dolby (Stereo): Cinema in the Digital Sound Age*. Bloomington: Indiana University Press, 2010.

———. "Understanding the Impact of Surround Sound in Multimedia." In *The Psychology of Music in Multimedia*, edited by Siu-Lan Tan, Annabel J. Cohen, Scott D. Lipscomb, and Roger A. Kendall, 365–389. Oxford: Oxford University Press, 2013.

Lastra, James. *Sound Technology and the American Cinema: Perception, Representation, Modernity*. New York: Columbia University Press, 2000.

Lev, Peter. *Transforming the Screen, 1950–1959*. New York: Scribner's, 2003.

LoBrutto, Vincent. *Sound-on-Film: Interviews with Creators of Film Sound*. Westport, CT: Praeger, 1994.

Marks, Martin M. *Music and the Silent Film: Contexts and Case Studies, 1895–1924*. New York: Oxford University Press, 1997.

Monaco, Paul. *The Sixties*. New York: Scribner's, 2001.

Morton, David Jr. *Sound Recording: The Life Story of a Technology*. Baltimore: Johns Hopkins University Press, 2006.

Neumeyer, David, ed. *The Oxford Handbook of Film Music Studies*. New York: Oxford University Press, 2014.

Ondaatje, Michael. *The Conversations: Walter Murch and the Art of Editing Film*. New York: Borzoi Books, 2002.

Pasquariello, Nicholas. *Sounds of Movies: Interviews with the Creators of Feature Sound Tracks*. San Francisco: Point Bridge Books, 1997.

Platte, Nathan. "Before *Kong* Was King: Competing Methods in Hollywood Underscore." *Journal of the Society for American Music* 8, no. 3 (2014): 311–337.

Rivlin, Michael. "Motion Picture Sound Re-recording and Mixing: Dawn of a Digital Decade." *Millimeter* 8, no. 5 (May 1980): 106, 111–115.

Sergi, Gianluca. "Knocking at the Door of Cinematic Artifice: Dolby *Atmos*, Challenges and Opportunities." *New Soundtrack* 3, no. 2 (September 2013): 107–121.

Slowik, Michael. "Diegetic Withdrawal and Other Worlds: Film Music Strategies before King Kong, 1927–1933." *Cinema Journal* 53, no. 1 (Fall 2013): 1–25.

Smith, Jeff. "The Sound of Intensified Continuity." In *The Oxford Handbook of New Audiovisual Aesthetics*, edited by John Richardson, Claudia Gorbman, and Carol Vernallis, 338–347. New York: Oxford University Press, 2013.

———. *The Sounds of Commerce: Marketing Popular Film Music*. New York: Columbia University Press, 1998.

Spring, Katherine. *Saying It with Songs: Popular Music and the Coming of Sound to Hollywood Cinema*. New York: Oxford University Press, 2013.

Thom, Randy. "Designing a Movie for Sound." *iris* 27 (Spring 1999): 9–20.

Whittington, William. *Sound Design and Science Fiction*. Austin: University of Texas Press, 2007.

Wierzbicki, James. *Film Music: A History*. New York: Routledge, 2009.

Wierzbicki, James, Nathan Platte, and Colin Roust, eds. *The Routledge Film Music Sourcebook*. New York: Routledge, 2012.

Winkler, Max. *A Penny from Heaven*. New York: Appleton-Century-Crofts, 1951.

Wright, Benjamin. "Sound from Start to Finish." Ph.D. diss., Carleton University, 2011.

Zak, Albin III. *I Don't Sound Like Nobody: Remaking Music in 1950s America*. Ann Arbor: University of Michigan Press, 2010.

NOTES ON CONTRIBUTORS

Vanessa Theme Ament is the Edmund F. and Virginia B. Ball Endowed Chair of Telecommunications at Ball State University. She is the author of *The Foley Grail* and is on the steering committee for Cinesonika, an international film festival and conference that celebrates sound and music in film and video.

Jay Beck is an assistant professor of cinema and media studies at Carleton College. He coedited *Lowering the Boom: Critical Studies in Film Sound* and is American coeditor of the journal *Music, Sound, and the Moving Image*. His current book project is *Designing Sound: Technology and Sound Aesthetics in 1970s American Cinema*.

Kathryn Kalinak is a professor of film studies at Rhode Island College and the author of numerous articles and books on film music, including *Settling the Score: Music and the Classical Hollywood Film*, *How the West Was Sung: Music in the Westerns of John Ford*, and *Film Music: A Very Short Introduction*. In 2011 she was named the Mary Tucker Thorp Professor at Rhode Island College.

Mark Kerins is an associate professor of film and media arts at Southern Methodist University. His work, focusing on multichannel sound, includes the award-winning book *Beyond Dolby (Stereo)*, journal articles, and anthology chapters. Kerins is also an active filmmaker with major label music videos and festival-award-winning shorts among his credits.

Nathan Platte is an assistant professor of musicology at the University of Iowa. His recent publications include *The Routledge Film Music Sourcebook* (coedited with James Wierzbicki and Colin Roust), *Franz Waxman's "Rebecca": A Film Score Guide* (coauthored with David Neumeyer), and articles in the *Journal of Film Music, Music and the Moving Image*, and the *Oxford Handbook of Film Music Studies*.

Jeff Smith is a professor of communication arts at the University of Wisconsin–Madison and the author of two books: *The Sounds of Commerce: Marketing Popular Film Music* and *Film Criticism, the Cold War, and the Blacklist: Reading the Hollywood Reds*.

James Wierzbicki teaches musicology at the University of Sydney. His research focuses on questions of modernity and the postmodern, on twentieth-century music in general, and on film music in particular. His books include *Film Music: A History* and monographs on Elliott Carter and the score for the film *Forbidden Planet*.

INDEX

118, 142; sampled, 141
intensified continuity, 151
International Alliance of Theatrical Stage
  Employees (IATSE), 108
In the Heat of the Night (1967), 60, 79, 80,
  81–82, 86; score and sound, 81
Iron Horse, The (1924), 44
Island of Lost Souls (1932), 48
It's a Mad, Mad, Mad, Mad World (1963),
  82
I Want to Live! (1958), score, 76

Jacobs, Lea, 48
Jamison, Barbara Berch, 63
Jane Eyre (1970) [telefilm], 91
Jaws (1975), 85; score, 97
jazz: in film scores, 76, 78, 81, 94, 117;
  fusion, 94; musicians, 80, 81
Jazz Singer, The (1927), 35–36; score, 179n64
Jolson, Al, 40
Jones, Quincy, 63, 67, 80–82, 94
Journal of the SMPTE, 86, 89, 91. *See also*
  SMPTE Journal
Joy Ride (2001), 152

Kalinak, Kathryn, 10, 206
Karas, Anton, 77
Katz, Mark, 66
Kaufman, Philip, 114
Kaun, Bernard, 56
Keighley, William, 41
Kerins, Mark, 13–14, 127, 152–153, 207;
  Beyond Dolby (Stereo), 148, 151
Kernell, William, 179n65
Kinetophone, 33–34
kineto-phonograph, 178n57
Kinetoscope parlors, 17
King, Richard, 137, 138, 154
King Kong (1933), 45, 48; score, 54
King Kong (1976), 189n59
King's Row (1942), 55
Kirk, Roland, 81
Knobloch, Mike, 137
Knopfler, Mark, 119
Korngold, Erich Wolfgang, 55–56, 97–98,
  182n98
Kroeber, Ann, 102–103, 114, 190n22

labor structures, in film production, 116,
  187n10
Lady in the Lake (1947), score, 76
Laemmle, Carl, Jr., 38
Langford, Barry, 61
Lasky, Jesse, 40, 41, 43
Last Picture Show, The (1971), 81; songs,
  95
Lastra, James, 22
Lawrence of Arabia (1962), 79
Lazarowitz, Les, 87
Lazarus, Arnie, 103
lectures, illustrated, 19, 175n17
Legrand, Michel, 94
Lev, Peter, 62
Levinson, Nathan, 45
Levy, Sol, 25
Lewin, Albert, 180n26
Lewis, John J., 19
library sounds. *See* sound effects libraries
license-free material, 32
Lindgren, Harry, 65
location shooting, 46, 47, 87; sound equip-
  ment, 52
Loews theater chain, 42
Long Day's Journey into Night (1962), score,
  78
Long Goodbye, The (1973), score, 97
Long Riders, The (1980), 131
looping, 48
Los Angeles Examiner, 46
Los Angeles Times, 46, 47
loudspeakers, 35, 89
Love Bug, The (1968), 85
Love Story (1970), 85
Lucas, George, 97, 101, 111
Lumière, Auguste and Louis, 18
Luz, Ernest J., 28, 176
Lynch, David, 103, 113, 114

MacDonald, Jeanette, 46
MacGowan, Kenneth, 179n4
Mad Max Beyond Thunderdome (1985),
  songs, 191n54
Madonna, 121
magic lantern shows, 3
"magic surround" effect, 124

Murch, Walter, 88, 99, 100–101, 108–110, 112, 125, 131, 188n47
Murder on the Orient Express (1974), score, 94
music, 5; awards, 164; composition, 65–66; computer-based, 141; descriptive, 25; electronic, 76; industry, 84, 90, 119, 122; as moneymaker for films, 95; for narrative films, 23–27; new wave, 119; piano, 24–25; popular, 76, 117; production crews, 143–144; publishers, 30, 32, 43; recording, 57, 90; recycled, 54; and sound effects, 62, 143. *See also* jazz; *musique concrète*; orchestras; rock 'n' roll; scores; songs
musical: genres, 60; instruments, for film scores, 24–25, 79, 94–95, 118, 142; styles, 60–61, 76–77, 81
musical directors, at film studios, 44
musicals, 45, 73
Music and Effects mix, 130
music coordinators [film and music product], 122
music cues, 27, 56
music departments, division of labor, 55. *See also under studio names*
musicians, 42–45, 63, 76–78; Broadway, 43; contracts, 78; freelance, 57; recorded on set, 45; on records, 76; studio, 57; unions, 42, 57, 78. *See also* accompanists; jazz musicians; orchestras
Musicians Guild of America (MGA), 78
music librarians, 56, 192n94
music libraries, 32, 56–57
Music Publishers Association, 30
music supervisors, 122, 123
music videos, 122–123
musique concrète, 66
M. Witmark and Sons [music publisher], 43
My Beautiful Laundrette (1985), score, 120
Myers, Stanley, 120

Nagra sound equipment, 87–88, 134
narrative: and pop songs, 122; and sound, 3–4, 13, 114–117; and speech, 107
narrative films, 21–24
Nashville (1975), 91, 92–93, *93*
National Lampoon's Animal House (1978), 97

Natural, The (1984), score, 119
Neale, Steve, 49
Neumeyer, David, 141, 142, 143
Newman, Alfred, 93
Newman, Randy, 119
new wave music, 119
New York theaters, 19, 175n21
Nickelodeon, The [trade journal], 28
nickelodeon operators, 28
nickelodeons, 22–25
nickelodeon-style: films, 23–27; theaters, 25
Night Visitor, The (1971), score, 95
"noise libraries," 48
noise reduction technology, 46, 88–91, 123
No Way Out (1950), 86

object-based mixing, 149, 195n73
Oliver! (1968), 90
O Lucky Man! (1973), soundtrack, 119
one-reel films, 28
opera stars, 43
orchestral: music, mixing, 64; scores, 117, 142
orchestras, 30, 57, 177; on set, 45. *See also* studio orchestras
orchestration, 32, 56, 98
orchestrators, 56
original scores, 31
Out of Sight (1998), 190
overlapping dialogue, 91–93
Owen, Reginald, 51

Pacific Rim (2013), 148
Page, Jimmy, 119
Paley, Andy, 121
Paradine Case, The (1947), soundtrack album, 73
Paramount, 42, 46, 49, 54, 70, 144; music department, 44, 54; music library, 56; sound department, 45
Paris, Texas (1984), music, 119
Parr, John, 122
Parsons, Luella, 43
passion play attractions, 19
Pasternacki, Stephan, 182n88
Pee-wee's Big Adventure (1984), score, 120